STAGECRAFT 1

A COMPLETE GUIDE TO BACKSTAGE WORK
WILLIAM H. LORD

SECOND EDITION

MERIWETHER PUBLISHING LTD.
Colorado Springs, Colorado

Meriwether Publishing Ltd., Publisher
Box 7710
Colorado Springs, CO 80933

Editor: Arthur Zapel
Typesetting: William H. Lord
Cover design: Tom Myers
Cover photo: James M. Vawter

© Copyright MCMXCI William H. Lord
Reprinting and distribution rights assigned to Meriwether Publishing Ltd. 1991
Printed in the United States of America
Second Edition

Library of Congress Cataloging-in-Publication Data

Lord, William H.
    Stagecraft 1 : a complete guide to backstage work / by William H.
Lord. -- 2nd ed.
        p.   cm.
    Includes bibliographical reference and index.
    ISBN 0-916260-76-3 : $12.95
    1. Theaters--Stage-setting and scenery.   I. Title. II. Title:
Stagecraft one.
    PN2091.S8L6   1990
    792'.025--dc20

                                                     90-26462
                                                       CIP

DEDICATION

Theatre continues to play an important part in my life — a life which has been shared willingly by my immediate family as they allowed and encouraged me to continue practicing. For that reason, I again dedicate this effort to my wife Cathy, and our daughters Jennifer and Louise.

INTRODUCTION

The theatre has been a world of fantasy since the Golden Age of Greek literature. Its agents in tragedy, comedy, musicals, and ballet unite to create for their spectators a medium of escape from the cares of the working day by what Coleridge has aptly termed "the willing suspension of disbelief." People for the most part credit the composer of the piece or the actors who interpret it for artistic success. But our greatest Poet has said that the stage is a place "where every man must play his part." This includes the technical director and his staff, a group vital to success but often overlooked by the audience. Were it not for these, utilizing wood, cordage, canvas, light, paint, and other equipment, the production would be bare indeed. The author of this solid book takes his readers behind the proscenium and provides comprehensive and expert insight into the activities there. He has designed a book of basics in the arts and crafts of technical theatre for beginners, but one not without value for the experienced.

Personnel and equipment are combined for the successful combination which produces the results required by the dictum of Plautus: "Those who live to please, must please to live."

William H. Lord brings impressive credentials to his task. He earned his Master's degree in his field at Northwestern University under professors of unusual competence; he has spent many years as technical director of productions at North Central High School in Indianapolis and in various civic theatres; in addition, he is widely recognized as a theatre consultant in technical matters and has had a hand in construction of most high school theatres built in Indiana in the past thirty years. Perhaps his most important qualification is his unrivaled knowledge and skill with tools and building materials of all kinds.

The 19 chapters of this book cover all that the aspiring stage worker needs to know about properties, scenery, painting, sets, lighting, and sound, together with their most effective employment. His firm command of his subject matter is shown both in the selection and arrangement of relevant topics. As benefits the artist-craftsman, his prose is clear, direct, and appropriate to the matter it conveys. No detail in technical theatre appears to have escaped the microscope of his attention.

The writer of this introduction, himself a former department chairman of a university department of speech and drama, declares with assurance that there is no rival for this book now in print.

George P. Rice, Ph.D., Jur. D.
Professor of Speech Emeritus
Butler University
Indianapolis, IN

ACKNOWLEDGEMENTS

As I prepare this revision of my original text, I must again express my gratitude to many individuals who have made this possible. Again, the greatest contribution came from my parents in the background, encouragement, and support which they offered.

My teachers: Miss Lenore Cupp from Bosse High School in Evansville, IN; Mr. Howard Hill of (then) Evansville College; and Mr. Theodore Fuchs of Northwestern University, each enriched and encouraged me in my theatrical efforts.

The number of friends in the industry continues to increase. As I meet the people involved in the development of supplies and equipment for the technical theatre industry, I am pleased that they are truly concerned about their products and the use of these. Many of these firms are credited throughout these pages as they have so kindly allowed me to use various samples of their illustrations. A current listing of many of the extant manufacturers is given in the appendix.

My colleagues at North Central have provided support and input. A special thanks to Doug McIntosh who, as a computer programming specialist, has suffered through my attempts to master the programs required to edit this book.

A very special thanks to Dr. George P. Rice of Butler University, now emeritus, who has encouraged me in many ways from the very beginning of this effort.

TABLE OF CONTENTS

05 - SOUND

06 - TOOLS

07 - LUMBER AND BY-PRODUCTS

08 - FASTENERS

09 - SCENERY CONSTRUCTION

10 - HARDWARE

11 - PLATFORMS, PARALLELS, STEPS AND RAMPS

12 - PAINT

13 - LIGHT SOURCES

14 - CONTROL OF LIGHT

15 - LIGHTING INSTRUMENTS

16 - ELECTRICITY AND DEVICES

17 - DIMMING AND DISTRIBUTION

18 - COLOR AND LIGHT

19 - PLANNING LIGHTING

APPENDIX

AUTHOR'S PREFACE

The original edition of this book was done in response to my concern about a need for a basic text to cover those first, basic elements for those who wanted to function behind the scenes in theatre.

In this edition, I have expanded on several of the ideas, techniques, and methods found in that first edition. These expansions come in response to comments and questions from many of the people who have been using the original. Today there are even more methods of accomplishing a given objective and many instructors will utilize different approaches than those suggested herein. It is not that there is a right or a wrong way of accomplishing a goal, it is that we take different routes to reach it. This myriad of solutions to problems is what makes involvement with technical theatre such an interesting experience.

The techniques, methods, and ideas expressed in this edition are things which we have used. I have tried to deal with the very elementary steps in our craft. In the bibliography at the end of the book I have listed many books and sources for specialized information. Many of the books are older, but still have some excellent information within their pages.

Today's technology, particularly in the domain of electronics, provides a rapid rate of change in equipment design and capability. For this reason,I have included the names of manufacturers who, at the time of publication, were, to the best of my knowledge, most active in their fields. Most of them publish catalogs, data sheets, and/or brochures dealing with their specific equipment. These are available upon request by writing to the manufacturer.

Flexibility continues to be the key word in technical theatre. When this is lost, productions suffer. A key to the fascination of live theatre is that every presentation of each production has novelty. New variables appear and fresh solutions to both old and new problems are devised. This is, to me, the reason why we cannot make positive and demanding statements about how something HAS to be done in theatre.

In her play HARVEY, Mary Chase wrote several delightful lines for the lead character, Elwood P. Dowd. One can be a credo for us in theatre: "Wherever I am and whatever I am doing, I have a wonderful time!" If you enjoy your work, so will those who are in your audience.

CHAPTER ONE

STAGES AND RIGGING

Whether actor or technician, your greatest ally in theatre is the *imagination* of your audience. Your job is to trigger that imagination. While this may be done in many ways and by methods of differing quality, the task must be done. To do it efficiently requires at least some knowledge of the facilities, materials, equipment, and techniques available.

The facility will vary greatly from theatre to theatre. The physical plant divides into three basic parts and each of these can be provided in different forms. Each facility will be a combination of parts, each of which will have its own strengths and weaknesses.

PARTS OF A THEATRE

The primary part of a theatre is its *acting area* – the only one of the parts actually required in order to present a theatre experience. The functions of this part are to set the actor apart from the audience, to divide his actions from reality, and to provide a degree of visibility and audibility for the performer. This is the area with which you should be most concerned since it is the focal point of the theatre experience.

The second part of the theatre is the *auditorium* – an area to provide some degree of comfort and safety for the audience, and to allow them to see and hear what is on stage. Some auditoriums are poorly planned and do little to provide these things. The more poorly planned the auditorium, the greater the task of the performer and the technician.

While optional, most theatres provide a *scenic background*. Taking many forms it may appear as: a curtain, either patterned or plain; a painted backdrop, depicting something real or symbolic; a constructed background; or a natural background as provided by many outdoor theatres.

FORMS OF THEATRES

The forms of the acting area are many. While they may be at any level in relation to the audience, they are usually a little above the lowest row provided for the viewers. These forms are usually named according to the amount of space occupied around them by the audience.

The *theatre-in-the-round* presents actors completely encircled by the audience.

Avondale Playhouse

In this form of staging, which is also known as *arena*, *circle staging*, or *center staging*, the stage directions are taken from a clock face. An area adjacent to one of the entrance aisles is designated as the location of the technical control equipment and this aisle is then designated as the "12 o'clock" position. Viewed from above the other aisles take on designations as 3, 6, or 9 o'clock. In this way the director can locate actors and scenery by reference to time position. While this form of theatre offers the closest actor-audience proximity, it also is probably the most limiting on scenery and lighting equipment placement.

Obviously there is no limit as to how many degrees of wrapping-the-audience-around-the-stage seating are used. For reference, however, theatres fall into categories by quarters. Thus the *three-quarter round* stage has seating around 270 degrees, while the *half-round* seats throughout 180 degrees. In either of these forms you can accomplish a closer relationship of actor-to-audience than in other forms, but since there is an area in which sight lines are of no concern, scenery begins to become more flexible.

Christian Theological Seminary

The Greek and Roman theatres which were almost three-quarter and half-round respectively, gave us some of our basic concepts of physical theatre and many of our terms come from them. These early forms shared such things as a seating area for the general public and an *orchestra,* which in the Greek theatre was a performance area used by the chorus. In Roman times it became the seating area for local dignitaries. Alleyways called *parados* were provided for the Greek chorus to gain entry to the orchestra.

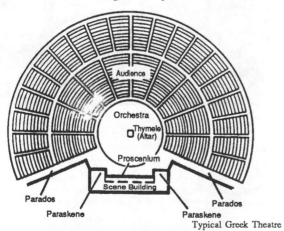

Typical Greek Theatre

In the center of the orchestra was a *thymele* or altar which the Greeks used for sacrifices. The Romans reduced this in size, placed it at the front edge of the stage, and used it as a display location for the laurel wreath to be given to the top performer.

Each had its *scene building* to provide storage for costumes and properties. These buildings had *doors* which aided in the dramatic story. One door represented the home of the protagonist (hero) while another was the home of the antagonist (villain) and the middle door represented a temple which, of course, was the home of the gods. Alongside the building were *paraskene –* towers added to the sides to make the scene building take on a "U" shape. Later a playing area was added to the face of each paraskene and called *proscenium*, the place in front of the scene.

The Greeks were the first to use scenic devices. The *periaktoi* were triangular shaped units which when placed side by side formed a flat surface for painted scenery. The shape allowed the units to rotate, thus giving simple "shifts" between scenes. The *eccyclema* was a cart or platform on wheels used to move items on and off of the playing area. This is the forerunner of our stage wagons and platforms of today. The Greeks also used a *deus-ex-machina*, or "god of the machine." It was a means of having a character "descend" onto the stage from the heavens, or used by the dramatist to rescue a hero from an impossible situation. Since the audience could see the machinery as well as the operation of it, it was very contrived or "fakey". This is the meaning which the term has in its use today.

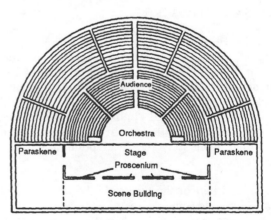

Typical Roman Theatre

The Roman theatre gave us a *sounding board* which was a top panel above the stage to help project sound into the audience area. It also brought us *awnings* to protect people from sun during performances and a huge *scene wall* which was an ornately carved permanent facade in front of which the actors performed.

When the audience seating is restricted to less than 180 degrees and no proscenium is present, we achieve the *open stage.* There is little structural restriction placed upon the stage or the acting area and the audience is seated as closely as possible. This gathering of the audience into less of an arc allows the use of scenic projections as a major scenic technique.

Indianapolis Children's Museum

If there is some physical, structural limitation placed upon the vision of the audience, the theatre will fall into the *proscenium* category. In the true proscenium theatre the actual presentation takes place behind the curtain line, or imaginary fourth wall, formed by the proscenium. In this form the audience is looking through a picture frame to see the action.

North Central High School, Indianapolis

In recent years, this fourth wall concept has been breached and the actors will play onto the front of the stage, thus allowing them to get as close to their audience as possible, "thrusting" the action toward the audience. Here the action behind the actual proscenium arch becomes less and we find ourselves presenting theatre on a *thrust* stage.

Of all forms of theatre it is this author's opinion that the proscenium form of theatre offers the most opportunity to the technician, the actor, and the audience. This is the form of theatre which utilizes the most talents from the technician. Some feel that it is more costly to build and equip than other forms and

cite this as a reason for eliminating it; but in the hands of a staff who wishes to be creative, a proscenium theatre can easily be transformed into any of the other forms, thus allowing experimentation. The majority of the stages in operation today are proscenium stages and since they offer the greatest opportunity to the technician we will talk mostly of their techniques and equipment.

STAGE TERMINOLOGY

Stages other than those in theatre-in-the-round must also have a method of indicating directions to the participants. Because early stages were sloped or *raked* (set at an angle to the audience's line of sight) so that the action farthest from the audience was actually higher than that closer, the rear portion of the stage is referred to as *up stage*. The area closest to the seating is *down stage*.

Since we are giving directions to persons on stage, reference is made as they face their audience. *Stage left* is designated as the actors' left while facing the audience; conversely *stage right* is to the actors' right.

By labeling the *center* portion of the stage, we have the complete set of words for identifying areas.

The nine basic areas of the stage are designated by indicating up or down first, then left or right, and finally center when required.

Up Right	Up Center	Up Left
Right Center	Center	Left Center
Down Right	Down Center	Down Left
	(apron)	

(pit)

Between the stage and the audience there is usually some form of *apron*. This is the portion of the stage floor between the curtain and the front edge of the stage. Its size will vary from nothing to a larger-than-stage area as found in a thrust stage.

Most proscenium type stages also provide an area between the apron and the audience for the location of musicians. This is the *pit* and may be nothing more than a floor area without audience seating, or an elevator floor which allows adjustment from stage level down to any point. Some of these pits are so small that they are more of a limitation than a usable area. Others are so large that the audience in the first row feels a great separation from the action. In the "up" position, the pit provides a thrust stage to

3

overcome this feeling of distance. If the lift is nonexistent, then fillers can be used to bridge this space.

Since the members of a musical group in the pit would be considered as part of the presentation on stage, the stage directions usually hold through the pit. At the pit wall we begin to deal with the audience which is facing the stage, thus the directions here begin to relate to the position of the viewing public.

The proscenium form stage with its associated rigging is the most complex of the forms. It contains some items which are unique to it while it shares some things with other forms. Its name is derived from the picture frame opening which allows the audience to look in on the action while it blocks off a view of the supporting mechanisms and personnel.

An imaginary line drawn across the stage even with the backside of this arch will form the *curtain line*. Centered in the proscenium opening and drawn from the front to the rear of the stage is the *center line*. It is from these two reference lines that locations for sets, lighting, and curtains are measured. The standard stage directions are used then to relate locations for purposes of movement. Some houses will establish a curtain line upstage of the edge of the arch, perhaps to clear some permanent obstruction. The exact location does not matter, it is only important that the line be decided upon to prevent technical confusion.

The *flooring* of a stage is often ignored. This material is very much a part of the technical work and can be either an aid or a hindrance. As an aid it will allow the technician to attach scenery, place pivots for wagons, or locate marks for the placement of scenery.

The upstage two-thirds of a proscenium or thrust stage floor needs to provide a means of attaching scenery. Quarter-sawn *fir*, a material with a close firm grain yet soft enough to allow penetration with nails, screws, or other attaching materials, is a recommended material. It has the capability to absorb a lot of punishment and recover somewhat. The floor, like other technical items, can be expected to wear out and have to be replaced.

In the downstage portion and apron, *maple* flooring creates the resonance to provide some sound for dancing. It also is a hard-to-damage surface. This portion especially should have the space below it filled with some insulating material to deaden the echo sound. Ideally, the entire stage floor should be thus insulated.

Some years ago attempts were made to utilize linoleum for stage floors. The attempts met with some degree of success in spite of the instability of the early large-sheet flooring materials. Recently, materials have been developed which will allow them to be used for either permanent installation, or for roll-up portable flooring. Such flooring answers the problems created by the earlier ground cloths used when a designer wanted to paint the floor for a show, yet allow traction for dancers and a firm enough surface that scenery could be rolled over it.

The finish of the stage floor is also important. To allow the lighting technician better control of his light the floor should be finished in a dark color and matte finish. This will eliminate much of the reflection and thus provide better light control.

The termination of the audience's sight is the rear "wall" of the stage. Often this is a neutral, smooth sheet of material used to indicate sky. The material may be a temporary fabric curtain or a permanent plaster or sprayed concrete wall. It may be flat or may curve in one or more planes. Regardless of shape or material, it must still produce illusion. Usually this is referred to as the *"cyc"* or cyclorama.

To aid the lighting technician, the best color is a slightly blued grey. This allows a maximum of color changes through the use of lighting. The paint used should be flat so as to cut down the glare reflected to the audience.

STAGE RIGGING

The audience sitting in the house is unaware of the amount of technical equipment backstage. Their vision is blocked by the proscenium and unless they are allowed to see a scene shift they will not realize the method by which the change is made. While there are other methods of shifting scenery, one of the oldest is the use of a flying system or raising the scenery up out of sight. A *working stage* (referred to in the 1985 Uniform Building Code as a "Professional Stage") is one which provides some means of *flying* or lifting scenery.

In a working stage house the stage "ceiling" provides a location for the mounting of *blocks* (pulleys or sheaves). The most complex is the *upright gridiron* which provides a steel framing with sufficient space above it, yet below the roof, for a person to move. The blocks stand above the gridiron level, hence the term upright.

The term *"gridiron"* is the label given to the collection of beams that provides this working "platform" and usually will support the blocks. If these beams also support the roof of the building thus causing the blocks to be hung below them. This is called an *underhung gridiron* system. More and more stages with fly space are being designed to have their blocks mounted on the roof beams and still provide a gridiron for technicians to use for maintenance and rigging.

Either of these forms will provide some area above the playing space on stage. This space is known as the *fly space* or *loft*. The area is used for the storage of items suspended out of sight yet ready to be used. Rigging is provided so that curtains or scenery may be raised to facilitate movement on stage, or raised completely out of sight. This is, of course, dependent upon the height relation of the proscenium and the gridiron.

On any stage which uses suspended items we find collections called sets of lines. A *set of lines* is a group of associated items which allows the suspension of a curtain or portion of scenery or some lighting equipment. A set, dependent upon the exact style of the stage, is made up of several things.

Each set will have a *batten* which is a metal pipe (it used to be a wooden strip) upon which the curtain is tied or the lighting equipment is actually hung. This batten must be supported. The suspension is done through the use of rope or cable although in some cases the batten may be suspended from a chain. If chain is hung from hooks or steel the set is *dead hung*, i.e.: cannot be raised or lowered simply.

The number of ropes or cables used for support will vary according to the length of the batten. They are called *lines* or lift lines. In order to give technicians points of reference along the batten the lines are named in their length relationship from the operating side. The line closest to the point of set operation is the *short line;* the line farthest away the *long line.* If there is an odd number, you will find a "center, short center, and long center."

Above an upright grid

Underside of an Upright Gridiron

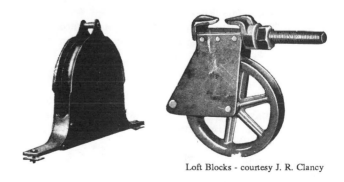

Underhung grid

Loft Blocks - courtesy J. R. Clancy

Steel cable lines should be checked over their length and at their fastenings every two or three years for signs of wear or loosening of clamps. Ropes should be checked yearly for fraying, wear, and drying out. If problems are found a professional rigger should be contacted to work on the system.

The lines of an operating set do not terminate at the grid as the dead-hung set did. Instead they continue through a series of single grooved wheels called *loft blocks*. There will be the same number of loft blocks as there are supporting lines and they usually will be set in a line parallel to the curtain line.

From the loft blocks the lines run horizontally, gather, and pass through a *head block* which is a single wheel with a number of grooves. Passing around the head block, the lines then drop back toward the floor.

In the case of a cable set, the lines will terminate in a steel frame called a *counterweight carriage* or *arbor* which results in a batten and counterweight carriage connected by cables. The newer carriages utilize steel shapes with a welded spine. This replaces the older cast iron tops and bottoms, some of which have failed under stress.

In a rope set the ropes drop to a *pin rail* which provides a convenient means of tying the ropes once the batten is pulled up to where you want it. The pin rail comes from the days of the tall rigged sailing ships where the lines supporting the sails were secured (belayed) by wrapping them around pins which were inserted through holes in the rails around the decks.

In order to raise or lower the carriage, and as a result the batten, an *operating line* is provided. This line is usually a 3/4" rope line which attaches to the top of the carriage, goes over the headblock, and comes back down again. Today these lines, also referred to as overhaul lines, are provided in manila (or hemp), polypropylene, as well as a cotton covered nylon rope. Each of these has its advantages and disadvantages.

As the rope drops down it passes through a *rope lock*. The lock is really only a brake or clamping device used to apply pressure to the rope so it will not move easily.

The lock is attached to the *lock rail*, can be adjusted rather simply, and should be set so that approximately 75 pounds of pull will cause the rope to slip. This is a safety factor so that an improperly balanced set will show by slipping through the lock.

Headblocks - courtesy J. R. Clancy

courtesy United Stage Equipment

Counterweight Carriage- courtesy J. R. Clancy

Pin Rail courtesy J. R. Clancy

6

Lock Rail courtesy J. R. Clancy

After passing through the lock the operating line goes around a *take-up-block* which turns the line so that it now travels up and is tied to the bottom of the carriage. This rope loop is used to operate the carriage, which in turn causes the batten to *fly* (raise) or *set* (come in). The line closer to the stage moves the same way that the batten will move. Pull down on it and the batten will go down. Pull down on the line away from the stage and the batten will go up. Note that you always pull DOWN to operate a set, not up since the mounting of the take-up block is not designed to take a lot of stress.

The operation of a counterweight system is relatively simple, but due caution must be taken. Prior to releasing the rope lock the *flyman*, the operator of the sets, should grasp the line above the lock and see if the set can be made to travel an inch or so. If it can, then the weight of the set can be controlled. If the set will not move slightly then a visual check must be made to make sure that the set is not fouled, that the load on the batten (estimated weight) matches the load on the carriage (estimated weight). This obviously is done in rehearsal and set-up so that during a production the flyman knows that the sets are balanced.

In setting up a show there will be communication with the crew on the loading platform to balance a set. Sets which are out of weight are either: *batten heavy* (not enough counterweight in the carriage, too much scenery, lighting etc. on the batten); or *iron heavy* (too much weight on the carriage).

Once the flyman is sure of the loading the safety ring on the lock is lifted. During work sessions or the first rehearsals in which the curtains are used, "heads up

number - -" is called giving the set designation so that people on stage will be aware of moving scenery. Obviously this is not done during a performance. By that time all the people on and back stage should be aware of what has to move and when.

On the counterweight sets which have to move during a show the flyman can use an *endless line trim clamp*, usually called a *knuckle buster*, which is really a

Endless line trim clamp courtesy J. R. Clancy

marker. This item is clamped to the onstage line of the operating line, just above the rope lock, when the set is in the proper playing trim. Many stages use tape as a marking device, but this is not positive and will sometimes catch in a lock and defeat both its marking potential and the efficiency of the lock.

With rope sets it is possible to use a *trimming clamp*. This is a device to hold the set of ropes together. This device also provides a method of attaching a sandbag to the set for counterbalancing. In this type of rigging the set must be kept a little batten heavy so that the batten will come down when the lines are released. Here, too, the operator should check the weight of the set prior to untying the lines.

Trimming clamp courtesy United Stage Equipment

While there are some who feel that a rope set is so old fashioned that it is no longer of use, it is still the easiest to move from one location to another on the stage. Most often you will find *spot lines*, single ropes used for support of one small item, rigged with rope. The cable set is by far the safest when properly installed, but it is expensive and difficult to relocate.

Items related to a working gridiron are a *loading platform*, a *lock rail*, and/or a *pin rail*. The loading platform provides a storage and access platform near the grid so that the counterweight carriage can be loaded with weight while the *grips*, stagehands who work on the floor, are placing curtains or scenery on the batten. The lock rail is a long piece of steel angle to which the rope locks are attached. In the case of rope sets a *belaying pin*, which is a hardwood or steel shaft some two feet in length and a little over an inch in diameter, is set through a rail thus called a pin rail. The rail may be located on the floor level or it may be elevated according to the operation of the given stage.

STAGE CURTAINS

Curtains are employed as a means of deciding when and what the audience is to see. The *main curtain*, *front curtain*, *house curtain*, or *act curtain* is usually the first decorative curtain on the stage. It is used to block off the view of the total stage. Associated with it may be a horizontal *grand border* immmediately behind it. This wide curtain is a little over half the proscenium height and is used to determine the height of the picture that will be presented to the audience. Some stages still have a *valance* which is a short curtain just in front of the main that permanently lowers the usable proscenium height.

What other curtains are to be used on stage depends upon the size of the stage and the budget for its operation. Usually included is a *cyclorama set* which is made up of a number of curtains providing a visual cave. Above the stage they will be *borders* or *teasers* which are wider than the playing space but short in height. These are used to mask the view of the audience from the *flies*, *fly space*, or *loft*.

The *leg drops* or side leg drops are tall but narrow pieces of fabric hung at the sides of the stage to mask the backstage areas. The set or pair of legs farthest downstage are usually referred to as *tormentors*.

Travelers are curtains which are placed on a track so that they can move horizontally. The farthest one downstage is usually the main curtain. Most often another traveler will be placed from eight to fourteen feet up stage of the main. It will be called the *intermission curtain* or *oleo curtain*. This is used to cover scene changes between full stage numbers while a smaller scene or act is being done in front of it. There is no limitation as to the number of travelers that can be installed on a stage. Some stages are rigged with traveler tracks on the leg drops to provide a fast way of changing the visual width of the playing space.

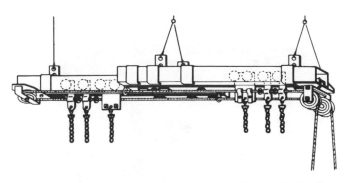

courtesy Automatic Devices Co.

To complete the cyclorama set the rear wall will be covered. In the older style of stage rigging the sides and rear were covered with curtains suspended into a "U" - shaped arrangement with the audience looking into the top of the "U". The advantage of this arrangement was that it provided a maximum of space backstage for storage and waiting. The disadvantage was the problem created for the movement of people and scenery on and off stage. In newer border/leg arrangements the legs and rear curtain are suspended parallel to the proscenium wall and the upstage unit referred to as the *rear curtain* or *rear traveler* or *back drop*.

The term *"drop"* applies to any curtain which, in its used position, touches the floor. Travelers are drops as are back drops, leg drops, and painted drops; the latter being large sheets of duck, muslin or canvas on which some scene has been painted.

LINE SCHEDULE

At the end of this chapter is a line schedule. You should have one for your stage to assist you in planning locations for shows. Yours may be more or less elaborate, but will provide you with the information you need to position sets and props on your stage.

KNOTS

A stagehand needs to know some basic *knots* to work on any stage. The more knots you know, the better off you are. To start you need to know how to tie a *bowline*, a *clove hitch*, a *half hitch*, and a *sheet bend*. These knots are shown in the dictionary as well as in other books.

BIBLIOGRAPHY
B-12, 14, 16, 23, 25, 27, 38, 39
P-1, 3, 5, 6
M-2, 17, 20, 24, 26

GLOSSARY

act curtain 7
acting area 1
apron 3
arbor 6
arena 1
auditorium 1
awnings 2
back drop 8
batten 5
batten heavy 7
belaying pin 7
blocks 4
borders 8
bowline, 8
center 3
center line 4
center staging 1
circle staging 1
clove hitch 8
counterweight carriage 6
curtain line 4
cyclorama set 8
dead hung 5
deus-ex-machina 2
doors 2
down stage 3
drop 8
eccyclema 2
endless line trim clamp 7
fir 4
flies 8
flooring 4
fly 7
fly space 5, 8
flying 4
flyman 7
front curtain 7
grand border 7
gridiron 5
grips 7
half hitch 8
half-round 2
head block 6
house curtain 7
imagination 1
intermission curtain 8

iron heavy 7
knots 8
knuckle buster 7
leg drops 8
line schedule 8
lines 5
loading platform 7
lock rail 6, 7
loft 5, 8
loft blocks 5
long line 5
main curtain 7
maple 4
oleo curtain 8
open stage 3
operating line 6
orchestra 2
parados 2
paraskene 2
periaktoi 2
pin rail 6
pit 3
proscenium 2, 3
raked 3
rear curtain 8
rear traveler 8
rope lock 6
scene building 2
scene wall 2
scenic background 1
set 7
set of lines 5
sheet bend 8
short line 5
sounding board 2
spot lines, 7
Stage left 3
stage right 3
take-up-block 6
teasers 8
theatre-in-the-round 1
three-quarter round 2
thrust 3
thymele 2
tormentors 8
Travelers 8
trimming clamp 7
underhung gridiron 5
up stage 3
upright gridiron 4
valance 7
working stage 4
"cyc" 4

North Central High School

Indpls., IN

Auditorium Line Schedule

Set No.	Dist. from Proscenium	Usual Contents	Notes
0	0'-3"	Fire Curtain	Automatic fall, also manual operation
1	1'-3"	Main Curtain	Light Blue, 20' high X 60' wide, fly or travel
2	2'-0"	Grand Border	Black, 10' high X 60' wide
3	2'-3"		
4	3'-2"	First Electric	4 color borderlight, 19 spot circuits repeat, 34' wide
5	4'-6"	Motion picture screen	18' high X 24' wide plus frame
6	side	Stage right light pipe	Double rack runs up/down stage
7	side	Stage left light pipe	Double rack runs up/down stage
8	6'-0"	Leg Drops	Black, 8' wide X 20' high
9	6'-6"		
10	7'-0"		
11	7'-6"		
12	8'-0"		
13	8'-6"		
14	9'-0"	Border Curtain	Black, 8' high X 60' wide
15	9'-6"	Leg Drops	Black, 11'wide X 20' high, on track
16	10'-6"	Intermission Curtain	Gold, 20' h X 60' wide, fly or travel
17	11'-6"	Second Electric	4 color borderlight, 10 spot circuits repeat, 39' wide
18	12'-6"		
19	13'-0"		
20	13'-6"		
21	14'-0"		
22	14'-6"		
23	15'-0"	Border Curtain	Black, 6' high X 60' wide
24	15'-6"	Leg Drops	Black, 11' wide X 20' high, on track
25	16'-6"	Traveler Track	Red, 20' high X 60' wide, fly, travel, tab, contour
26-27		NOT RIGGED	
28	17'-6"	Third Electric	4 color borderlight, 39' wide
29	Rope set	Stage left diagonal	
30	18'-6"		
31	19'-0"		
32	19'-6"		
33	20'-0"		
34	20'-6"	Border Curtain	Black, 6' high X 60' wide
35	21'-0"	Leg Drops	Black, 11' wide X 20' high, on tracks
36	22'-0"	Traveler Track	Black, 18' high X 60' wide, fly or travel
37	23'-0"	Fourth Electric	4 color borderlight, 39' wide
38	24'-0"		
39	Rope Set	Stage right diagonal	
40	24'-6"		
41	25'-0"		
42	25'-6"		
43	26'-0"		
44	26'-6"		
45	27'-0"		
46	27'-6"	Border Curtain	Black, 6' high X 60' wide
47	28'-0"	Leg Drops	Black, 20' high X 11' wide, on tracks
48	29'-0"	Fifth Borderlight	3 red, 6 blue, 3 green, 39' wide
49	Rope set		
50	30'-0"	Rear Traveler	Black, 20' high X 60' wide, fly or travel
51	31'-0"		
52	31'-6"		
53	32'-0"		

CHAPTER TWO

SAFETY

A stage and auditorium are points of concern to most fire departments, fire inspectors, and insurance underwriters. The auditorium is a gathering point for a large group of people, most of whom will be in less than familiar surroundings. The stage is not usually on the daily route of the building cleaning staff and, due to the uses of the stage, dust, dirt, debris, and small items from previous productions will gather.

The scenery shop, costume spaces, props areas, and the stage itself also present possible locations for personal injury due to the nature of the work done, materials and equipment handled, and the fact that the individuals involved are not always totally familiar with them.

While not all the materials used on stage and in the shops are flammable they lend a less-than-neat appearance and will cause the casual observer to feel that the area is unsafe. The area may well be unsafe since many use this situation as an excuse for having a messy stage.

FIRE SAFETY

By nature of the area a stage is prone to collect dust, and dust in great quantity in the air does contribute to possible fire. It settles on curtains, scenery, the floor, and can thus contribute to the deterioration of the *flameproofing* – if flameproofing has been used. Any stage using rope at any point in the rigging produces a problem in the flaking off of bits of manila or hemp as the rope is used. If these flakes are allowed to pile up under the lock or pin rail they produce a tinder pile which can be ignited by a glowing cigarette or a spark.

It is for this reason that smoking on stages is strictly forbidden in most locations. The individual cigarette as it is smoked is not the primary problem. The problem occurs when the unsmoked portion is carelessly discarded.

People also confuse *fireproof* and flameproof. Very few items, if any, are fireproof. Get anything hot enough and it will change form, i.e. burn. Even the nose cones of re- entry vehicles for space exploration have their limitations as to how much heat they can take and for how long.

Flameproofing merely means that in its original state the material was so treated. It will resist bursting into flame when brought into contact with a hot item such as a stage lighting instrument. The material will usually char and smoke, but that is all. Age causes deterioration of flameproofing compounds; thus stage curtain manufacturers and scenic houses who treat their scenery are quick to indicate the estimated life of their compound. For the most part, this life is five years on new stage curtains, less on scenery.

To do the job properly a curtain must be re-flameproofed when it is cleaned. Cleaning and reflameproofing stage curtains is getting to be so expensive that one is better off to look into getting a new curtain. Research continues to find a flameproofing compound that will stay in the fabric through the cleaning process.

On most stages there are some provisions made for fire safety. These provisions are often ignored or misunderstood. Crews often do not know where fire safety items are, what they are for, what their limitations are, or how to operate them. There are five types of provisions.

SAFETY DEVICES

Because the stage is a real fire hazard area and since the audience is watching the stage, the first concern is to get the stage separated from the audience. This is done (according to local building codes) usually with an asbestos *fire curtain* which is immediately behind the proscenium.

Due to the concerns over the use of friable asbestos many people panic at the thought of its use in a stage curtain. The key here is "friable" which is defined as "easily crumbled." Most of the fire curtains made are sealed one way or another. The OSHA concern is for the manufacture of the asbestos curtain (which was ceased in 1987), not its installation or use. Building codes for the most part now recognize a reinforced fiberglass material which is used as a replacement for these curtains.

A fire curtain is designed to descend automatically in case of high temperature on stage to seal off the proscenium opening and block the vision of the fire. With a fire out of sight there is less reason for panic, and the curtain will hold fire long enough for the audience to leave the hall. Fire curtains vary in form and manufacture, dependent upon the layout of the stage and again, the requirements of the local building codes. Some curtains provide for manual operation which allows the use of the curtain to block the opening before and after a performance, or to provide security for a set and its props while something else is taking place in the house.

A second set of fire safety provisions is usually coupled with the installation of the fire curtain. These are the *stage ventilators*, or *smoke vents*, and are rigged to open automatically at a given heat level. They act just as a damper in a chimney above a fireplace. When the damper is open, the smoke and flame go up and out. If the damper is closed, the smoke and flame go into the house. In case of fire and the closing of the fire curtain the ventilators provide a route of travel for the superheated air which is responsible for so much damage and for the spread of fire. Some ventilators will be found which can be operated manually in addition to the automatic trip. They can be used to release the build-up of hot air in the loft during performances in warm weather when no air conditioning is present.

A third type of fire safety device is the *fire extinguisher*. It is a visually familiar item and is often seen around buildings. Unfortunately, relatively few people know how or when to use one. Fire extinguishers are devices of limited use and call for knowledge on the part of the user. Each type of extinguisher is different in method of operation so each person working on a stage should be familiar with the location and exact method of operation of the particular extinguishers in the area. Some must be turned upside down to operate. Others will operate only in the upright position.

Most important is the rating of the extinguisher. Rating indicates the class of fire and relative effectiveness on that fire. *Fire classifications* are: Class A–cloth, wood, paper, etc.; Class B–flammable liquids; Class C–electrical. In addition to the letter of class indication, there is a number rating which designates relative effectiveness. The larger the number, the more effective the extinguisher.

FIRE EXTINGUISHER/ AGENT CHARACTERISTICS

SUITABLE FOR USE ON TYPE OF FIRE	AGENT CHARACTERISTICS	Available Sizes	Horizontal Range	Discharge Time
WATER A	Basically tap water. Discharges in a solid or spray stream. (May contain corrosion inhibitor which leaves a yellow residue.) Protect from freezing!	2½ Gal.	30 to 40 ft.	1 Minute
ANTI-FREEZE SOLUTION A	Basically a Calcium Chloride solution to prevent freezing. Discharges a solid or spray stream. Leaves residue. Non-freezing.	2½ Gal.	30 to 40 ft.	1 Minute
LOADED STREAM A B	Basically an alkali-metal-salt solution to prevent freezing. Discharges a solid or spray stream. Leaves residue. Non-freezing.	2½ Gal.	30 to 40 ft.	1 Minute
MULTIPURPOSE DRY CHEMICAL ★ A B C OR B C (A CAPABILITY)	Basically Ammonium Phosphate. Discharges a yellow cloud. Leaves residue. Non-freezing. Some extinguishers utilizing this agent do not have an "A" rating — however, they are designated as having "A" capability.	2 to 30 lbs.	5 to 20 ft.	8 to 25 Sec.
PURPLE-K DRY CHEMICAL ★ B C	Basically Potassium Bicarbonate. Discharges a bluish cloud. Leaves residue. Non-freezing.	2 to 30 lbs.	5 to 20 ft.	8 to 25 Sec.
KCL DRY CHEMICAL ★ B C	Basically Potassium Chloride. Discharges a white cloud. Leaves residue. Non-freezing.	2 to 30 lbs.	5 to 20 ft.	8 to 25 Sec.
POTASSIUM BICARBONATE/UREA DRY CHEMICAL ★ B C	Basically Potassium Bicarbonate/Urea. Discharges a white cloud. Leaves residue. Non-freezing.	11 to 23 lbs.	15 to 30 ft.	8 to 31 Sec.
REGULAR DRY CHEMICAL ★ B C	Basically Sodium Bicarbonate. Discharges a white cloud. Leaves residue. Non-freezing.	1 to 30 lbs.	5 to 20 ft.	8 to 25 Sec.
CARBON DIOXIDE B C	Basically an inert gas that discharges a cold white cloud. Leaves no residue. Non-freezing.	2½ to 20 lbs.	3 to 8 ft.	8 to 30 Sec.
HALOGENATED AGENT B C	Basically halogenated hydrocarbons. Discharges a white vapor. Leaves no residue. Non-freezing.	2½ to 5 lbs.	4 to 8 ft.	8 to 10 Sec.
DRY POWDER SPECIAL COMPOUND ★ D	Basically Sodium Chloride or Graphite materials. Agent is discharged from an extinguisher in a solid stream or is applied with a scoop or shovel to smother combustible metal. Leaves residue. Non-freezing.	30 lbs.	5 to 20 ft.	25 to 30 Sec.

★ NOTE: Available in stored pressure or cartridge operated types.

A NOTE: Pump tanks available.

Soda-acid extinguishers which are found in many schools and public buildings are for use in fighting Class A fires. They are similar in looks to *water* filled tanks which have been pressurized with air. Either projects its contents with such pressure that it would spread a burning liquid and, the fluids being conductors of electricity, are not recommended for use on liquid or electrical equipment fires. Water is present in each and would dampen and weight paper, wood, fabric, and the like, so the material would not blow away in the force of the stream.

CO_2 and *dry powder* type extinguishers do not expel liquid. Either the gas expelled by the CO_2 or the powder of the dry type would have a tendency to blow burning bits of material around. Both of these work by forming a "blanket" of gas which forces oxygen away from the flame thus causing it to go out. Neither gas nor dry powder conducts electricity, thus allowing the use of either on electrical fires.

A newer chemical type, a very efficient extinguisher, uses *halon*. It is a more effective material to use in that it works to eliminate the fire faster and cleaner than the others. But it is a more expensive method.

A fourth fire safety consideration usually found on a stage is a *fire alarm system*. Participants should be aware of this system, where its stations are located, and whom it notifies. Some systems simply provide an audible internal building alarm while others also alert the local fire department.

In case of fire summon help first. The first few moments of a fire tell how bad it will be and the longer start it has, the harder it is to fight. Attempting to control a small fire with a hand extinguisher and failing will only encourage the fire with a good start. Firemen would rather get a call on a small fire and arrive to find that after they had been called the flame was extinguished.

A fifth method of protection required in stages and shops by some local codes is the automatic *sprinkler system*. Examples of such systems may be seen in most department stores. They consist of individually activated sprinkler heads which will release a heavy flow of water when the temperature in the immediate area reaches a designated level. Many of these systems also have a built-in alarm which notifies the local fire department when any water flows in the system.

Many public buildings also contain wall-mounted *fire hoses*. These, like fire extinguishers, have limitations. Most of the fire hoses, for instance, must be entirely removed from their racks or reels and the valve manually opened before they can be operated. A kink or fold in the hose can limit its operation, and if there is sufficient pressure to flip this kink out the moving hose would probably have sufficient power to cause injury to anyone it struck.

Fortunately fire today is relatively uncommon on stages. Better enclosures on lights and better flameproofing materials have helped. Since a stage is most susceptable to fire, it is wise for the personnel working in the area to be familiar with the equipment at hand and what to do in case fire starts. Planning eliminates panic.

INDIVIDUAL SAFETY

Our other point of concern is for personal safety. Because tools are being used, pieces of scenery constructed and moved, items perhaps flown or hung overhead, and battens moved up and down, the stage and related areas are points of concern for safety.

In chapter six on tools a number of safety practices are mentioned. As an overall rule workers in this area should wear leather *shoes*, not sneakers. Leather will provide MUCH more protection than cloth when something is dropped, a platform rolled over toes, or a board with nails is left where one can step on it. Nothing takes the place of care, but we need all the help we can get.

Some sort of *eye protection* should be worn while using saws, drills, or even hammers, and while erecting a set or hanging scenery. The tools named all throw chips and the other work causes the crew members to look up a lot where there is liable to be dust, dirt, or other foreign matter falling.

Ideally the set-up and strike crews should wear *gloves* to guard against splinters, exposed hardware, or other items likely to cause injury. Rigging system operators should also wear gloves to help eliminate rope splinters and rope burns.

While operating any motor driven tool be sure that clothing is secured. Properly fitted *shop coats* not only protect your own clothing; they also provide an additional layer of protection.

Society is becoming more aware of the hazards to humans caused by *chemicals*. Individual chemicals can pose problems but the combination of elements also can be dangerous. The worker needs to read the label carefully on any liquid being used and if unsure of its possible danger, get a professional opinion. Danger is present if you inhale fumes. A great quantity of ventilation needs to be provided when spraying paints, mixing compounds for fiberglass or Celastic, or even when applying commercial paints.

Of equal concern is chemical burn on the skin or in the eyes. A scene shop can contain as many dangerous chemicals as a chemistry laboratory so care MUST be exercised.

Several safety monographs, pamphlets, catalogs, and brochures are available. The United States Institute for Theatre Technology (U.S.I.T.T.) has a commission on Theatre Safety and publishes most useful information. In addition you may check to see what company holds the insurance on your facility and ask them to send someone out to do a safety seminar for you.

BIBLIOGRAPHY

S- 6, 7

GLOSSARY

CHAPTER THREE

PRODUCTION STAFF AND CREWS

During the performance of a production the audience is aware of the actions and capabilities of the performers on stage. As an observer does not see all of an iceberg, the major portion of it being under water, the audience does not see all of the work that goes on before and during and after the performance. This supporting work is done by a great number of participants, often greater than the number in the cast. All of these unseen people on backstage and other production crews, help toward the goal of triggering the imagination of the audience.

A charting of the total production takes on the look of a diamond with the cast at the center and the whole thing balancing on the audience point.

The people working backstage and those who worked with the production prior to its actual presentation are all members of the production staff and production crews. Their individual jobs vary from theatre to theatre due to the difference in talents available and the demands of each situation. In the professional form of theatre an individual is hired for personal talent or capability. In many amateur theatres today people are chosen for given tasks only because they want to try it – with or without any background of experience or training. In educational theatre individuals take on the tasks because they want to learn.

Many educational theatres are arranged so that a student can provide physical presence without much, if any, mental operation. A job is undertaken simply to do the job. If this happens, the educational theatre is really non-existent.

The philosophy of an educational theatre should be to train through guided experience each individual who expresses a true interest in theatre. This true interest is evidenced by a desire to become involved in each and every facet of the total operation. Through this involvement the participant can gain knowledge of the requirements of each position. Through this knowledge one can work to do a single job better in

relation to those around when he finally chooses his own specific section of theatre.

While job descriptions differ from place to place due to local requirements and the personal abilities of others on the staff, this chapter is an attempt to outline broadly the tasks and draw some conclusions about the staff and crew responsibilities. An overall view of the totality of the project is shown by the six-week production schedule which has been included at the end of this chapter. In addition copies of some of the forms used to assist in training students and maintaining records are printed. Forms will be found at the ends of several chapters.

PRODUCTION STAFF

PRODUCER

The *producer* in a commercial theatre can be considered a professional gambler. This is the individual who decides to do a show and proceeds to gather money to finance the venture. Since the producer is often heard more than seen the responsibilities are often not fully recognized. The initial work of selecting a script, choosing a director, and hiring a designer is more than meets the eye. If the producer has chosen well, then the job is only to be a guiding hand to coordinate and to make command decisions.

In educational theatre the drama or theatre department is actually the producing agent. Money to be spent comes from the department treasury and profits derived will be put back into the treasury. The selection of personnel for the staff is done either by the department head or by the director – and often these two are one and the same person. There is the possibility that one person may be given the title of producer, but more often than not he will have less actual responsibility than a professional producer.

PRODUCTION RESPONSIBILITIES

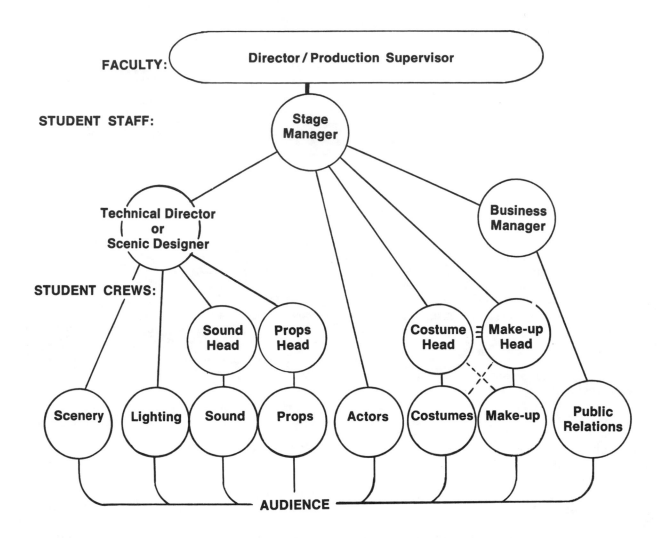

DIRECTOR

A *director* is the interpreter of the play as a whole; the one who is concerned with the total picture and decides just how to arrive at that total. The director determines the concept of the production; that is if it is to be realistic, stylized, expressionistic, or fantasy. The director instructs the actor as to the type of character to be portrayed and tells designers of costumes, lighting, and settings what their crafts are to create. The director in essence is calling for individual pieces which must be carefully shaped, cut, and then fit together as a finished product.

If the director is to direct rather than aim or choreograph a show, there must be a background of knowledge and understanding of all of the crafts with which he is dealing. Decisions must be made

affecting the interrelations of the blocking with the setting, lighting, sound, props, and costumes. This ability comes through training and experience, not through appointment.

In educational theatre the director most often maintains control of the production throughout its presentation while in professional theatre the control is relinquished to the stage manager at dress rehearsal. The reason for this goes back to the fact that the educational theatre director has the primary responsibility of teaching. The observation of the experiment and the reporting of its result are necessary steps in the job of educating the participants in the production. While the friends of the participants may love what was done, the director has to look at the relationships as a whole. After observation the responsibility is to be candid.

The director's job is somewhat like that of the tailor. The producer has found a pleasing script (bolt of cloth). There is a style of production (a pattern) that the producer would like to use. End result is that a tailor (director) is hired to cut the fabric according to the pattern and put it together to fit the particular situation.

Often with the true producer not present in amateur or educational theatre the director will treat the script and its directions as gospel. From the book will come the set diagrams, lighting cues, and the lines and stage directions. It is sort of like buying a ready-made suit; it fits and covers, but not really as well as a tailor-made item. What the director and cast are doing is a copy or imitation of an earlier presentation–not a production of their own.

PRODUCTION SUPERVISOR

In some instances a second administrative level person will be available. This person is known as the *production supervisor*. The implication is that responsibility for the physical plant (auditorium, stage, and shop areas) as well as the crews dealing with these areas will be assumed to relieve the Director of direct concern for these details.

STAGE MANAGER

Second in command to the professional director is the *stage manager*. This position is often misunderstood and in educational or amateur theatre is given to just anyone who happens to be available. To really do the job the stage manager must have a working knowledge of all of the elements of the production.

The stage manager must be able to: coach actors should the director be absent; intelligently discuss any technical problem with any staff member; take many of the relatively minor decisions and problems from the director's busy schedule. A stage manager must know when to make a decision and when it must be referred to the director.

During rehearsals the stage manager fabricates the *prompt book* – a copy of the script which includes the marking of all of the blocking, business, and cues. In addition to keeping attendance and contacting those not present, other tasks include noting the possible locations for all technical cues and marking actor warning cues if used.

The major responsibilities during the performances of the show will be to check attendance, call "half-hour" thirty minutes prior to curtain time, "places" at curtain time, then call cues as well as keep track of the progress of the show.

As the person in charge of the performance the stage manager will often be the one to indicate to an actor that there was an entrance missed or that cues are slow, that lines are muffed, etc.

This is a position of utmost responsibility – indeed it is the top student staff position in educational theatre and one which should be filled by a person who has experience in many other production areas.

After the show the stage manager collects all of the various cue sheets and show records and places them with the prompt script. This will provide an accurate, complete record of the show.

The experience of stage management is additional education toward the end of being a totally oriented theatre individual. Having taken instructions as a crew member, learning lines and blocking as a performer, the stage manager must be prepared to give some direction and take the responsibilities that come with decision making.

ACTOR - RELATED CREWS

Holding the position indicated as the top point of the diamond of responsibility the stage manager has direct control over the *actor-related* areas of a production. This includes the performers and things directly related, such as costume and make-up.

The cast itself is the only crew actually seen as such. They are the ones around which the production work revolves and it is toward their support that the rest of the machinery operates. The job of the *actor* is also the only one which is the same in educational, amateur, or professional theatre: to interpret the character.

The *costume crew* and *make-up crew* may be separate or combined, dependent upon the number in the cast and the complexity of the work required. Some educational theatres treat make-up as an actor craft much as the professional theatres do. These schools call for the individual to do his own work, thus learning the process. Others provide a make-up crew thereby teaching the actor as well as the crew member. There is no right or wrong method, only a difference in teaching technique.

Costuming is often done in the same manner. A problem occurs if each actor, or more probably a mother, does the individual costume. This can produce a lack of visual continuity in the production. An individual often loses sight of the total effect and strives to stand out as an individual rather than contributing as a member of a total production.

Many books deal with acting as well as with costume and make-up therefore we shall not go any deeper into these areas which are the core of the diamond.

The audience-related and the stage-related crews form the sides of our diamond.

AUDIENCE - RELATED CREWS

BUSINESS MANAGER

The *business manager* is responsible for the finances and all of those elements of the production dealing directly with the public. Often this area is called *public relations*. Encompassed are publicity tickets, and ushering. Some of these facets must be addressed perhaps even before casting or rehearsals begin since there is often a time lag between submittal of material to a printer and the finished product.

Dependent upon student enthusiasm and participation, public relations can be handled by a single crew or by separate crews. Either way can work, but the comments herein will be directed toward a single public relations crew headed by a business manager.

The overall *publicity* project is to make known to all persons who might be interested that the show will be performed. Use an adaptation of the journalistic approach by answering who, what, when, where, and how much. A decision on the general publicity approach must be made, then specific duties and deadlines assigned to each crew member. Posters must be designed and ordered early. Releases, cast and crew lists and a show synopsis need to be prepared and distributed. If radio or TV spots are used the stations need to have the public service materials quite far ahead, so the announcements need to be written and sent.

One of the best methods of selling *tickets* for a non-reserved house is to have the tickets printed with sequential numbers. They are then packed into groups of ten tickets each. A member of the crew should appear at rehearsals and crew calls as soon as the tickets are available — usually two weeks prior to the show — to sign out the packets for cast and crew members to sell to their friends and acquaintances. These are to be signed for on the *Ticket Distribution* form (Form B-1). Tickets and/or money are to be turned in at the latest the day after the show closes. (Copies of forms are located at the end of this chapter.)

At this time the crew will need to distribute posters announcing the show and start local announcements about the production. Since this will be about two weeks before the show it is also a good time to make arrangements for the change for the box office.

The business manager needs to assign, train, and supervise those who will sell tickets at the door. These are the people who make the first public contact and present an initial attitude to the audience.

If a person purchases a ticket from a sassy or sullen ticket salesperson this experience can be carried to the seat. The actor has to overcome this attitude without even knowing that it exists. It is indeed unfortunate but it often happens because the ticket salesperson does not realize the importance of the position in the total operation.

Each seller is responsible for completing the *Box Office Report* (Form B-2) for the portion of the sales period. Our box office normally opens forty-five minutes before curtain time and closes just prior to the first intermission. At that time the box office staff retires to the office to count tickets turned in to get a house count, and to tally the sales and balance the books. The daily box office report is completed and the deposit prepared. Note of the deposit is made on the *Deposit Report* (Form B-3).

The crew members who are not working in the box office will form the *usher crew*. They need to be present, neatly attired, ten minutes before the house is to open. They, like the ticket sellers, must project a positive, pleasant attitude as they deal with the individual patrons. For non-reserved seating these crew members must be available before the show to take tickets and distribute programs. For reserved seat houses they must also know the seating layout so they can be efficient guides. They also need to be in place during intermission(s) to answer questions for the audience members and guide them to rest rooms or refreshment stands. At the end of the show they need to do a visual check of the seating area for lost items and then secure the doors.

Quite often the ushers for school plays will utilize the time during the final performance to go around and remove the advertising posters and any other show-related items which have been posted in the building and immediate area. The business manager can make sure that the technical director has turned in the *Production Costs* form (Form B-4) so that the *Production Accounting* (Form B-5) can be completed.

This crew will utilize days after the show to complete the financial records of the show, get all of the ticket packs and/or money returned from the individuals, and clear all posters and other publicity items missed earlier. This completed, the crew can be dismissed.

TECHNICAL DIRECTOR / SCENIC DESIGNER

The stage related crews are headed by the *technical director* or *scenic designer*. The exact title is determined by the background of the individual and the precise nature of the job to be done.

To be a scenic designer one must have sufficient background in architectural drafting, decorating basics, and an understanding of scenery construction and painting. The designer will produce plans and sketches for the production, have them approved by the director and then supervise their construction and finish.

If there is no one available to design the show internally, then the design will come form another source and a technical director will be used.

The technical director takes someone else's designs and supervises their construction, painting, erection, operation, strike, and storage.

Whether actually designing the sets or not, this staff member must be experienced enough to envision the exact methods of erection of the set or the placement of a prop during the time that the set or prop is being built. This is the only way that the production can be assured of a smooth transition from building to physical placement on the stage. Problems of fitting, painting, or operation must be worked out as much as possible prior to the time the units are actually placed on the stage since stage time is usually at a premium and is wasted when the stage crew has to make a great number of changes or must compensate for some unforeseen situation.

In general the jobs of either the scenic designer or technical director are parallel once the set is designed. Either needs to be very familiar with the play, then be able to: check stock and order any supplies needed (paint, lumber, hardware, etc.); select crews from the *Crew Sign-Up Sheet* (Form O-1) and post crews and calls (*Crew Call*, Form O-2); plan training sessions for those crew members who might need them; schedule work for calls including clean-up and proper storage of the tools at the end of each call; assign crew positions for the running of the show; supervise the running of the show; strike and store the set; supervise the final clean-up of the shop; inventory stock and order what is needed; figure the costs of the scenic part of the show; evaluate the crew members, then compile all of the plans, cue sheets, and other materials to be delivered to the stage manager.

With responsibility for the properties, sound, scenery and lighting crews this staff member needs to be familiar with what each of these crews does and techniques they use. During the technical and dress rehearsals one needs to be in the house with the director and/or production supervisor to take notes for the crews, then plan work sessions to take care of any defects.

STAGE - RELATED CREWS

The four stage-related crews handle properties, sound, lighting and scenery.

PROPERTIES AND SOUND

The responsibilities of the *properties crew* and *sound crew* are covered later in this book by a chapter dealing with each.

SCENERY (STAGE) CREW

The *scenery crew* is responsible for building, painting, erecting, operating, striking, and storing the set(s) for the show.

No doubt there will be crew members who "specialize" in some of the things covered in chapters six through twelve in this book. They will be of value to the supervisor since they can share their expertise with others on the crew. There will be a lot of construction, painting, and detail work to get the sets ready. In the case of a musical or variety show this may include the sewing and painting of backdrops.

There will be manual labor involved during construction as well as during set-up, running of the show, and strike. All of this is most important to the show and, while it seems mundane, is really one of the factors of differentiation between a below average, average, or above average production.

LIGHTING CREW

Chapters thirteen through nineteen all deal with the things which members of the *lighting crew* need to know. They must transfer this information into working knowledge of their own facility and equipment.

Members of the lighting crew need to inventory all of their color media, check their instruments and replace any burned out lamps, clean lenses and / or reflectors, if necessary, and check over the cables available to them. Each member of the crew should be familiar with the control system to know its capabilities and limitations.

If you are working a musical or variety show you need to know follow spot operation if one will be used in the show.

The lighting must be planned to be sure that it is coordinated with the scenery to be used for the show so that there is as little conflict in used space as possible.

AUDIENCE

The *audience* is the bottom point of the diamond, the point upon which the entire project balances. Our diamond-forming lines of responsibility diverge from the director and encompass the staff and crews before they converge again on the audience. This is the point of judgment and if any part of the operation is too heavy or too light, the balance will be missing.

The audience bears a responsibility, especially in educational theatre. It seldom accurately discharges this responsibility. People should be frankly critical of the production and should state what they think. "You were good" is a usual comment.

This is a pleasing reaction but it gives the actor no point of relation to the rest of the production. As in team sports theatre is a group effort and but for the presence of others the individual performer would be incomplete.

This message often seems to be lost on members of the audience as they run backstage after a show to congratulate their friends, then leave the theatre talking among themselves about parts which could have been better. Why not share honest views with the cast and crew members? Why not see what the problem was with a given cue which looked slow? These presentations are done to sharpen the skills of the participants, whether in educational, amateur, or professional theatre, and through recognition of effect upon the audience that whetting is accomplished.

BIBLIOGRAPHY
B - 8, 9, 11, 12, 16, 22, 23, 25, 30, 31
P - 1, 4, 5, 6

GLOSSARY

Six Week Production Schedule

North Central
High School
Indpls., IN.

Production

Form

O-3

Week Before Show	Costumes	Make-up	Public Relations	Scenery	Lighting	Sound	Properties
6	Casting, crew sign-up Mon - Wed. All crews posted on Friday						
5	List & Measure	Plan	Cast/Crew lists, Synopsis	Plan	Read Show	List what is needed	List what is needed
4	Build, Gather, Fit	Inventory Order	Letters to Schools, Program copy	Build	Plan	Gather	Collect, Build
3	Build, Gather, Fit		News releases, TV/Radio	Build	Inventory color media	Tape	Stand-ins for all
2	Build, gather		Posters out	Build	Clean, Hang	Tape	Run with all
1	Ready	Train crew	Daily announce-ments	Set-up	Gel, Focus	Run with rehearsals	Run with rehearsals

PRODUCTION WEEK: All crew members are to plan to see the show from out front during technical or dress rehearsals. No crew members are to be out front during performances.

	Costumes	Make-up	Public Relations	Scenery	Lighting	Sound	Properties
TECHNICAL REHEARSAL 1st HALF:							
	Finish	Apply	Noon Sales	Touch-up Set cues	Set cues	Set cues	Complete plot
TECHNICAL REHEARSAL 1st HALF:							
	Finish	Apply	Noon Sales	Set cues	Set cues	Set cues	Polish
DRESS REHEARSAL							
	Dress	Apply	Noon sales	Run	Run	Run	Run
PERFORMANCES							
	Dress	Apply	Box office, Usher	Run	Run	Run	Run

STRIKE: All crew members help clear, clean, repair, return, store all items in their proper locations

Ticket Distribution

North Central
High School
Indpls., IN

Form
B-1

RETURNED:

Ticket Block	STUDENT NAME	Home Room	Tickets	$.$$	Batch	Tally
01-10						
11-20						
21-30						
31-40						
41-50						
51-60						
61-70						
71-81						
81-90						
91-00						

PURPOSE OF THIS FORM:

**To list the students assigned the numbered packets
of tickets for their personal sale.**

USE OF THIS FORM:

Ticket Block						
01-10						
11-21						
21-30						
31-40						
41-50						
51-60						
61-70						
71-80						
81-90						
90-00						

To the left of the 01-10 series, add the hundreds digit.

Students sign for the ticket packets.

**Upon return the business manager notes the amount
of money and the number of tickets returned.**

**We use individual envelopes for ticket returns so we
have written record of the return. Envelopes are
opened and recorded in batches as they come in.**

TOTALS THIS PAGE

CARRIED FROM PRIOR PAGE

CUMULATIVE TOTAL

Box Office Report

North Central
High School
Indpls., IN.

Production

Form
B-2

Dates:_____ Day:_____ Ticket Price (s):_____

Sales Session		Show 1		Show 2		Show 3		Money	Sellers
		A	C	A	C	A	C		
	STOP								
	START								
	SALES								
	STOP								
	START								
	SALES								
	STOP								
	START								
	SALES								
	STOP								
	START								
	SALES								
	STOP								
	START								
	SALES								
SHEET RESOLUTION:								Cash	Checked by:
Stop									
Start									
SALES									

PURPOSE OF THIS FORM:

To track ticket sales at each box office session.

USE OF THIS FORM:

The form is designed to track tickets for three shows, with adult and child tickets for each show.

Assuming that you have numbered tickets, enter the starting number for each type in the proper space.
At the end of the session enter the stop number, then subtract to find the number sold.

Multiply by the ticket price to determine sales amount.

Check against the money on hand.

The same process will allow a full day check.
(we sell during five lunch periods then evening

Deposit Report

| North Central High School Indpls., IN. | Production | | | | | | Form B-3 |

Deposit Number	Date	Dollar Value of Tickets Sold			Batch Number	Total Deposit	Receipt	
		Noon Sales	Door Sales	Envelopes			Number	Date
1								
2								
3								
4								
5								
6								
7								
8								
9								
10								
11								
12								
13								
14								
15								
16								
17								
18								
19								
TOTALS =								

PURPOSE OF THIS FORM:

To tally the deposits showing source and amount from each source.

USE OF THIS FORM:

Columns are self-explanatory.

For student sales note that you can track the amount taken from each group (batch) of envelopes.

To close the show accounting total each column, then add horizontally to cross-check.

Use the "NOTES" section to indicate any discrepancies.

NOTES:

Production Costs   (scene shop)

North Central High School Indpls., IN.	Production	Form B - 4

Date:_____Charge to:_____Acct. #_____

NOTE: All items become or remain the property of North Central Stage Crew.   TOTAL BILLING:$

1. Stock expendable items (nails, screws, bolts, tool depreciation, etc.)		
2. LUMBER		
3. FABRICS		
4. PAINT:		
5. SOUND / VIDEO:		
6. COLOR MEDIA:		
7.		
8.		
9.		
10.		
Total		

PURPOSE OF THIS FORM:

To track the materials used for a show, and their cost

USE OF THIS FORM:

Enter indication of what and how much was used, then its cost.

For the sake of simplicity we have established a stock cost for the first entry so we are covered for our shop materials.

The total amount is charged against the show (See Production Accounting Form B-5).

Production Accounting

North Central
High School
Indpls., IN.

Production	

Form

B - 5

Show Dates   Paid Attendance   Comp. Attendance   Total Attendance

_____   _____   _____   _____

_____   _____   _____   _____

_____   _____   _____   _____

Show Totals: _____   _____   _____

RECEIPTS: Student Sales:_____   List Special Sales:

Lunch Hour Sales:_____   A:_____

Door Sales:_____   B:_____

Special Sales:_____   C:_____

TOTAL RECEIPTS.......................$_____

EXPENDITURES:

Accompaniment	$_____
Books	$_____
Choreography	$_____
Costumes	$_____
Custodians	$_____
Make-up	$_____
Orchestra	$_____
Printing	$_____
Piano Tuning	$_____
Props	$_____
Publicity	$_____
Royalty	$_____
Scenery	$_____
Security	$_____
Sound/Video	$_____

PURPOSE OF THIS FORM:

To provide an overall look at the expenses incurred for a show.

USE OF THIS FORM:

Enter attendance figures at the top.

Enter receipts in spaces provided.

Enter expenses as used in the production.

Do the math required to determine profit or loss from the show.

TOTAL EXPENDITURES. . . . . $_____

NET PROFIT . . . .$_____

Crew Sign - up

North Central
High School
Indpls., IN.

Production	Form O - 1

CALLS:

TECH:
DRESS:
SHOWS:

CREW: _____

CREW: _____

NAME	Home Room	Year Grad	NAME	Home Room	Year Grad

PURPOSE OF THIS FORM:

To provide a means of determining which students are available and interested in working a crew.

USE OF THIS FORM:

Indicate the general calls proposed, and the dates and times of production week.

Post on the call board for a period of time to allow all who are interested to see.

CREW CALL

North Central High School Indpls., IN.	Production	Form O - 2

CREW_____ POSTED BY_____ DATE_____

Crew Members   Crew Calls

PURPOSE OF THIS FORM:

To indicate which students will work a crew, and the exact call times.

USE OF THIS FORM:

List from the sign-up sheet the names of those whom you have chosen to work the crew.

Students accepting the assignment will initial their names so you are aware that they have seen the calls.

Please Initial Your Name

CHAPTER FOUR

PROPERTIES

The Properties Crew provides all properties for a show. It is faced with a four-step job as the show begins. The crew must determine what is needed, get it, maintain it, store it, and finally return it.

This crew needs to be formed early and start work just as soon as the actors begin rehearsals. It is important that each member of the crew read the script so there is an awareness of not only what props are needed, but how these items fit into the show.

It is the responsibility of the crew head to check carefully with the Director to assure proper color, style, size, shape, type, and period of the individual items. The Technical Director will assist in procuring items once the crew can identify the requirements.

At the first full crew meeting the Props Head assigns at least one member of the crew, preferably two, to each rehearsal scheduled. A list of the assignments should be given to the Stage Manager, one posted on the call board, one given to the Technical Director, and one kept by the crew head. The entire crew should work on making the initial Properties List (Form P-1). Sample forms are found at the end of this chapter.

The crew head is responsible for seeing that each crew member is supplied with a time card and that it is filled out for each call attended. The crew head posts calls for the crew and assumes responsibility to cover any absences. A minimum of 36 hours notice should be given for a call.

DETERMINING PROPS

Starting with the first blocking rehearsal and continuing for the run of the production, there must be at least one representative of this crew at each cast call in order to complete a listing of all the props needed in the show. The prop list is formed by carefully checking the script and its props listing. In addition carefully listen to rehearsal to list required props not shown as well as those mentioned by the

director. List these item on the *Properties List* (FORM P-1).

The crew members work with the Stage Manager to assure that there are chairs available and set in place to represent furniture. Furniture should be plotted on the *Property Set-Up Plan* (Form P-2). At the end of the rehearsal leave the updated forms for the crew head to check prior to the next call so the working list may be current.

DETERMINING - DEFINITION

Simple definition of properties is difficult. My attempt may leave confusion because this is a complex and changing area. Definition indicates to the properties crew the things for which they are responsible. Concisely, anything that looks portable to the audience, is a prop.

We are aware of the fact that a grand piano is much heavier than a canvas covered wood frame called a flat. People know that grand pianos come with wheels on them and therefore are considered portable. On the other hand a flat which has been painted to look like a brick wall should trigger the imagination to believe that it is permanent. Therefore the flat becomes scenery, the piano is a prop. Sometimes the use to which an item is put during the show will help label it.

Through mutual agreement the properties people may have the scenery crew build a bookcase into a wall. The books in it would remain props while the bookcase just became a part of the scenery. The definition is really immaterial, it just helps clarify responsibility.

DETERMINING - PURPOSES

As with any other thing on stage in view of the audience, a property must fulfill a purpose. By proper selection and use each prop becomes meaningful. This is why it is important that the properties crew members make sure that each item is just what the director had in mind so that it will perform its function.

There are three *purposes* of properties, and a given prop can and should fulfill more than one of these at a time.

The first is *to dress* the stage. Each property in itself will help make the stage picture more complete. A book may be required, but in its size, shape, and perhaps even color, it can help work toward a total picture. Many props are used simply as set dressing. They are not handled, moved, or used in any way by the actors. With these the concern is that they fit into the picture. Other props must be handled, used, or perhaps consumed. (They must fulfill all their responsibilities well.)

The second purpose of a property is *to interpret*. By its own character it interprets style and/or mood of the production. It also gives some insight into the background of the characters.

The furnishings of a home tell something about the residents. A stage set should be no different. Careful thought, selection and placement on the part of the properties crew will provide the audience with some insight into the characters the moment the curtain goes up.

The third purpose of a property is *to aid* the actor in his characterization, movement, or business. Business, the little things that an actor does to create the character he is portraying, is most important. If a prop does not function as it is supposed to, the illusion is broken and the actor is not aided. An umbrella that does not open easily, a trunk or suitcase with a sticky latch or a latch that fails to open will distract the audience and perhaps break the character of the actor.

The properties crew members must be aware of these purposes and keep them in mind throughout the show. With care and concern expressed in the finding of a specific prop, then care and concern must be utilized in maintaining it during the show. This is the reasoning behind the stage rule that people do not use the props unless they are doing it in the show. A broken chair, misplaced sword, or consumed food does not interpret, dress, or aid. These problems occur because of thoughtless individuals who do not understand what is going on.

DETERMINING - CLASSIFICATIONS

The labeling of classifications of properties provides an aid to the crew in checking their lists to make sure that they have covered all the necessary elements.

Set or scene props are those that are primarily to dress the stage. Pictures on the walls, draperies at the windows, books on shelves, articles of furniture including rugs, vases of flowers, all are examples of stage dressing. Some will simply be placed on stage to provide atmosphere while others may be handled or used by the actor.

If an actor actually carries or handles an item, it becomes a *hand prop*. Letters, telegrams, food, dishes, and any item of clothing which is carried but not worn, are examples of hand props. If an item of clothing is to be worn, then it must be obtained in a given size. In that case it becomes a costume. If it is to be only carried and size is of no concern, then it is a property.

The creation of *visual effects* by a means other than use of rays of light is also a project of the props crew. This includes rain, snow, smoke, and steam, or wind. Whether these are evident offstage through a window or appear on stage on an actor's clothing, they do aid, interpret, and dress and thus are classified as props.

Since *sound effects* also fulfill the three purposes they are often listed as a props responsibility. This is a carryover from the days when such effects were created manually, usually backstage. If an effect is done manually, it will probably be done by the properties crew since they are on stage and available to do the job. If the effect is electronically reproduced, chances are that the sound crew and associated tape decks will be off in some corner or even at the rear of the house. We will not cover sound here since there is a later chapter devoted to it.

GETTING PROPERTIES

During rehearsals the remainder of the crew with the crew head should be gathering items known to be needed. Thus begins the very large and exhaustive "treasure hunt".

Many theatres have their own prop rooms so this is the place to begin the search. Discovery is sometimes difficult because the last crew may not have done a proper job of storing their props. Remember this when it is time to put them away from your show. Props not readily available in the theatre must be borrowed, made, rented or purchased by the crew.

Set, scene, or hand props can be *borrowed* from homes, offices, or establishments which deal in the sale or repair of the item. The project of borrowing the props is the most usual since the greater portion of the educational or civic theatres are on limited budgets. To nurture greater cooperation in the lending of props it must be remembered that merchants are in business to sell. If sales can be encouraged by your borrowing, you are more likely to get the desired item. Program notes; "...through the courtesy of..."; signs in the lobby; acknowledgments; all help sell. Indicating to a merchant that his items will be seen by an estimated (total number of audience during the run) people will help you get your request fulfilled. Remember that there is little you can do to change the attitude of a merchant who has lent something before and it has been damaged, returned late, or returned by a rude student. The person lending you the prop is doing you a favor.

In many locales agencies such as Volunteers of America, Salvation Army, Goodwill, and others will lend larger items that have been given to them for salvage. Often smaller items they have are within the budget and can be purchased, but the larger items or seldom-used articles which take up so much storage space can be borrowed.

With many materials readily available today in plastics, fiberglass, woods, etc., the other possibility is to *make* the prop. If members of the crew are at all inclined toward model building, this can be a real opportunity to be resourceful and creative.

Properties that need to be built are usually designed as part of the total setting by the scenic designer. The item has been researched for size, shape, color, and materials, making sure that there is a total concept of the requirements of the item. Sketches are made, then a plan drawn.

Many common resources are available for use, balsa wood, clay, plaster of paris, papier mache, and plastic wood are some of the well-known materials. Other things more specifically suited for specific projects are: Celastic – a resin-impregnated fabric which, when softened with a (toxic) liquid and shaped, will dry hard and hold its shape, is waterproof and can be painted and works like wood; Cloth-mache, the cousin to papier mache, in which the paper is replaced with strips of cloth, is much more durable and will not split due to changes in temperature or humidity like the paper often does; Plaster cast material, like the doctor uses for casting broken limbs, works extremely well for joining odd items, for applique (third dimension) work on door frames or picture frames, is easily worked, and not too expensive.

The final step in building an item is to apply a finish. This has become easier recently with the availability of finishing materials in spray cans. A check of the hardware store shelves will provide finishes in almost any texture and degree of reflective quality. A combination of various finishes may be used to provide a desired look.

If a prop is so very unique that it will probably never be used again, you might *rent* it. If it is so common that it will be used often, buy it. If a prop is rented several things must be done. Check the pricing carefully. Many times the extended rental price will total almost the purchase price. If this is so, the item might be purchased and offered at a reduced rate to other groups in your area to help all concerned. Make sure the rental or purchase cost has been checked from as many sources as possible. If the property is mechanical, make sure that it does the required job in the manner that required. If the show has to be changed to accommodate the prop, then the prop is not the right one. If you are renting, assure yourself that you have a complete listing of the defects and damages to the unit on the rental invoice before you leave your source with it. This will save trouble in the long run.

If it becomes necessary to *purchase* items, the crew head must first check with the Technical Director indicating possible source(s) and projected cost. Money or a purchase order is obtained, then a receipt is brought back with the item(s). Any purchase over $5.00 probably will have to be approved by either the Director or the Technical Director.

VISUAL EFFECTS

Methods of getting or "doing" *visual effects* are many and varied. Only a few of those which have worked best are mentioned here.

The presentation of *smoke or steam* usually brings dry ice to mind. If proper equipment is available, fine. To provide any quantity of smoke or steam from this source it is necessary to have a container of hot, preferably boiling, water which can be kept hot. Dry ice will give off the visual vapor when immersed in water only until a covering of regular ice forms around the dry ice cake due to the temperature. To avoid this encasement the water must be kept hot. Since the resultant vapor is cold, it will drop toward the floor. The quantity and density of this covering will depend upon the temperature and air currents of the stage area, and the amount of movement. Obviously, if only a small quantity is needed, simply use a pan of hot water and a small amount of dry ice.

Dry ice is so low in temperature that it will cause rapid dehydration of the skin coming in contact with it. This is a burn and it can easily be a second-degree burn. A lesser point of caution is that dry ice will sometimes cause metal to "scream" if contact is made. Use the proposed equipment in several rehearsals to assure the effect desired.

Commercial smoke machines are available. These units have a heated area into which a liquid is sprayed. Pressure is provided in the unit in various ways, sometimes by plunger and sometimes by pressurized containers of the fluid. In this manner the amount of smoke can be controlled. Usually a basket adjacent to the nozzle is provided to hold dry ice. The smoke passing through this cooling chamber will thus fall to the floor level. It will not lay as well as dry-ice fog will.

Control is very important in the use of smoke and steam; therefore, it must be turned off and on at will. If it is necessary to fill the entire stage area probably more than one source is indicated. Air movement in the stage area will also affect the smoke/fog so rehearsal must be held with special care as to what doors are open, what blower speed is being used by the air handling system, etc.

Earlier units utilized an oil based liquid which had an odor reminiscent of insect spray. Later units use other liquids. Find one in which the odor is not too offensive and the quantity of smoke builds up quickly and disperses rather rapidly when the power is turned off.

Snow is another effect often desired. Producing an even, well distributed fall is the problem. Cut-up paper or confetti works fairly well but is difficult to get up off the floor. Shredded Styrofoam produces a most acceptable snow effect.

A "snow machine" is rather easily made by taking a strip of fabric about three feet wide and placing tie laces along each side. This will tie to adjacent battens and form a stage-width trough. Cut slits diagonally along a center line half-way between the tie-laces, the slits being six to eight inches in length.

Set the battens level and fill the trough with paper and when one batten is raised or lowered the paper will sift through the openings and provide a rather even fall.

For "snowing" Styrofoam use a piece of netting with about half-inch openings, and 6 inches wide. This is sewn between 18 inch pieces of fabric and suspended as the unit was for the paper. It is filled with the Styrofoam shreddings and the result is a sifting of the material. The Styrofoam seems to be better since it sweeps up easily and will stick to clothing in much the same manner that real snow will.

Rain is perhaps more of a problem than it is worth. A means of getting rid of it must be worked out at the same time that a method of producing it is prepared. To deliver the effect of rain only a narrow band the width of the audience vision need be produced. This can be done by cradling a length of pipe under a batten. The pipe has been carefully drilled with holes all at the same angle along the length of the pipe. The angle is important so that all streams of water are projected in the same plane. One end of the pipe is capped and a "T" handle and valve are supplied at the other end. The pipe must be level in its entire run. The holes are turned up and the pipe filled with water. On cue the valve is opened and the holes turned down and the rain will fall the full width of the stage. A trough below will catch the water and carry it off stage. Obviously there are problems and coordination is tricky. This is why a large rain effect is seldom seen on stage.

One of the most dangerous yet most called for effects is that of the *flash pot*. Usually smoke is to accompany the flash so the use of a flash bulb will not produce the desired effect. This effect requires a controlled explosion, and for this reason it is best if you rent or purchase a commercial flash pot.

If this cannot be done, then one way is to secure a container made of steel. An electrical junction box 6" X 6" X 4" does well. It is equipped with a heavy duty porcelain lamp socket with about two feet of fiberglass covered cable leading from it. A hinged cover of heavy screen or perforated metal is placed over the top. Keep in mind that you are creating an explosion, and what you want is a CONTROLLED explosion.

From a pad of fine steel wool take a pinch of about a dozen strands, and enough diameter to fill the bottom of the receptacle and make electrical contact with both the side and center metal. Onto this steel wool pour a half-teaspoon of black powder. This is done backstage with the short power lead disconnected. The person placing the pot on stage takes the load end of the extension which will feed the pot with him thus assuring that no one will accidentally turn on the circuit while he is bent over it. With the filling completed and the cover on, the short connection is made and then the person returns to the control point to make sure that the power is off. Connect the extension and the device is set.

Another method is to use a black 2 inch pipe cap. The cap is bolted to a 4"x 4" electrical box which will contain a doorbell transformer. The cap has a small hole drilled in the side just large enough to insert an electric match – the kind that is used to set off model rocket propellant charges. Add a 3 inch long nipple to the cap. With the match connected to the output of the transformer and the head of it covered with either the black powder or commercial flash powder, the steps are taken to safely connect it to its power source.

Any flash pot is capable of throwing sparks. This must be kept in mind if the pot is placed near curtains, scenery, or in a location where someone in a flammable costume might stand nearby. There are other methods of creating smoke, snow, rain, and flashes, but these are ones which we have tried and have found to be most effective. Be aware that this is probably the most dangerous thing used on stages today. EXTREME CARE MUST BE TAKEN in the use of flash or smoke pots.

MAINTAINING PROPS

As props are gathered it is necessary to store them. The use of large storage cabinets on wheels is a good idea. It allows a secure space easily transported from rehearsal to storage area when the props are not in use. If the rehearsal space is secure and is not used by others during the practice period then a prop table may be used. When not in use it should be covered.

Props must be brought to the rehearsal area on or before the date established by the Director. By that time we must have the final prop, or a stand-in for it and the knowledge of from whence the final prop is coming. As the actual prop for the show is obtained, it is to be approved by the Director.

From this point on there is to be one prop crew member for each box present at each rehearsal to open the props box(es) and set out the props. It is important that from this time on water is available in any situation calling for the actors to drink. The crew members are to check and update the list of props in their care, noting where each is to be placed at the start of each scene and where it is to be retrieved at the end of the scene. This is all done on the *Property Set-up Plan* (Form P-2). These forms, one completed for each box or table for each scene, will assure that any crew member can run the show efficiently. Each day at the end of the rehearsal all props are returned to the prop boxes, checked in, and locked. The updated forms are to be left for the crew head to check prior to the next rehearsal.

As crew members work rehearsals they are to alternate sides so that they become familiar with the total operation. During production week all crew members need to report at least 45 minutes prior to each tech and dress rehearsal. If required, all members may be called for all shows, again usually at least three-quarters of an hour before curtain time to have everything set and checked. For performances the crew members are to be in neat, dark clothing. Call is over when hand props are back in the cabinets, furniture is covered, and any clean-up required is completed.

It is anticipated that crew members will work three or four days a week during the rehearsal period, the entire week of the production, and on strike days, and that the crew head will be present almost daily.

RETURNING

It is often difficult to keep the props crew members at task to finish one of the most important parts of this entire crew project – *returning* the props.

You can make the job easier for future props crews if you will clean, repair, refurbish, and properly store all of the items you have used. Of course this includes the things you have retrieved from your own prop storage as well as those which you have been able to borrow or rent from others.

Take time to repair any item which has been broken or which has malfunctioned during its use.

PROPERTIES

The crew is finished only when all props have been
properly returned to their specific locations or owners
and all prop records have been turned over to the
Stage Manager.

 BIBLIOGRAPHY
B--1, 2, 3, 6, 8, 16, 20, 21, 22, 23, 25, 27, 31, 41
P--1, 3, 5
M--18

GLOSSARY

Properties List

North Central
High School
Indpls., IN.

Production:	Form P-1

Property	Description	Source	In

PURPOSE OF THIS FORM:

To provide an organized method of listing the props needed for a show.

USE OF THIS FORM:

The props crew members transfer information gleaned from the playbook, rehearsals, talks with the director and designer, to get as complete a list as possible.

The list needs to be copied so that those crew members not attending rehearsals may gather the props on the list.

As the props come in they need to be available for the performers to use.

Properties Set-up

North Central High School Indpls., IN.	Production	Form P-2

Act _____   **Scene** _____

SET DIAGRAM:

PURPOSE OF THIS FORM:

To provide a plan for the specific location of all props prior to each scene.

USE OF THIS FORM:

In the upper portion sketch a floor plan of the scene. Indicate the precise location of all furniture and of any props which need to be preset for that scene.

In the lower sections provide a listing of all the props needed for that scene on that side as well as any special information needed.

OFF STAGE LEFT:	OFF STAGE RIGHT:

SPECIAL PROPERTIES LOCATION:

CHAPTER FIVE

SOUND

Sound is a technical area that has gone almost unnoticed, yet has made great advances in the past few years. It is usually mentioned with thought only toward the amplification of voices. Sound can serve the director well as an aid in creating mood through the use of sound effects and music. Regardless of the use of the system, it need not be as confusing as it seems. Anyone who understands the relationship of the basic components of his home record player or stereo can be trained or can self-train to handle production sound.

The members of a sound crew define, secure, record, and/or produce all sound effects, mood, overture, and intermission music, and/or amplify the production as required by the script and/or the director.

Crew members should read the script and attend early rehearsals to assure familiarization with the show, its needs and requirements. Within the first week of rehearsal a conference with the director should be held to determine the type of music or effects, the requirements for live or taped effects or music, and their possible sources. Questions arising in the taping or creation of effects or music or in the equipment used or techniques tried need to be compiled and taken to the technical director.

In the case of musicals or other productions requiring the use of microphones, determination as to what microphones to use and where to place them needs to be made as soon as possible. The crew head must be sure that all of the crew members have been trained in the use and understanding of all of the equipment to be involved in the production.

The sound crew is to provide, set and strike operational buzzers, phones, or other sound making equipment for rehearsals as well as performances. The Stage Manager, actors, or prop crew members may be instructed in the set up and use of on-stage equipment for rehearsals so a member of the sound crew does not have to come to each rehearsal.

For technical and dress rehearsals as well as for performances all equipment should be in place and tested at least one half hour prior to performance. The sound crew should also be responsible for the operation of closed circuit TV, video-taping of shows, and set-up as well as the testing and maintenance of intercommunications systems.

PURPOSE

All sound systems have the same purpose: the amplification of sound and its distribution evenly to the audience. The word "evenly" indicates the level of quality that is difficult to reach since sound levels deteriorate rapidly as you move farther from the source.

SYSTEM PARTS

To accomplish its purpose any system contains three basic parts and their functions are the same regardless of how elaborate the set-up is. First, some form of *pick-up* is needed. This device takes sound, from one form or another, and turns it into electrical impulses. Carried by wire or cable, the impulses go to the second part; a control device. Usually this is an amplifier with volume control and switching capability. From here the electrical impulses are taken, again by wire or cable, to the third part; a reproduction device. At this point the electrical signal is transformed back into sound. The operation of a system consists of selecting and utilizing specific parts in their relationship to reach the stated end.

PICK-UP

The most common pick-up device is the *microphone*. It is also probably the most misunderstood. Each type of microphone is different in the manner in which it changes audible sound into electrical impulses. Some methods of change are more sensitive than others, thus one type of microphone will be more sensitive than another. The names of the types indicate their method of making the change: dynamic, ribbon, condenser, crystal, ceramic, and carbon, to name a few. Add to these two new items: the Pressure Zone Microphone (PZM) and the Phase Coherent Cardioid (PCC) microphone.

Microphones also differ in quality. Quality is the capability to faithfully respond to a great number of pitches (frequencies). High quality microphones will respond to a wide range of pitches. Lower quality microphones such as the one in the telephone, have limited production of low and high tones and only respond to middle range pitch. The wider range microphone will cost more.

Pick-up patterns of microphones also vary. This is due to the design of the housing and of the element inside which actually makes the transition from sound to electricity. These patterns are designated as: uni-directional (1-way), bi-directional (2-way), omni-directional (spherical), cardioid (heart shaped), or shotgun (emphasized one-way). Variations of these patterns are available and the specific pattern of any given microphone is shown in its accompanying literature.

Locating a microphone to provide the most efficient pick-up is a technique that needs to be studied carefully. There are more and more articles being published today than ever before because we have become more aware of sound as an area for study, experimentation, and perfection.

Impedance, or statement of the character of electrical output, of microphones differs. Low impedance microphones can send their signals farther along a wire than the high-impedance microphone. In either case a special cable called "shielded cable" is used. This cuts down on the amount of electrical interference from nearby devices.

The *phonograph cartridge* in the pick-up arm is also a pick-up device. Like the microphone, it is produced in different types, and qualities, and the same type designations apply as with the microphone. The "frequency response" which is the capability to respond to the different pitch levels is charted. The end result is the same as in the microphones – a pair of wires transmitting electrical impulses.

Tape heads are devices on tape players which read magnetic impulses from the metallic coated tape run past them. These impulses are changed into tiny electrical charges. There are fewer variables in tape heads than in microphones or phonographic cartridges.

An *antenna* is a pick-up device used for either a radio or television set. It is receiving waves from the atmosphere and turning them into electrical impulses.

CONTROL

The second major portion of the sound system is used for *control*. Usually this provides for the amplification or increase of electrical pressure and the switching required to select source and path. Actually volume and direction are the two things that can be controlled. Through switching it is possible for the operator to take a number of sources and mix or balance them before sending them on. Through amplification the operator can determine quantity of sound.

Stereo sound provides a method of "locating" the source. Higher volume from the right will place the evident source there. This can be used to help an audience locate a soloist who is on the stage in a large group of people.

Consoles are built which provide a great number of choices to the technician. The operator can mix signals from several microphones, record players, and tape players as desired. To do this mixers or pre-amplifiers must be installed. The *mixer* simply combines signals while the *pre-amplifier* does add a degree of amplification before the sound is sent on to the main amplifier.

REPRODUCERS

The last portion of a system is the *reproducer*. This device is used to turn electrical impulses into sound. This may be audible sound from a loudspeaker, visual evidence of recording such as is found on a phonograph record, or invisible as found on a tape.

Audible sound comes from a *loudspeaker* or *earphones*. Either of these, like microphones, comes in different sizes and types. Each of the units has its own particular purpose and use for which it was designed. Sound is like light in that when it is projected from a unit it can, to a certain degree, be focused. It will also reflect off of some surfaces. More precise control of sound is desired where echo would create problems, just as we need tighter control of light where reflection would be inadvisable.

Loudspeakers are available in *horn* or *driver* styles which are quite directional. The other style is the regular more-or-less directional *cone* speaker. Extreme limitation of area covered can be accomplished through the use of earphones, which are really small speakers. A pair of earphones is called *"headphones."* If they include a microphone with the assembly so that the wearer can carry on a conversation with someone else, the unit is referred to as a *"headset."*

Systems may provide a number of reproducers to which the sound may be sent. While all of these choices tend to confuse the casual observer, they are provided to offer flexibility in the operation of the system. The system still operates in the manner designated in the "System Parts" paragraph of this chapter.

The antenna on the transmitter portion of your wireless microphone system is a reproducer.

Variables available in the components are tremendous. From the variables comes a good choice and opportunity to select the right piece of hardware to do the required job.

SOUND SYSTEM USES

The uses for sound systems in an auditorium are many. The most obvious of course is the *public-address* system which transmits the sound from the stage to the audience. In the acoustically better auditoriums of today this system may be one of the lesser used systems in the house.

Similar to this system is the *monitor system*. A *cue* or monitor system provides microphones in the auditorium to pick-up stage sound as well as audience reaction and feed it to dressing rooms and other backstage locations where the performers and staff cannot otherwise hear what is going on.

With the more elaborate technical operations of today there is a need for communication among the crew members. The *stage managers' system* provides this. It is usually an *inter-communications system* which allows each person to transmit as well as receive information.

To help create an illusion, sometimes a sound effect must be created audibly backstage instead of in the house. This calls for a set of speakers backstage so that the sound will mix with the actors' voices during the show. A *sound effect system* which is separate from the house public address system is best. It is conceivable that the director might wish for the intermission music to be played through the house system since the curtain is closed while the other effects will go through the sound effect speakers. Both sets of speakers may be used for effects such as thunder.

Signal systems are found in many auditoriums. These are systems which provide audible or visible signals in the form of tones, sounds, or by indicating lights which in turn must be translated by the individual. Some examples are: school bell systems (which should have some means of silencing bells in the house lest "Romeo, wherefore art thou?" be answered by a ringing bell); fire alarm systems, and clocks. A system that should be included is some kind of signal system as a recall method to let the audience know when intermission is over.

Unfortunately, cost instead of need is the deciding factor in the installation of most sound systems. A group is better off getting less quantity – but better quality – then adding to it. A potential high-capability system can be filled out as time and money allow.

The operator of a sound system in an auditorium should be equipped with visual reference markings on the control knobs. He should also be well enough aware of the capabilities of the equipment that he can be fairly certain of the amount of sound in the house. Since for most lecture-type programs the microphones and loudspeakers will be in their normal positions, the level of sound possible from the system will be the same.

An operator faced with a lecturer who cannot or does not project his voice can only do so much. A constant attempt to increase the gain or volume will only result in a howl from the system as it creates *feedback*. Unfortunately, most people think that this is caused by the person speaking being too close to the microphone. It is really the result of a microphone picking up the output of a loudspeaker and causing it to be re-amplified. It is also the mark of an inexperienced or poor operator.

For any production using sound effects a cue sheet should be prepared indicating which pick-up device is to be used, what its operating level is, and which reproduction device is used. A *sound effects cue sheet* serves two purposes. The first is to remind the operator of what is to be done. The second, and perhaps the most important, is that it allows some other person to take over should the original operator become unavailable. Preparation of any cue sheet takes time and care, but this is part of the planning and resultant learning that is a major part of educational theatre.

As indicated earlier, the creation of sound effects is no longer as great a problem as it once was. There are now a number of good sound effect discs available and what they do not have, a person can record by taking a portable tape recorder to the source of the sound.

Quite often taped effects do not reproduce to sound like the real thing. Here again, imagination is our ally. A careful analysis of the required sound for quantity and quality may suggest a substitute. A recording may have to be made at one speed and played at another to get the desired response. Recording of several items may have to be blended. This analysis, interpretation and experimentation is the thing that makes the creation of sound effects a challenge. It is often much more rewarding than buying the commercial sound effect discs that are available for many of the shows today.

If you are to record effects, make sure that there is an adequate supply of splicing tape, splicing leader, razor blades, extra tapes, cassettes, etc. in the booth or work area. Make sure that all tapes are labeled clearly with the show name, cue number, what the tape is, and that all old labels are removed or obliterated. Previously used tapes should be bulk erased to eliminate unwanted signals.

Finally, the sound crew must be responsible for strike. At that time any defective items should be repaired or at least marked and brought to the attention of the responsible person. All recordings used should be returned to their proper homes, and specially made tapes labeled clearly for possible future use. Clean the sound booth area and turn in the cue sheets to the Stage Manager and you will have completed your assignment on sound crew.

BIBLIOGRAPHY
B-- 16, 27
P-- 1, 3, 5, 6
S-- 3
M-- 11, 27

GLOSSARY

Sound Effect Cue Sheet

North Central
High School
Indpls., IN.

Production

Form
S-1

Page _____ of _____

Cue	Page	Sound or effect	Source	Input	Level

PURPOSE OF THIS FORM:

To provide a listing of effects and sources so the sound technician has a specific list, or another technician might run the show.

USE OF THIS FORM:

In early discussions all effects and music must be listed, then during technical rehearsals the order is set and levels marked.

Dress rehearsal provides a final check for volume level, length of sound, etc.

CHAPTER SIX

TOOLS

Simply having a number of tools available in a scenery shop will not guarantee high quality work. A tool will work only as well as the operator is able to use it. The operator will be limited if the tools are not good tools. In tools as in other areas, choose the well-known reputable brands. They will cost more initially, but they will be more satisfactory in the long run. It is more desirable to purchase a few good tools on a limited budget and build up the stock as time passes.

For purposes of discussion divide tools into five categories according to their general function. In addition to knowing how to hold and move a tool, a concept of its possible uses is important. The operator also must recognize what actions will cause damage to a tool, and what its limitations are.

CATEGORY 1 -- CUTTING TOOLS:
Tools which are designed to either divide or shape material by removing a portion of it. Saws, files, and planes are included in this category.

A study of hand saws reveals a number of different forms, each with a slightly different purpose. The saw will have a handle and a blade. The tip of the blade is farthest from the handle and the heel of the blade is closest. Blades are made of a good grade of steel to stay sharp but they will kink very easily. Care should be taken when setting the saw down even for a short period of time so that it is not stepped on or anything placed on the blade. One edge of the blade is cut so teeth are formed.

courtesy Millers-Falls

The *crosscut saw* will have from 7 to 11 points (teeth per inch). The number of teeth will usually be printed on the side of the blade or stamped into the heel or the handle. The teeth have a sharpened front edge and are spread slightly. This spread is known as the "set" of the saw. The set of the teeth determines the width of the *kerf* -- the path of the saw from which the wood

has been chipped to allow passage of the blade. The crosscut saw is used when cutting across the grain of a piece of wood.

The *rip saw* looks like the crosscut saw but has 6 or fewer teeth per inch. It is also made with a wider set. This provides a wider kerf since the lumber has a tendency to spring together when it is cut with the grain. In spite of the kerf width a screwdriver or thin piece of material may have to be placed into the kerf to hold it open in green or wet wood.

courtesy Millers-Falls

Saws with greater than 12 points are usually back saws. This is considered as a piece of finish equipment because the greater the number of teeth the smoother the cut. A *back saw* is so named because it will also have an added heavy metal spine along the top edge of the blade. This spine stiffens the blade and provides a method of guiding it. The back saw is usually used in conjunction with a *miter box*. Miter boxes can be made of wood, but the better ones are steel frames which allow adjustment to set the blade of the saw at varying angles to the wood. Miter boxes are usually used in finish carpentry such as molding or cabinet work but are valuable in the scene shop as a means of making the precise cuts at the ends of pieces of lumber used for flat frames.

The *keyhole saw* provides a narrow blade capable of cutting cross or with the grain and is used for cutting curved lines. The coping saw or scroll saw uses a very thin, narrow blade to cut intricately curved lines in thin material. These have been replaced to a large extent by the electrical portable saws today.

To work properly any saw blade must be sharp. By placing the toothed edge of the blade between the thumb and index finger and then running these fingers along the length of the blade it can be noted that there is a slight drag where the teeth are sharp. In areas where the blade is dull the fingers will slide very easily. Most saws will be sharp at the ends since few people actually use the length of the blade in cutting, as they should.

Proper use of a hand saw calls for a long, smooth stroke with the wrist providing downward pressure. The shoulder, elbow, and wrist should be in a line with the saw blade and the line that is being cut. In this manner the saw will move in a straight line and will cut a straight line. While the wrist provides downward pressure, it also must keep the saw in the proper relation to the surface of the material. The finished cut must be checked for proper angle and dimension, not only in relation to the edge of the material, but also to the surface.

In more modern shops the portable electric saw, called *sabre saw* or *portable jig saw*, has taken the place of the *coping saw.*

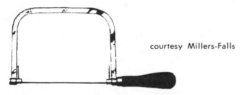

courtesy Millers-Falls

While the electric saw is well suited for cutting curved lines, it must be used carefully to produce anything close to a straight, true, cut. The electric saws provide a basic unit which has attachments to help hold a true course along the surface of the material. It is faster and requires less physical exertion. If the cutting process is rushed, then there is the probability that the blade, which is attached at one end only, will drift from side-to-side on the lower portion of the cut. In many cuts this is of no consequence, but the operator should be aware of this. Since the saw is faster, it also makes a mistake more quickly, hence must be used carefully.

When using the electric saw it is best not to use the switch lock provided on most models. This lock keeps the saw running regardless of finger pressure on the trigger. (Other saws will have a slide type on-off switch.) The trigger type switch provides a safer arrangement than the positive action switch. Make sure that there is nothing in the path of the blade either above or below the work. Remember that the power cord will be moving with the saw and can get into the path of the blade. Secure your material to the working surface so that pressure can be kept on the saw. Too little pressure will allow the blade to bind in the material and the saw will jump. Binding will also occur if too sharp a corner is made.

Saws mentioned so far are designed for cutting wood and softer building materials. Others are designed for cutting metals. In the instance of the electric saw the blade is changed to a blade with more teeth per inch.

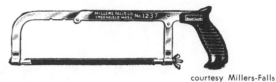

courtesy Millers-Falls

The *hack saw* consists of a heavy frame which supports a blade having from 24 to 36 teeth per inch. This saw is for cutting metal. With such small teeth it is impossible to achieve sufficient set to get a wide enough kerf to allow blade passage. For this reason the cutting edge of the blade is manufactured so it curves back and forth while the remainder of the blade is straight.

Each of the saws chips out a portion of the material being worked. It is possible to shave a very small amount of material off of an end or an edge by placing a long scrap of material with the piece to be cut and use the scrap piece kerf to guide the blade along the end or edge of the material from which a small amount is to be taken. There are other instances where the small amount can be removed with a chisel, plane, or file.

courtesy Stanley Tools

Chisels, whether for wood or metal, are used to gouge out a shaped hole, or for shaving off a thin portion of a surface. Wood working chisels will have a flat, smooth back and an angled face. When sharpening a chisel the back is not filed. The face is filed at an angle to provide as sharp an edge as possible. If the back is filed, it is no longer possible to easily control the depth of the cut. If the chisel is driven into wood to cut a rectangular hole, a properly sharpened tool will cut a rather smooth side. The cutting edge should be kept sharp. Being sharp it will be thin and collision with a nail or other foreign material will result in dulling. Check material carefully for such possible obstructions.

The metal chisel is shaped the same on both sides; therefore, there is no front or back. It is heavier and bulkier since it will be used in harder materials.

One method of smoothing a surface or thinning a piece of wood is to use a *plane*. The plane is comprised of a frame which holds a chisel-like blade and controls the amount of blade exposed for cutting. It is used more often in cabinetry and other finish work, but at times is found in scene shops. For a number of years it was the only method of smoothing surfaces or rounding the edge of a board.

Smoothing and rounding could also be done with a wood file called a *rasp*. A rasp is a very course file and leaves identifiable marks in the surface. Most of its work has been taken over by a cutting/shaping device which was designed like the cabbage grater found in a kitchen. One of these is the Stanley *Surform*.

courtesy Stanley Tools

Its thin blade with holes set at an angle, provides a series of small planes, each of which will curl off a small sliver of wood. The result is a fast cutting tool leaving a relatively smooth surface.

Sometimes there is need for smoothing metal or sharpening a tool. For this a *file* is used. The term "file" indicates that the device is made for cutting metal. Files are made in a number of ways -- their manufacture differing in the angles and depth of the scoring made across their surfaces. Manufacturers' catalogs and some local hardware stores can show you many differences and help select the best suited for a specific job. Files are made with flat, round, and/or curved surfaces.

As tools are added and more small or close work is done, some other shaping tools might be added. The block plane is smaller than the universal plane mentioned earlier. In the absence of power tools the spokeshave and the drawknife are both good for shaping shafts of wood.

courtesy Stanley Tools

A *utility knife* or mat knife is a must for a shop. Often referred to in error as a "razor blade knife," this tool provides a thicker blade which can be turned to use either end. A good, solid handle opens to provide storage for additional blades. Because of the thicker blade breakage is not likely.

Any tool with a cutting edge should be kept sharp. A sharp tool will cut material as it is supposed to. A dull tool will have a tendency to skip off of material and this encourages accidents. Storage of tools should be in such a manner as to protect the user from the edge, and the edge from the user.

CATEGORY 2 -- BORING TOOLS:
Tools for cutting round holes in materials.

"Drills" is the usual catch-all term used for tools in this category and is, at best, confusing because it is often used to refer to both the device driving the cutter and the cutting device itself. Remember that it takes two items to bore a hole - a bit to cut the hole and a device to propel it.

The propelling device or drill will be equipped with a holder to allow you to attach the cutter. This holder is called the "*chuck*" and you will find some which are designed to be opened and closed by hand, others which require a chuck key. For the sake of safety it is best to disconnect any electric drill prior to using a chuck key.

The oldest boring tool is the *brace*. Used with its associates, the auger bit and the expansive bit, it can cut holes of varying diameters. Being hand-powered, its precision capability is great. It is still the preferred tool for working expensive woods and cases where both the start and the exit of the bit from the material must be exact and smooth. The brace provides a chuck to hold the bit, usually with the capability of locking to drive in either direction of rotation, or a ratchet to cause the bit to move with the handle one way, but to remain still when the handle is moved the other direction. This allows the boring of a hole next to an obstruction such as a wall.

courtesy Stanley Tools

The *auger bit* has a tip which looks like the familiar wood screw. This will help pull the cutting edges into the wood. Two small cutting edges like chisels are located at the outer or maximum diameter of the bit. These will score the diameter of the hole while two surfaces perpendicular to the bit length chip out the wood. Both cutting edges and chipping edges must be sharpened for best cutting action. Auger bits are made in graduations of 1/16th inch and the number stamped into the tang of the bit is its diameter in 16ths.

courtesy Millers-Falls

The *expansive bit* is similar to the auger bit, but has only one cutting edge and one stripping edge. This is included on a single "arm" which can be adjusted or expanded, hence the name, to set the diameter of the hole that is to be cut.

A later boring tool is the *hand drill* or eggbeater drill. This drill will hold bits capable of cutting metal, although bit breakage is a great problem. The term "eggbeater" is most descriptive because the tool looks and operates like the kitchen eggbeater. Bit breakage is caused by allowing the axis of the drill to shift while the crank is being turned. This happens most often in hard materials or in wood of varying density, where the bit will turn easily for a while, then tighten up, causing the drill to shift and perhaps break the bit. It is possible to use a nail in place of a drill bit and throw the nail away when finished.

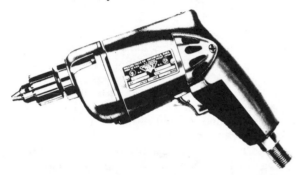

The modern replacement for both of these hand-operated boring tools is the *electric drill*. A variety of capabilities is offered with speed controls, reversible motors, and now the rechargeable drill. With speed control a screwdriver blade can be placed in the chuck and used. If the drill is operated too fast, the blade is liable to jump out of the throat of the screw and damage the material surface.

There is a screw driver unit available which has a sleeve that fits around the blade and drops over the head of the screw to maintain alignment even at higher speeds.

The electric drill, like the hand drill, must be kept in a single plane while working. This is often difficult since most of the "pistol grip" designs cause pressure exerted to shift the drill body. You can overcome this by holding the drill so that the trigger switch is operated by the ring or little finger instead of by the index finger, thereby allowing you to place the pressure straight down the axis of the drill and bit.

Other variables of the electric drill are its chuck size and the power of the motor. The chuck size will indicate the largest bit diameter that can be accommodated. The power of the motor will be the limiting factor in how long the drill can be used without overheating and how difficult a job can be done.

There are many accessories available for the electric drill – devices to enable it to be turned into: a portable saw, a sanding machine, a table saw, to drill at right angles to the drill, and to speed-up or slow down the bit speed.

For boring either the speed bit or the twist bit is used in the electric drill. The *speed bit* is a flat metal shaft with a sharp spike at the end, and cutting or chipping edges on the tip of the spike and the lead sections of the bit. These are designed to chip out material at high speed and will jam if operated too slowly. These bits are available in increments of 1/16th inch, and the diameter of the hole is stamped on the flat of the bit. Seldom do they actually cut a round hole since they will tend to go around hard spots in the wood rather than through them.

Twist bits are designed for use in metal or wood. They provide two cutting edges which must be at slightly different angles to the center line of the bit to operate. They are more difficult to sharpen and often are over-heated to the point of losing the edge. This is especially true in drilling deep holes in wood as well as in metal. Twist bits come in many sizes and their diameter is usually stamped into the shank near the portion that fits into the chuck. This diameter may be either in fractions of an inch or in code number or letter, either of which takes a chart to decipher. The numbered drills are accurate to 1000'ths of an inch.

CATEGORY 3--DRIVING AND PULLING TOOLS:
Tools for inserting or removing hardware for joining materials.

Hammers are comprised of a handle and a head. Each of these parts is available in a number of forms. The most common hammer in a scene shop is the claw hammer. The head of this hammer has a driving face and a pulling claw. Its weight is variable. The heavier the head, the more force applied to the head of the nail during driving. The quality of the steel used in manufacturing the head sets the price and the length of life.

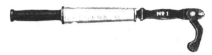

The *curved claw hammer* jaw is almost parallel to the face to provide greater leverage for pulling nails.

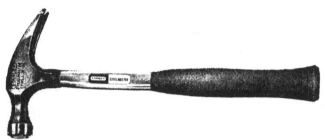

If the jaw of the hammer head is almost 90 degrees in relation to the face, it is called a *rip claw hammer* and will allow a "chopping" stroke to wedge between boards to separate them. Either claw can be used for either job, but their design allows simpler accomplishment of their specific tasks.

The head of the hammer should be forged and the face practically flat. In driving a nail heat is created by the collision of face with nail. This heat will cause an untreated face to swell over a period of time. This swelling can also cause pieces of the driving face to chip off, especially when driving large nails.

Handles are also variable. Many carpenters prefer a wood handle while others like steel or fiberglass with a rubber or leather grip. The steel shank hammer will not break even under severe abuse such as trying to pull too large a nail. This is the reason it is found in many school shops.

For pulling longer nails the leverage of a claw hammer can be increased by placing a small block of wood under the head in order to increase the angle of the handle with relation to the nail. Once the handle of the hammer is parallel with the nail, most of the pulling power is lost and there is undue strain placed on the joint between handle and head.

If the head of a nail is set flush with the surface of the wood and there is no way to lift this head, and there is no concern about the condition of the surface when the job is completed, a *nail-puller* can be used.

The nail-puller is made with one floating jaw and one solid jaw. The handle extends to provide leverage for pulling as well as a means of driving the jaws. By locating the jaws just outside the diameter of the head of the nail, then extending the handle after making sure that the grip of the other hand is safe, the handle is brought down to drive the jaws under the head of the nail. The handle is re-extended and pulled to one side and the nail is lifted. Later, when scenery and scenery hardware are discussed, it will be found that this is the only tool that will pull a clout nail.

For prying apart boards, pulling large nails, or acquiring great leverage to lift something, a number of choices are available. They are all in the same general name of tool, the wrecking bar.

A small, steel bar curved at one end with a claw at that curved end, is a *crow bar*. Its larger, usually 18" to 36" long, cousin is a *ripping bar*. A longer steel shaft with a squared end that has been cut to a chisel-like point is a *wrecking bar*. In manufacturers' catalogs these various terms become intertwined and any of the three terms is often applied to any of these tools with size (length) being the stated differential. This is the only form of tool that cannot be abused. Since there is no adjustment, no cutting edge, no precise form, and the design is made to transfer brute force, the individual can use the tool as he sees fit.

A new addition to this category is the *"Super Bar."* It is a flat piece of steel, curved and angled at one end, and is available in several sizes.

The stapler is a relatively recent addition to tool cabinets. Before its manufacture scenic items which had to be fabric covered required a great quantity of tacks. Now, instead of placing the individual tack and striking it with a hammer, a method is provided to drive a series of holding staples which have lined up automatically.

courtesy Bostitch-Textron

There are two forms of stapler. The *staple gun* uses a spring compressed by gripping the handle to drive the staple. A good commercial grade gun will have sufficient spring pressure to fire a staple some 20 feet through the air. This is necessary to drive the staple into wood. The force is sufficient to penetrate flesh at close range, so care must be taken in the use of the gun. Guns are also available which use electricity or air pressure to fire the staple. They are even stronger and therefore can be more dangerous to the user as well as those nearby.

courtesy Bostitch-Textron

The *staple hammer* looks like a hammer but its handle is filled with staples which are ejected into material by the force of the blow. The staple hammer will drive a staple into most any surface struck.

Staples are lightly glued together to form a "line," and are available in different sizes and weights. For the most part they are not interchangeable between devices of different manufacturers and in some cases not between guns and hammers. Staples can be removed after use by slipping a screwdriver blade under the top bar of the staple and prying up. If one leg happens to break off, a pair of pliers will lift it. It is important that staples be removed from any material that is to be used again. A staple which is slightly above the surface of some material is capable of causing a cut. A single leg broken off or protruding from a surface is like a small knife blade and can inflict injury. Material can be checked by running a soft cloth over the surface. It will drag on any staple part projecting.

An adjunct to driving tools used in scene building is the *clinch plate*. It is simply a piece of steel of any convenient size that is used to turn the end of a clout nail. The clout nail is explained in detail in a later chapter. The clinch plate can be flat sheet, a piece of

angle, or any other shape providing a small flat surface.

CATEGORY 4 -- HOLDING AND TURNING TOOLS: Tools for gripping and/or rotating pieces of fastening hardware.

Tools designed for turning the head of a bolt are wrenches. There are several kinds including monkey wrenches, combination wrenches, pipe wrenches, and socket wrenches. There are others, but the one found most often in scene shops is the *adjustable wrench*.

courtesy Millers-Falls

It, like other shop tools, provides a multitude of uses through its variables. Some refer to this as the "Crescent Wrench" naming it after the tool company which was among the first to manufacture the tool. It is unique in that the jaw faces are always parallel – the very thing that makes it so effective in gripping the head of a bolt or nut.

Many people depend upon one of the different types of pliers for turning bolts or nuts, but the usual result is the tool's slipping and chewing up the head so that tightening or removal is more of a problem than necessary. The slipjoint or *combination pliers* are the ones most often used.

courtesy Stanley Tools

Like most multi-purpose tools, no one job is done well. These pliers will grip flat-sided surfaces as well as cylindrical shaped objects fairly well and in addition are equipped with adjoining flat surfaces to act as wire cutters for soft wire.

The slip-joint allows the jaw surfaces of these pliers to adjust slightly to grasp flat surfaces. If the jaws happen to meet the surface, maximum holding power will be obtained. Unfortunately, this is the exception rather than the rule. If the surfaces do not meet, the tool may do more harm than good by slipping and marring the surface. All pliers depend upon the human hand and its grip to keep them closed. Because of our muscle design, the hand is not the most efficient gripping device.

A great many other types of pliers are manufactured. Some are designed for a single purpose, others have multiple use. The *lineman's pliers* provide a gripping surface for twisting splices in wires, a cutting edge for trimming wires, and a set of flat surfaces between the handles used to crush insulation on a conductor prior to removing the insulation to make a splice. None of the surfaces will function well for other purposes.

The *diagonal cutting pliers*, sometimes called "diagonals," or "dikes," are made for cutting only. Their jaws are sharpened the full length and will provide a means of getting into electrical junction boxes or other limited spaces to cut wires. They provide no surfaces for crushing or holding.

The *Channellock pliers* are invaluable tools in the scene shop. There are a number of tools of similar style, but pliers trademarked Channellock are stronger and more sure than the others. The handles adjust to a number of positions, each giving the jaws a different range of sizes to hold. These jaw spacings allow a good, firm, easy grip on a variety of things, including pipe. They can be used in lieu of pipe wrenches since they will grip, but have other uses as well, whereas a pipe wrench has a very limited use in a scenery shop.

For continuing pressure in holding materials during building, temporary holding on sets, or even forming handles to pick up large sheets of plywood, clamps are available.

One of those suggested for use in a scene shop is the *"C" Clamp*. Deriving its name from the shape of the steel frame, it is used to hold objects of rectangular shape. The open part of the "C" is variable, the maximum opening being the indicated size of the clamp. The opening is adjusted by turning a threaded rod, thus tightening a swiveling foot at the end of the

rod against a flat portion of the frame, or against material gripped between.

The *hand screw* is composed of two pieces of hardwood connected by two threaded rods. By turning the rods the pieces of wood may be brought closer, spread, and/or set at slight angles to each other. The entire wood block can be used as a clamping surface for jobs over which the pressure must be spread evenly. The uses of this tool are limited only by the ingenuity of the user.

Screwdrivers are primarily used for turning. It is possible to get them with magnetized bits or with holding devices to hold the screw or bolt in position while it is being started into the hole.

courtesy Stanley Tools

The standard is the *flat blade screwdriver* for the slotted screw or bolt head. It offers a parallel sided slot into which the blade is set. Three things are necessary for a proper driver fit; first, the end of the blade should be exactly the width of the slot in the head of the screw or bolt; second, the driver should have a flat tip which will seat against the bottom of the slot; third, the sides of the driver blade should seat firmly against the sides of the slot. Since there is no standard for width or depth of slot, it is seldom that the driver really fits.

courtesy Stanley Tools

A more efficient but more expensive arrangement is the *Phillips-head driver*. In these an "X" shaped pattern in one of 4 sizes has been used. The size of the slot is not related directly to the width of the head but instead to the size of the driver. In addition, the "X" provides almost twice the bearing surface for tightening or loosening, thus making the screw itself more efficient. The Phillips "X" is also set on center. Thus the use of an electric or other speed driver is safer since the tip of the blade cannot easily escape from the slot and damage the surrounding material.

Recently other head forms have been introduced, primarily into the automobile industry. Heads with square, hexagonal, clutch, and Torx shaped slots are appearing more and more. Each comes in several sizes and requires a specially matched driver bit.

courtesy Stanley Tools

The *Yankee screwdriver* provides a method of driving or removing screws which is mechanically between electric and manual screwdrivers. Available in several sizes, the operation is achieved by having a shaft with a double helical grove fitted inside the handle. Using the switch on the side of the handle the operator can choose a position allowing the shaft to rotate left, rotate right, or lock, when the handle is moved up or down. Downward pressure on the handle then causes the driver to set or extract the screw. For initial loosening or final tightening the lock is set and the tool is used as a standard driver. Both regular blades and Phillips blades are available for this tool in various sizes. In addition some will hold bits for drilling wood and other bits will no doubt become available.

The Yankee provides a quick mechanical method of driving or extracting screws without providing electrical power. It is rather expensive in relation to the other tools.

The inner shaft is spring loaded and the spring is strong. Care should be taken to assure that the tool is not stored with the shaft locked in the up, or retracted portion. In this position the spring exerts enough force to allow the blade to penetrate a piece of cardboard if the lock is released while the blade is about an inch away. The shaft is locked in retracted position by a ring at the lower end of the handle.

The screwdriver blade or drill bit is held in place by a slip collar at the bottom end of the shaft. Pulling up on this collar will release the blade or bit.

It is extremely important that the shaft of this type driver be kept absolutely straight. For this reason the Yankee should never be used to pry. Do not leave it lying around where it could be stepped on or have materials placed or dropped on it. If the shaft is bent, the driver will not operate.

CATEGORY 5-- MEASURING AND MARKING TOOLS:

Tools for determining length, width, or thickness, or for drawing patterns or shapes.

The *yardstick* is probably the most familiar measuring device. In a shop it may do well as a straightedge – although few of the free ones are straight – and it will measure rather accurately until the end is worn or broken off.

courtesy Stanley Tools

A *steel tape* is also familiar, but unfortunately its care is not. These are made of a flexible but brittle metal. The tape itself rolls easily into the coil within the cartridge for storage and when out of the case will curve, roll, or even accept being tied into a knot. Don't fold, crease or bend it sharply because it will snap. If left on the floor and stepped on in such a manner as to fold the tape lengthwise, it will begin a split that will eventually reach the side and leave a sharp point or cutting edge. Most of the tape cases today allow you to replace the blade. The blades are available in hardware stores and include the instructions for changing.

courtesy Stanley Tools

Tapes are available in many markings. A brick mason can get a tape that is emphasized in units which he uses, multiples of four inches. Carpentry tapes, the ones usually found in hardware stores and in scenery shops, are highlighted in sixteen inch multiples. Usually one edge is marked in cumulative inches while the other is in feet and inches. To eliminate confusion get accustomed to giving all dimensions in feet and inches.

Because most scenic items are constructed with 90 degree corners, a series of squares for marking and fitting corners is required. The largest of these is the *carpenter's square* or *framing square*.

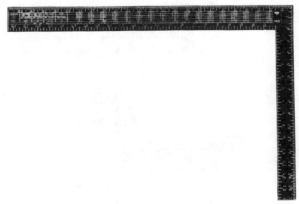

courtesy Millers-Falls

With its longer sides it provides a most accurate check on a corner. Its name is derived from the fact that it is equipped with a number of markings imbedded in its faces which provide the figuring for much of the work a carpenter or framer does.

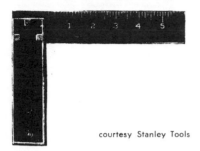

courtesy Stanley Tools

The *try-square* is smaller and one leg is thicker than the other. This provides a thick handle with a blade projecting at a 90 degree angle. The blade is usually 6" or 8" long and is used for trying the angle after sawing, or for guiding the pencil while marking a proposed cut at the end of a board. Like any square it is a good idea to test the accuracy the first time it is used in any work session. Draw a line across the board, then place the square on the opposite side and draw a second line. They will coincide if the sides of the board are parallel and if the square is in alignment.

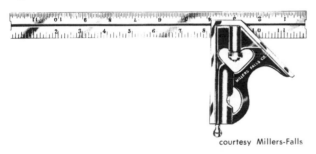

courtesy Millers-Falls

The *combination square* provides a pre-set angles at 45 and 90 degrees. In addition, the blade is allowed to slip within the handle and can be locked in the desired position. By allowing a given length to protrude from the handle, placing a pencil at the end of the blade, and running the handle along the edge of a surface, you can efficiently draw a line which is parallel to the edge of the surface. Most of these also have an oil-filled glass tube serving as a small level.

courtesy Stanley Tools

The *bevel square* provides a tool to copy angles. The tool resembles a square but the angle relation between handle and blade can be changed. The blade can be set at any angle to the handle and can be

changed in length then locked in position with a single-wing nut and bolt combination.

Small circles may be drawn with a compass. On stage it is often necessary to scribe a much larger circle than a compass will handle. A nail, length of string or wire and a pencil are sometimes brought into use, but the precision of the result is always in question.

If a set of *trammel points* is used, a perfect arc or circle can be made. One of the parts is a clamp with a pointed shaft which will be set into the center point. The other section is a clamp which will hold a pencil at slight angle. These units are clamped onto a beam – which is a board of the required length. Since the beam will not stretch, the radius remains constant.

courtesy Stanley Tools

If a long straight line between two points is required, the best tool is the *snap line*. The original "chalk line" was nothing more than a ball of string and a piece of chalk. Today a unit with a plastic or metal case around a spool of string works very well.

Several different colors of powdered chalk are sold but, dry scenic paint works very well to fill the case of the snap line. By stretching the line between two identified points then picking up the middle of the line and letting it snap onto the surface, you will have marked a straight line with chalk dust.

Whatever tools are stocked in your shop, and whatever tools are used, use each only for the purpose for which it is intended. Materials used in the manufacture of tools look much the same but they differ greatly. Misuse of a tool can cause irreparable damage and/or breakage to the tool or injury to the user or those nearby. If a tool malfunctions, or is damaged in any way, please report it to your supervisor. If left unreported, it is of no value to the next person who needs to use it and you probably have not learned anything about it.

(Tool illustrations courtesy of STANLEY TOOLS)

BIBLIOGRAPHY

B- 16, 18, 21, 22, 25, 27, 28, 29, 32
P- 1, 5
M- 2, 5, 16, 17, 18, 21

GLOSSARY

(Be able to identify all tools and their proper uses which you have available in your tool cabinet or in your shop.)

adjustable wrench 48
auger bit 45
back saw 43
bevel square 51
brace 45
carpenter's square 50
Channellock pliers 49
Chisels 44
chuck 45
clinch plate 48
combination pliers 48
combination square 51
coping saw 44
crosscut saw 43
crow bar 47
curved claw hammer 47
electric drill 46
expansive bit 45
file 45
flat blade screwdriver 49
framing square 50
hack saw 44
hand screw 49
kerf 43
keyhole saw 43
lineman's pliers 49
nail-puller 47
Phillips-head driver 49
plane 44
rasp 45
rip claw hammer 47
rip saw 43
portable jig saw 44
miter box 43
ripping bar 47
sabre saw 44
snap line 51
speed bit 46
staple gun 48
staple hammer 48
steel tape 50
Super Bar 47
Surform 45

trammel points 51
"C" Clamp 49
hand drill 46
try-square 51
Twist bits 46
utility knife 45
wrecking bar 47
Yankee screwdriver 50
yardstick 50

CHAPTER SEVEN

LUMBER AND BY-PRODUCTS

Steel and plastics are used more and more in the making of scenic units. Most of the work in schools, however, is still done with *lumber* and lumber by-products. Lumber is material sliced from a tree with no forming, gluing, or other modification. For *lumber by-products* the raw material is wood, but after being initially cut, the wood is re-formed into a size, shape, or configuration that could not have come from a tree.

LUMBER CLASSIFICATIONS

Lumber is first classified as hardwood or softwood. The *hardwoods* (e.g.: hard maple, walnut, oak, hickory) are used for furniture, floors, and trim in construction. The hardwoods are stronger, heavier, more difficult to work with, and much more expensive. The trees take a longer period of time to grow. They cannot be planted and harvested quickly as a crop which is how some of our softwoods are now being grown.

The *softwoods* are the ones generally found in construction of homes, buildings, and scenery. Some examples of softwoods are fir, pine, hemlock, soft maple, and basswood. These trees grow rather quickly and in large numbers, resulting in a greater supply and a lower price. The softwoods are lighter, easier to work, and more flexible than the hardwoods.

The lumber used in scenery is more critical than that used in buildings or homes. In commercial construction the framing or skeleton is sooner or later covered by other materials. Blemishes or warping does not show in the finished unit. Strength is gained by pieces of material supporting each other and by carefully locating the fasteners. Scenic units are of simpler construction using single layers of lighter materials and light-weight coverings.

LUMBER GRADES

In addition to being rated hard or soft, lumber is graded. This is the industry evaluation of its visual quality as well as physical characteristics. The judgment is made on the basis of the number of knots in a given amount of space (surface), and how solid the knots are. A knot is caused by the layers of wood of the trunk growing around a limb. Clear lumber is more valuable than knotty; hence, in the tree farms the lower limbs are trimmed as soon and as much as possible. The tree is thus left to grow a tall, straight, relatively limbless trunk from which can be taken a maximum number of clear boards.

Lumber grading differs slightly from one mill to another. The top grade is "B and Better," although theory says that it is possible to label Select A, B, or C. If the "B and Better" is too expensive, the C will probably do. It should have few knots and what there are should be tight.

The second level of grading is "Common." This is also divided into three parts: No. 1, No. 2, and No. 3. Common 1 has knots spaced a little more closely than in Select C. Common 2 contains many knots but is structurally sound. Common three is sometimes called "Crating Grade" because of its tendency to warp, its great number of knots, and its tendency to break due to the defects.

Of all the grades only a few satisfy the requirements of scenery building. Basic requirements are of equal concern: the material must be straight; it must be light in weight; and it must not split either during construction or during the life of the unit.

Ideally, then, scenery is constructed of lumber which is straight, strong, and light. The kind which is best is Idaho or Northern White Pine. There are other kinds of white pine, but they are heavier by sometimes half again as much due to the greater water or resin content. Other pines, such as Sugar Pine, have too much resin and will gum the blade of a saw very quickly. Douglas Fir and California Redwood split more easily. Cedar is brittle and varies greatly in hardness from one piece to the next.

Due to warping characteristics, spruce, hemlock, and most firs are unsatisfactory. Other variations of pine, such as Ponderosa, Yellow and California White, are not the best for scenery because of their moisture content, but are used rather widely because of their low cost.

Lumber is relative and the choice is made recognizing the weaknesses and strengths in relation to the cost. Do not purchase the cheapest lumber available. If the time is going to be taken to build a set, it is better to build less set and have it last longer. Pieces can be added in the future. A well-built frame of proper material should last ten to fifteen years. (We have some built in 1958 and they are still sound!) This is worth the greater investment over a unit which can be used only once. Even if the unit is to be used only once, make sure that the material will offer the strength needed.

LUMBER SIZING

Sizing is of concern in figuring the actual use of lumber. There are two lumber sizes in use: mill size and full size. The usual lumber purchased is *mill size*. Reference is made to dimensions of thickness and width, but the actual measurement of the material is 10% to 15% less than the stated size. It is presumably cut this way so that it is modular; that is, the lumber plus the other building materials attached to it during construction will make up a given total. This sizing is of more concern to the carpenter cutting and using the material than it is to the person ordering it.

Compensation in pricing has been made between mill and full size. You indicate in full size terms what is desired, the clerk talks in full size terms, but the lumber delivered, unless specifically stated otherwise, will be mill size.

Full size lumber is available, but usually at a premium price. If *full size* is required, then be very careful in ordering to make sure that it is understood the order is for full size.

Scenery building seldom requires full size lumber. The additional wood dimension adds weight without adding a relative amount of strength. With problems created by having to find full size lumber added to understanding the order, mill size becomes the simplest and the most used.

LUMBER MEASUREMENTS

In dealing with lumber and lumber by-products, selection will encompass three quantity measurements; board foot, square foot, and the running foot, the latter sometimes called lineal foot.

The *board foot* is the basic unit of measure for lumber. This measurement deals with all three dimensions of the piece: width, length, and thickness. All three are necessary to figure board feet.

The board foot is a unit of lumber equal to a piece 12" X 12" X 1". Thickness and width of lumber are always expressed in inches. Dependent on the length, it is sometimes simpler to express it in inches, sometimes in feet and inches. It is suggested that you standardize on one way of doing it – preferably feet and inches – to eliminate confusion. The two formulas below differ due to the measure used for designated length:

Length given in feet (& inches)

$$\frac{T'' \times W'' \times L' \text{ (in feet)}}{12} = \text{Board feet}$$

Length given in inches

$$\frac{T'' \times W'' \times L'' \text{ (in inches)}}{144} = \text{Board feet}$$

Lumber yards will often price lumber by hundred or thousand board feet. Moving the decimal point will give the single board foot price which is then multiplied by the number of board feet to get the cost of the lumber.

The *square-foot* measure considers only the width and length of material since the thickness of the material is pre-determined or is of little or no consequence. The formula is length times width, with both measurements expressed in the same units. If the expression is in inches, divide by 144 to get square feet. The square foot is the unit of measure used for coverage by paint or wallpaper since thickness is not a criterion. Lumber by-products are sold by the square foot. Their thickness is established and surface measure is the variable.

Sometimes lumber is sold by the *running foot* or *lineal foot*. In this unit of measure the thickness and width have been established and only the length is expressed. In asking for delivery of 70' of 2" X 4", the width and thickness are defined and the length is the unit on which the pricing is based. This is the pricing unit used on fabrics since they come in a given width, and thickness is no consideration. The most common item of lumber to find in this pricing is decorative molding which is a shaped board with length consideration only.

LUMBER BY-PRODUCTS

Mills take wood from a tree in many ways and form it into building materials which can be classified as *lumber by-products*. These will range from slicing thin sheets of wood from the circumference of a tree trunk section to grinding chips and bits of wood then gluing and pressuring them into a unique shape or size.

Lumber by-products are used on stage for *decking* or *profiling*. Decking is material used to cover a large, usually horizontal, surface. Profiling is the addition of a shaped cutout edge to a regular piece of scenery to change the outline or profile. Many kinds of by-products are available now and more are being introduced. Each will have its good and bad features. The basic size of a sheet of by-product is 4' X 8', although some can be obtained in larger sizes. If an order is placed for "one sheet of ..." the sheet will be 4' X 8'. The thickness will have to be specified. All dimensions of by-products are full size and dimension stated is actual dimension received. Some examples of by-products available are given here.

Homosote is the only one of the materials that is easily available in larger-than-normal sheets. Made of material that resembles a well chewed heavy paper, tightly compressed, it presents a rather easily workable material that has a medium resistance to breakage. The edges of a decorative cut-out will not chip off as on other materials, but will flatten or roll. It accepts paint well and is most easily available in 15/32" thickness, although it is also made in 5/8" thickness.

Upson board is made of a number of paper layers glued together and compressed. It is available in 1/8", 1/4", and 3/16" thicknesses, the first being the called "E-Z Curve." It cuts easily with a utility knife, especially in the thinner sheets, and will break rather easily. Really a heavy cardboard, it is subject to warping when painted. Some of the warping can be overcome by painting the backside with water just after the front side is painted, then placing a sheet of weighted material over it while drying. This is the least expensive of the profiling materials.

Masonite is available in either tempered or untempered form. The tempered masonite presents an extremely smooth, hard surface and is used by some outdoor advertising companies for billboards due to its resistance to warping. The untempered material is a little less tightly packed but is not as brittle. Either accepts paint well with a minimum of warping. Masonite can be purchased with a " screen back." It looks as though a piece of screen wire was placed in the press with the material during the manufacture, then the material compressed leaving a screen pattern. This presents an excellent slightly rough, matte surface. It has been used for flooring when the original flooring became so rough, cut up, and splintery that dancers could not perform on it.

Chips and bits of wood are mixed with glue and placed under heavy pressure to manufacture *particle board*.

Plywood, as described, is a sandwich of lumber sheets. To gain strength for the relatively thin material the grain direction of the layers is alternated. The outside sheets will have the same grain direction; therefore the primary strength of the sheet can be noted just as with a piece of lumber – the grain offers the greatest strength when it is across the line of the load. The material splits more easily with the grain than across it.

Plywood is available in several thicknesses, the most popular being 1/4", 3/8", 1/2", 5/8", and 3/4". These are actual or full dimension. Likewise, it is available in different face grades. These are labeled A, B, C, and D from best to poorest quality. Plywood carries a two-letter rating: A-D indicating that it is top quality on one side and low quality on the other. The "A" side will be firm and free from blemishes, while the "D" side may even have holes left in it where knots have fallen out. The usual lumber for face sheets is fir.

If you are going to use plywood for a situation where a load will be imposed in a very small area, you need to be aware that in regular plywood the internal layers may have holes in them and the face surface can easily be broken. To get solid interior layers you need to get marine plywood – and you will pay a lot more for it.

If lumber other than fir is used for the face sheets the material is referred to as *veneer*. The inner material of standard plywood is the same – inexpensive and "D" grade. Due to the alternate grain direction layering it becomes quite strong and forms an overall sturdy backing for a thin sheet of expensive wood. In this way the industry can use a piece of expensive wood over a less expensive supporting material. The look is that of expensive wood, the cost is less. Veneers are used at times in the building of stage furniture or small sections of decorative paneling.

Plywood is a little more expensive and a little heavier than the other profiling materials, but it is a lot stronger. For profiling pieces which will get a lot of use, particularly in a traveling show, plywood will return an investment several times because it will hold up under hard use.

55

While the A-D variety is the most common, the
material can also be obtained in any combination of
the four letters. C-D or D-D is also called plyscord
and is rough on both sides. This is used for flooring,
surfacing material which will be hidden under
carpeting or tile, roof decking to be hidden by
shingles, and other places where strength is needed
with no visual quality. Plyscord is of value on stage
for storage shelving, platform sub-flooring, or basic
framing for props and scenery.

BIBLIOGRAPHY

B-- 16, 18
P-- 1, 5, 6

GLOSSARY

board foot 54
decking 55
full size 54
hardwoods 53
Homosote 55
lineal foot 54
lumber 53
lumber by-products 53, 55
Lumber grading 53
lumber sizes 54
Masonite 55
mill size 54
particle board 55
Plywood 55
profiling 55
running foot 54
softwoods 53
square-foot 54
Upson board 55
veneer 55

CHAPTER EIGHT

FASTENERS

Materials are of value only if they can be fastened together to form the scenic item required. To accomplish this there are a number of hardware items available. The ones listed here merely represent a few of the great number of devices available in hardware catalogs. If, as a scenic technician, you are curious enough you will get a supplier's catalog and look through its pages to see the many items made for different fields of labor. With these in mind the next time you have a strange or difficult job to do, you can perhaps identify something that is designed to do that job, but is not normally thought of as a stage scenery item.

NAILS

The most obvious of the fastening type items is the nail. Like many other things, it is taken for granted until the time arrives to ask for a specific nail. The descriptive process often fails since one nail does look a lot like another. Nails basically have two variables – length and the diameter of the shank. For use backstage only two types of nails will normally be found – the *common nail* and the *box nail*. The difference is in the diameter of the wire used to manufacture the nail.

The common nail is made from a thicker piece of wire in relation to the box nail which comes from a thinner wire. The box nail came into being for the fabrication of wooden packing boxes. In fastening lids onto the thin dimension of the sides of the boxes, the lumber of the side often split due to the thickness of the nail. To keep this from happening, a series of nails with the same lengths as the common nail were made, but of a thinner wire. The common nail with its heavier shank is thought of as having a slightly greater holding power, but the difference is so slight that most cannot tell.

The length of a nail is usually expressed in *"D"* or *pennyweight*. Saying that a nail is "5D" or "5 penny" is the same thing. From 2 to 10 D the nail's total length is calculated; 1/4" for each D or penny, plus 1/2". Thus a 2D nail is 1" long, the 6D nail is 2" and the 10D, 3". Nails less than 1" long are referred to in inches and there is no pattern above 10D. Box nails are found only in the 2D to 10D lengths.

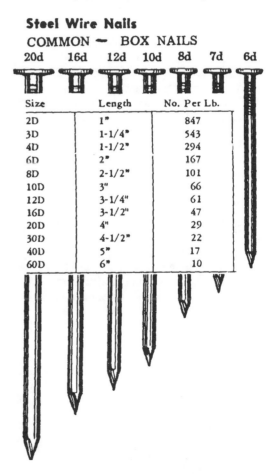

Steel Wire Nails

COMMON ~ BOX NAILS

Size	Length	No. Per Lb.
2D	1"	847
3D	1-1/4"	543
4D	1-1/2"	294
6D	2"	167
8D	2-1/2"	101
10D	3"	66
12D	3-1/4"	61
16D	3-1/2"	47
20D	4"	29
30D	4-1/2"	22
40D	5"	17
60D	6"	10

The holding power of a nail is dependent upon its penetration into the second piece of material. One should always nail through the thinner material into the thicker. Ideally the nail must penetrate a high percentage of the second material to provide maximum holding power.

Casing nails and *finishing nails*, which have minimal heads, as well as many other types are available; however, they have a limited use in a scenery shop. Wallboard nails which have large heads to provide a good holding area are perhaps of the most value for fastening profiling onto a frame. The clout nail can be used for this just as easily if it is long enough and does clinch.

For temporary fastening during construction, or even during the set-up of a setting, the *scaffolding nail* is helpful. Manufactured in the same dimensions as the common nail, the "scaf" nail provides one head to hold against the lumber surface while leaving a second head exposed to provide an easy access for the claw of a hammer when it is time to disassemble the set. Care should be taken as to where the scaffolding nail is used because the second head protrudes about a quarter of an inch and can snag clothing, scenery, and/or people.

To make a most secure joint, some people use a nail longer than the material is thick, and bend it over or clinch it. This is unsightly and time consuming unless the situation and the nail are made for such action. The nail for such a joint is the *clout nail*. It is one of the few items made specifically for the theatre industry.

Made from a soft, blued steel and tapered to a chisel point which is wider than it is thick, the clout nail comes in 1-1/4" and 1-1/2" lengths. Its purpose is to penetrate the strengthening cornerblock or keystone, then the lumber of the flat frame and to turn back into the lumber and roll. More will be said about this nail and its use in the chapter on flat construction.

CORNER FASTENERS

In order to hold a corner joint of any kind until a more secure fastening can be applied, the *corrugated fastener*, sometimes called a "wiggle nail," is often employed.

It can be obtained in lengths from 1/4" to 3/4". This is the amount the fastener penetrates the wood. Its other dimension will have either four or five waves. If this type of fastener is set in a direct line with the grain, or if it is driven with too much enthusiasm, there is a tendency to split the wood.

Another fastener for the same job is the *Skotch fastener*. It is a small rectangular plate with 8 "legs" sheared from it. They are curved so that they will pull the joint together as they are driven into the wood.

The tendency of this item is to fall over on its back when it is left in a work area. This leaves 8 small, sharp, painful, legs pointing up, which makes it less safe than other fasteners. In place it does a superior job.

SCREWS

In situations where a joint needs to be taken apart easily and the lumber is to be used again, or hardware is to be attached to the lumber, there is need for a fastener that will allow this and still hold well. One fastener is the *wood screw*. This is a metal shaft equipped with a rather coarse thread which increases slightly in diameter from the tip to the shank. This thread causes the screw to work its way into the fibers of the wood, force them apart, and hold extremely well. Whereas the nail only forces open a cylindrical hole, the screw threads slip between the fibers as well as opening its own hole.

Wood screws have two variables: length and diameter. The length is given in inches and/or fractions of an inch. Screws are manufactured in multiples of 1/8". The length is measured from the tip of the screw to the point where the head will be flush with the wood surface when the screw is in place. The diameter is measured at the widest part of the screw, excluding the head.

Wood screws are typed by head shape. The most common shapes are: flat – the head finishes flush with the wood surface; oval – the head rises slightly; and round - the head presents a hemispherical extrusion above the surface.

Rather new to industry is the *drywall screw* or *multi-purpose screw*. This type of screw has a flared or trumpet head. Formed from tempered steel with a Phillips head and very coarse thread, these are designed to be driven with electric drills or screw guns. They are commonly found in 1-1/8", 1-5/8", 2", and 3-1/2" lengths and can be used again and again. They are taking the place of nails in a lot of scene shops. Care must be taken with them since they are tempered and will at times shatter.

Other fastening devices utilize screw threads which cut their own way into wood. The *lag screw*, sometimes referred to as the *lag bolt*, provides a square or hexagonal head to be turned with a wrench.

It is really an extremely heavy-duty screw. The smooth portion of the shaft may be formed into a hook or an eye. As an example, the *screw hook* and the *screw eye* are both used on screen doors. They are handy and should be stocked in several sizes. Reference for purchasing any of these units is made to total length and diameter of the shaft.

Another type of screw is the *sheet metal screw*. It is used to fasten pieces of relatively light-weight metal to one another and can also be used for wood working. While it looks like a wood screw, its threads maintain a constant diameter over its length, and it is threaded its entire length. For it to penetrate, a starter hole must be drilled which is the diameter of the solid portion of the screw. Like other screws, it is typed by head shape and sized in diameter and length.

A "*drill & tap screw*" is also available. This screw has a tip designed as a drill bit. It will drill its own entry hole in light weight metal.

BOLTS

While screws force their own holes into material, another fastener must have a hole pre-drilled. This is referred to as a bolt. It is designed with a shaft of outside diameter equal through its total length. It is grooved helically, called threading. It fits into another piece of metal grooved, called tapped, to fit. The receiving portion is the nut.

Bolts have three variables being sized by length and diameter, both dimensions being given in inches or fractions of an inch, and also in the number of threads per inch. Therefore, all three measurements have to be checked, especially if a match is being made to an existing part. Certain types of bolts have a generally accepted thread number, but specials are made in every size and form.

The *carriage bolt* offers a head which is slightly rounded and has a square section of shank just below it. This allows the square section to be driven into a round hole to keep the bolt from rotating while the nut is being placed on it. It was designed to help the one-person operation when both ends of the bolt could not be reached at once. The threading of most carriage bolts is only about 1-1/2" long, so the length of the bolt must relate closely to the thickness of the materials being fastened together.

The *stove bolt* is threaded on its entire length and is available in both flat and round head design. Usually made from a very soft stock, it is often used when there is doubt as to just how long a bolt has to be.

The nut is placed on it and the extra length can be twisted off easily. When the end is twisted off it jams the threads slightly and will help hold the nut on. Jamming threads will happen if you tap the threaded end of any bolt to take it out. If you must drive a bolt out leave the nut on the tip end to start the bolt out then catch under the head with a claw hammer, wrecking bar, or pliers.

Other types of fasteners with screw or bolt threads are available. Again, the total length, diameter, and number of threads per inch are the variables. Some examples are the *eye bolt* and the *hook bolt*.

ADDITIONAL FASTENERS

A type of fastening "device" to come onto the scene is *duct tape*. Developed for the heating/cooling industry, this tape was originally designed to seal joints in ductwork. It is available in many widths and colors as well as in various qualities. The best seems to be the fabric backed variety with a strong adhesive.

Known as "gaffers tape", it is available through theatre supply houses as well as from the local hardware store. Cheaper brands do not hold well.

Duct tape has taken over the older more primitive forms of quick-fix methods. Earlier we used bailing wire, stove pipe wire, pinch clothes pins, and coat hanger wire. These are all still available and may be the solution to a problem at some time.

Two things I keep around a shop are rolls of *binder twine* and of *venetian blind cord*. Both are strong and can handle quick jobs calling for small diameter rope to secure or activate something. Available in black known as "*trick line*" the venetian blind cord has a lot of uses from making tie-laces to trip lines.

Recently 3M Company has arranged with one dealer in the Midwest to handle its line of heretofore commercial *adhesives*. DESIGNLAB in Chicago makes available a series of spray-on adhesives which allow the technician to attach almost anything to almost anything. There are quite a number of different adhesives and care must be taken in selecting the right one. They will be glad to help.

BIBLIOGRAPHY

B- 10, 16, 18, 30, 32
P- 1, 5, 6
M- 2, 5, 17, 18

GLOSSARY

CHAPTER NINE

SCENERY CONSTRUCTION

Construction of scenery is too often taken either too lightly or, contrarily, considered to be so difficult that a group of students or volunteers cannot attempt it. If properly planned for a group that is willing to use the proper tools, and some care in the work, scenery construction need not be a great problem.

PLANNING

The first step prior to any construction is the formation of plans. A *plan* is the placement of intent and information in as complete a form as possible, so as to provide a clear and complete picture of that which is to be done. The steps listed in planning can be altered in their order. The use of the steps is only to help provide communication between the planner and the worker.

The evolution of a set of plans usually begins with a *sketch*. A sketch is a rough, freehand resemblance of the total project. Although early sketches may not look exactly like the finished item, they provide a stepping-off place. The sketch can be done rather rapidly, therefore providing a point of conversation among parties. This conversation will cover capabilities, limitations, and may mention details in some cases. The sketch will usually present only a view from one location.

From the sketch, a set of *scaled drawings* is prepared. Scaled drawings are detailed and drawn so that all items are shown in their size relation. An item that is to be 8 feet high and 4 feet wide will be drawn twice as high as it is wide. These sheets transmit all of the detailed information regarding size, material, methods of fastening, and any special instructions. Because there is more information presented and more exactness of detail, there will be more views.

VIEWS

The *plan view* of an object illustrates how it will look to someone above it. We talk about the floor plan of

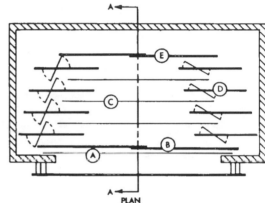

PLAN

a house or building. This shows the layout of the rooms, the door placement, stairways, etc. For the plan the drawing is made as the area will appear 4'- 5' above the floor. By drawing the view at this level the openings for doors and windows appear. The plan view will show less detail than some of the other views.

Sections or a *section view* is that which will be used to show construction methods as well as vertical measurements. A section looks at an item after it has been mentally cut in two and the front part removed. An apple, cut in two, provides a section view. The framework of a building under construction often will present a physical structure exactly as its section view showed.

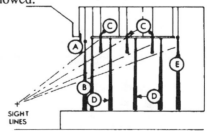

SECTION A-A

Sections can be drawn as longitudinal or cross. The *longitudinal section* looks at the long dimension of an item – like slicing a banana lengthwise. The *cross section* cuts through the short dimension--chopping the banana in two.

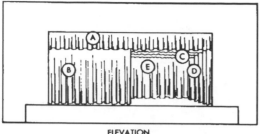

ELEVATION

A third view is the *elevation*. This is what the object would look like if the viewer backed away and looked at the finished project. For purposes of illustration the elevation often flattens out curves or angles in a wall, but it will look like a photo of the finished surface.

At times a fourth view may be considered necessary to transmit information. This is the *isometric view*. This is an exterior or finished view, as is the elevation, but is taken from above and off one corner at an angle. In this way you are looking at the only three dimensional view offered. The isometric view is seldom labeled with anything other than the most general measurements. You cannot take accurate dimensions from this view.

Often, in addition to the construction views, a *rendering* of the object is made. This will show, in color and relative scale, what the finished object will look like. When compared with a photo of the finished object, there should be a striking resemblance. Such a rendering is the type of drawing which presents the designer's ideas for color to the painter.

Drawings should be carefully prepared and should be made to *scale*. Obviously full-size drawings cannot be made of everything, so a representational scale is chosen. In scale a small unit of measure is designated as being equal to (representative of) a larger one. To aid in this tools called *scales* are manufactured. They look like regular rulers, but are marked off in the primary unit for that scale and these primary units are numbered consecutively. If working with a 1/4" scale, the primary lines will be 1/4" apart and numbered from 1 to whatever the scale is long enough to show. In this manner a line can be drawn representative of a line 20 feet long going from 0 to 20 along the scale.

Since a very slight error in line length could represent a great change in dimension it is wise to mark every dimension on each drawing. This eliminates the possibility of error in drawing as well as error in reading.

FLAT CONSTRUCTION

The basic unit of scenery is the *flat*. A flat is a covered wooden frame used for scenery. The covering may be most anything; the frame is the most important part of the unit. Through the years a number of construction features have evolved for flats. If the basic construction methods of a simple, rectangular flat are known, then almost any shape can be built using the same (or at least similar) construction features.

A flat will have two dimensions: height and width. If the theatre stocks a "set of flats" they will, within that set, be the same height. Various widths of flats are made in order that they can, in combination, make up a great variable of total widths. This helps make the designer's job easier. Flats used to be somewhat limited in their height and width so that they could fit into railroad baggage cars for transit from one city to another. From this limitation came the professional tradition of the 5'-9" maximum flat width. Newer transportation methods have overcome this limitation and allowed wider flats. The limitation now is the strength of the material used in the construction of the frame.

Check the two required dimensions, height and width, on the plans and start construction.

The first step is selecting lumber. For flats up to and including 6' X 14', a 1" X 3" material, often called "screen stock," is most often used. Even as this is being written, such material is becoming scarce. The local lumber yards indicate that they have 1" X 4", but the use of this will add about 25% to the weight of the frame. The builder and planner will have to decide if the added weight is acceptable, or if they want their lumber supplier to split 1" X 6" for them. A word of caution here: most of the 1" X 6" with which I have worked is not well seasoned and tends to curve and/or roll as it is being split into 1" X 3".

With a quantity of lumber on hand sufficient to build the flat, match the pieces to make sure that they are all the same width. If they are not, then assure yourself that this is kept in mind as the various board lengths are measured. The length of most flat pieces is dependent upon the width of an abutting piece. Sort the strips according to how straight they are. Ideally they should be perfectly straight, but this, too, is getting harder to obtain. Use the straightest pieces for the longest runs.

Due to the interdependence of some parts upon others for their proper length, you need to cut the *rails* first. The rail is the board which forms the top and/or the bottom of the flat. It will be as long as the finished product is to be wide; therefore, it is the only piece whose exact measurement is known. The lumber for the rails should be as straight as possible since there is usually no intersecting lumber to hold them straight in the finished frame. Before cutting make sure that the end of the piece of lumber is square. If the end is split or cut at even the slightest angle, mark it square both horizontally and vertically and re-cut it. Then the length can be measured off and cut properly. Square ends on all boards in flat construction is a must. The ends must be squared vertically as well as horizontally if the joints are to be firm and tight.

With the rails cut, it is possible to determine the length of the *stiles* – the long, vertical side pieces of the flat frame. The stile is cut the height of the flat minus the two rail widths. Since the rail is to run the full width of the flat and the corners are not to overlap, the stile must be shorter than the finished height, therefore the formula. Again, check the ends of the lumber to make sure they are square. Since a rectangle is being constructed, check the two finished pieces against each other to make sure that they are precisely the same length. A fraction of an inch on one rail or one stile will throw the entire frame out of square.

To assure accuracy mark one length at a time. If two lengths are marked at the same time there is seldom allowance made for the width of the saw kerf. With the mark in place make sure that the cut is made on the waste side of that mark. The saw should erase half of the pencil mark to assure accuracy. Leaving a narrow pencil line on the good piece of lumber will indicate that it was not cut short.

To save figuring mark the finished height of the flat on the stile lumber. Using the two rails that have been cut, lay them side by side on the stile side of the height mark. Mark at the collected width and this will indicate the " ... height of the flat minus two rail widths."

The same method can be used to arrive at the length of the *toggles*. A toggle is a horizontal board used to

keep the stiles from being pulled together when a fabric covering is placed over the frame.

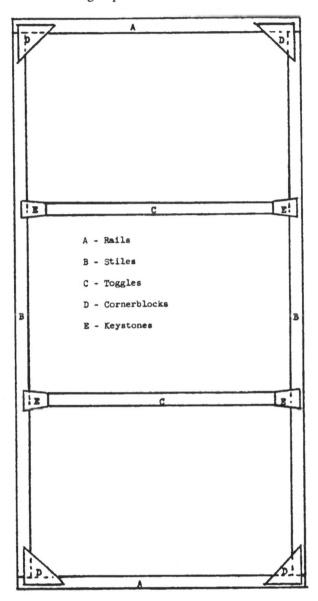

A - Rails

B - Stiles

C - Toggles

D - Cornerblocks

E - Keystones

Toggles are placed no less than 4' and no more than 6' apart, dependent upon the kind of lumber available. If a 12' flat frame is made of good, straight, strong lumber then only one toggle will be needed. If average lumber is used, provide two toggles. Flats shorter than 12' need only one toggle; taller flats should have two. Once the toggle(s) is cut, the primary materials are prepared for the frame.

Secondary materials needed are four *cornerblocks* and, a pair of *keystones* for each toggle. All are cut from 1/4" plywood. The cornerblocks are right isosceles triangles and, while size varies, 10" sides work well. Grain parallels a side, not the hypotenuse. Keystones are used to reinforce the joints of a toggle with a stile. Commercial keystones are cut in the keystone shape – one end wider than the other. The narrow end is the width of the toggle, the wide end one-and-a-half times that, and the length twice the narrow end. The grain runs the length of the keystone. More efficient cutting can be done with a rectangular keystone which is twice as long as it is wide. Very little strength is sacrificed by this shape.

Some scene shops use *corner braces* in their larger flats. These appear in flats over 5' wide and 12' in height, although they could be used in smaller units. In the smaller flats they add more weight than necessary. When used they are placed in pairs, one angled across the top stile/rail joint and another across the bottom, both on the same side of the flat. They are mitered at 45 degrees on each end and should intersect the rail near its center point. They are joined to the rail and stile with either an adapted corner block or keystone, care being taken to hold the edge of either at least 3/4" back from the edge of the lumber.

An area large enough to lay out the materials is the next requirement. In a permanent shop facility a lot of uses are found for a *template*. This is a table with a firm top that is the size of the largest flat normally built for the adjoining stage. The template is constructed in such a manner that the top is a perfect rectangle and is made of a material into which nails can be driven. Homosote makes an excellent top surface material. It provides a good splinter-free working surface which can be replaced after a period of time. Under the Homosote is a 3/4" wood surface which holds the nails as they are driven in.

Lay out the materials in their general relation and nail down one stile using scaffolding nails so they can be easily pulled later. The rails are laid in place; then the opposite stile. Next, check the exterior frame for

square. If both rails and both stiles are of equal length, the resulting frame must be either a rectangle or a parallelogram. The rectangle is required because

it has to be placed on the stage floor and against other flats. If the frame is a parallelogram, then it will not fit against ALL other flats. The check for square can be done by using a long tape measure or a long board. The two diagonals of the unit must be equal. If they are equal, the shape is a rectangle. If they are not equal, the shape is a parallelogram.

In laying out the stiles and rails a check must be made again to confirm that the boards are straight. If there is any bow in the stile, make sure that it bows out, making the flat look a little fat. When the joints are made with the toggles, the stiles will be pulled into line. There will be additional inward pressure exerted when a covering is applied to the frame. The rails cannot bow at all. If there is any bow or twist, it is best to replace them. The first ones cut can be used later for toggles since they are less critical in their place.

Once the frame is arranged with the corners tight and square, then nail down the other three sides temporarily. Make sure that the scaffolding nails are located at least two feet away from the end of any board so that the clout nails can be set properly. Set the cornerblocks in place. The *grain* of the block must go across the line of the joint. It makes no difference which side of the ply is up, since it is the grain direction that counts. If the grain direction is set parallel with the joint, there is the possibility of the plywood snapping. The cornerblock, as well as EVERY item placed on the back surface of a flat, must be set back from the edge of the wood the thickness of the lumber being used for the frame construction. This set-back distance allows flats to be used to make an outside corner with the flats fitting tightly.

The clout nails are placed into the blocks according to the pattern shown, but not driven all the way in.

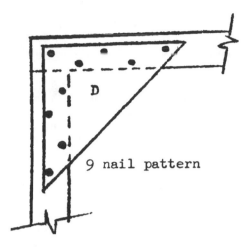

9 nail pattern

With all four corners started, check again for square. If the frame is square, then the clout nails are set by placing a clinch plate (flat piece of steel) under the wood and driving the nail all the way in. Since the clout nail used is 1/4"longer than the total thickness of the lumber and the plywood, the end of the nail will strike the plate and roll.

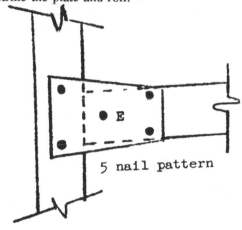

5 nail pattern

In placing the clout nail, the flat of the chisel point is lined parallel with the grain of the lumber (not always the same as the grain of the ply) so that when the nail rolls it will grip around the grain fibers instead of between them. If the nail rolls between the grain fibers, it will force them apart and perhaps split the lumber.

With the outside frame secure, place the toggles in position. If, as indicated earlier, the stiles were bowed slightly, then the scaffolding nails on one rail will have to be pulled. This will allow the width of the frame to be adjusted to the desired measurement and will assure tight joints at the toggles. Tight joints here are important since they will assure the edge of the flat will stay straight and will provide the support necessary when the covering is applied.

The keystones, like the cornerblocks, must be set back from the edge of the lumber the thickness of the

lumber. Nail the keystones to the stiles first, then pull the stiles together until they touch the ends of the toggles; then place the rest of the nails. Make sure that the points of the nails are placed in the proper direction and that the nails have clinched. By pulling the remainder of the scaffolding nails the frame can be removed from the template.

5 nail pattern

A flat frame can be built without a template. The frame can be laid down on the stage floor so that the pieces can be nailed in place. If only a concrete surface is available, the corners may be set by using a carpenter's square and making the cornerblock nails penetrate only part way. By placing all the nails in the stile portion, and only the corner nail into the rail, the whole unit will easily shift into alignment. Using the same measurements of diagonals as before, the unit can be squared and the remainder of the nails put into place. Concrete will not work as a clinch surface; a metal clinch plate must be used.

The determination of height and width of a flat or a set of flats is strictly a designer's decision. There is no absolute standard, although there are habitual measurements. Your flats must be high enough to represent the visual area, but not so tall as to present problems in storage or movement. For ease in building it is suggested that the height be an even foot measure, although odd-dimension building is not impossible.

The concept of a stock of variable flat widths is to allow different wall-section widths. Having four to six flats of each of several sizes, it is possible to select from stock most of the flats to meet the designer's requirements. These can be supplemented with whatever odd-sized or odd-shaped units have to be built, painted, and erected. This approach shortens the preparation time for a show.

A suggested inventory would include 1', 1'-6", 2', 3', 4', 5', and 6' wide "regular" flats. In addition, flats with openings in them for doors, windows, fireplaces, and arches would be built. Other flats included might be a series of plugs; small flats of the exact size to fill a space from the top of a door or arch opening up to the top of the rest of the flats; or a three-flat folding unit with a 6' center flat that has a 5' X 5' opening for a window, then has a 3' flat hinged to each side. This provides a 12' wall section with a large window.

It is possible and perhaps most practical to build and stock flats of several different heights. This will provide a supply of backing flats for a tall setting, plus the option of using the shorter flats in rooms other than an auditorium. If different heights are decided upon, it is a good idea to make the hardware spacing on the back of the flats to work out in a module measurement so that different heights may be lashed together. This saves time in set erection as well as providing some additional options on flat utilization.

As an instance in the determination of flat height let us look at an actual problem. The proscenium is a little over seventeen feet and there is a fourteen foot high door between the stage and the shop. Scenic units are often placed on casters but flats have to provide door clearance. Allowing an inch at the floor and an inch at the top, the tall set measurement is located at 13'-10". Because the group had performed in another building prior to the construction of this one, there was a set of twelve foot flats on hand. In addition to these a set of 8' flats has been added to provide the materials for one-act plays and for classroom use. For musicals or other multiple set shows the twelve and eight foot flats work with the fourteens as backings or even small wagon sets.

It should be noted that the scenery hardware, which is discussed in a later chapter, is placed on the 12' and the 14' flats in such a manner as to allow these flats to be set side-by-side and lashed together.

The basic scenic unit, the rectangular flat, in its construction allows some easy deviations. When a door is required, there are two possibilities. One: a *plug* can be built. This is a small flat which is the width of the door frame and fills the space between the top of the door frame and the top of the flats. The other is to build a *door flat*. The latter seems to give better support both to the door and the adjacent units. It differs from a regular flat in that one toggle is placed at the top of the door frame opening, generally at 7'-0", and from this two stiles are run down to the bottom rail. The bottom rail is removed within the door opening and a piece of strap iron either 3/16" or 1/4" thick is obtained. The iron should be as long as the flat is wide and as wide as the thickness of the lumber used in the frame. This is called a "*sill iron*" and is held in place by countersunk wood screws into

the bottom rail so as to stiffen the entire flat frame. A *fireplace flat* is built in the same manner, but with a smaller opening.

For a *window flat*, place two toggles spaced to form the top and bottom of the window opening. In any special flat the joints will have to be reinforced with cornerblocks placed outside the opening for door, window, or fireplace. The set-back rule for reinforcement and hardware items should be observed here, too, since the addition of profile or thickness materials is often required.

Construction methods for odd-shaped flats or irregular pieces will follow the same general rules of construction; only the need for different types of joints may arise.

JOINTS

The standard today for most flat construction is the *butt joint*. This is the simplest joint to make. The square-cut end of one board is placed against the side of another piece of lumber. Since the carpenter is only involved with cutting one end, there is only one variable.

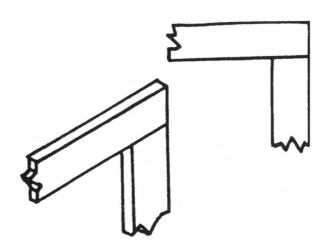

This joint is the weakest of the corner joints, but this is made up for through the use of the cornerblock. This joint also prohibits the end grain stile from touching the floor while the flat is being moved. If the end-grain comes in contact with the floor, there is a possibility of splitting the material.

The *miter joint* is a little harder to make, but it is also a little stronger. In this joint both pieces of material must be cut so that their angles equal 90 degrees. With the proper tools and ability this can be

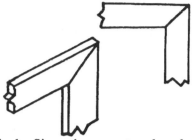

accomplished. Since there are two boards being cut, there is twice the opportunity for error over the butt joint. This joint is the type used in construction of picture frames or other items using contoured materials.

Professionally equipped shops still furnish scenery with a *mortise-and-tenon joint*. Special equipment is used to cut a rectangular hole in the rail. The stile is cut with a protruding tenon that will precisely fit into the mortise, or hole.

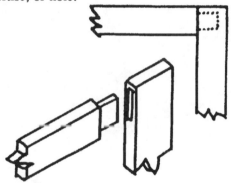

The joint is glued and reinforced with a cornerblock and is, for all practical purposes, permanent. This is the most difficult to make and, based on wood-surface to wood-surface contact, the next strongest for corner use.

The *lap(ped) joint*, like the miter, has little use in any standard flat. It is a little less difficult than the mortise and tenon in that it can be cut with normal hand tools and care. It is probably the strongest of the corner joints and, if cut to the proper dimensions, it will provide a smooth corner. This joint requires two surfaces on each board to be true, but they are cut at right angles so they can be done with hand tools.

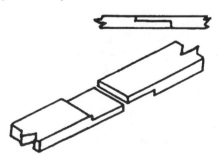

RUNNING JOINTS

Joints used to add lengths of lumber together to get a longer board are called *running joints*. The lap joint can be used as a running joint as well as a corner joint.

The strongest running joint is the scarf joint. This is a long diagonal cut along the thickness of the lumber. It is the strongest, the most invisible, and is used by carpenters in finish work.

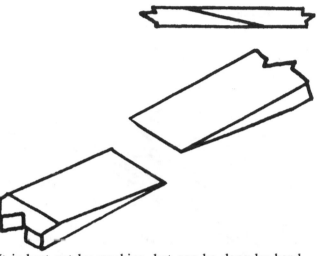

It is best cut by machine, but can be done by hand. Lap two pieces of material about 12"-16" and clamp them together. Draw a diagonal from the outside edge of one piece to the outside edge of the other, then cut along that line with a hand saw.

When battens were made of wood and long lengths were needed, there was a question as how best to accomplish this. Visual beauty was of no concern and the thickness of the finished unit made no difference. Ease of construction and strength were the two primary considerations. The scab or *scabbed joint* was the result.

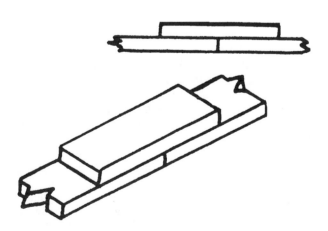

The scab is a piece of material nailed over an end-to-end butt joint. By using two layers of ten or twelve foot lengths of lumber and placing them so the joints stagger some five to six feet apart, a long, strong, batten could be fabricated easily. This is still used in some theatres especially at the bottom of a drop sandwiching the fabric between the layers of lumber. The scab joint is often used for fast repair on a flat if a stile, rail, or toggle breaks after the flat is painted for a show. The break can be restored to its original line and the scab added to the back of the break until the show is over and permanent repair can be made.

In addition to the end-to-end joints and the angle joining mentioned above, boards are joined side-by-side. To gain strength and minimize warpage, flooring is usually made with a tongue on one side and a matching groove on the other to provide a *tongue-and-groove joint.*

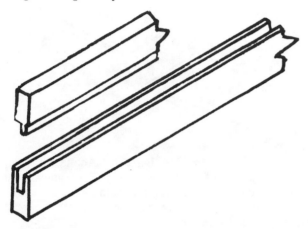

Both the tongue and groove run the full length of the board and when the flooring is laid with the matching accomplished, a smooth surface with great strength results. To add even more strength and warp-resistance the ends of the boards can be cut in the same tongue-groove manner. This is called "*end matching.*"

COVERING

Once the frame of a flat is made, the next step is covering it. The grade of fabric selected for the *flat covering* depends upon the use to which the unit will be put. For commercial use, where initial price is of less concern and durability is the prime consideration, *canvas* is used. Canvas is a strong, dense material that does not stretch easily. It is also rather expensive.

Duck is a little less expensive and is woven of smaller diameter thread, thus is a thinner fabric. The weave uses fewer threads per inch, hence its density is less than that of canvas and it tears more easily.

Muslin, which comes in several grades or weights, is the least expensive, tears most easily, and is the thinnest. Its cost is about one-third to one-half that of canvas and it lasts about one-third to one-half as long.

For use in educational theatre where the emphasis is on training and where the students do not always carry projects to the finished degree one would like, the use of muslin is recommended. It stretches more easily and shrinks when painted providing a tighter cover on a flat. It lasts a shorter time than the other coverings, but each time recovering is done more people are trained, thereby accomplishing the primary emphasis.

Canvas or duck may be used, of course. They are more expensive initially and to make this cost acceptable they must be repainted several times. Prior to any repainting the old paint should be scrubbed off, a dirty job at best. It is one that really can not be done with the newer scene paint binders. These fabrics must be stretched more tightly since they will not shrink like the muslin.

To cover a flat frame you should first tear a piece of fabric a couple of inches longer and wider than the frame to be covered. Note: TEAR. The weave used in muslin, duck, and canvas, allows the fabric to be torn straighter than it can be cut. The cut piece will often look crooked but that is due to the method used in rolling or folding the bolt of fabric in the processing. Measure along one side – known as the *selvage*. Clip the selvage and tear across to the other, then clip the second selvage.

Lay the frame to be covered with its smooth side up (opposite the cornerblocks and keystones). Place the covering material over this and fold back the sides and ends so as to expose the stiles and rails. The fabric will be glued only to stiles and rails or to the edges of an opening.

The glue chosen should be sufficient to hold the fabric in place tightly, but should not make a bond which is impossible to break. When dry, a pull across the glued surface line should hold, while pulling the fabric up and away from the surface should let it come free. Plastic Resin glue (Elmers) does very well.

A bead of glue about the size of a pencil is spread along the stiles and rails. Using the fingers or a wet block of wood like a snow plow, spread the glue out so that it is distributed across the width of the board.

The order of placing the fabric onto the frame differs from shop to shop. Some start at a corner and work across the stile and a rail from there. Others start at the mid point of the flat stretching across, then work first toward one end, pulling down and out, then down the other end. Whichever method experimentation tells is best for the individual is right. The object is to get a tight covering with no wrinkles.

Staples or tacks may be placed at intervals to help hold the covering until the glue dries. Place these on the edges of the lumber, not the face of the flat. After the fabric is stretched and laid in place, it must be set solidly onto the surface. To accomplish this sprinkle

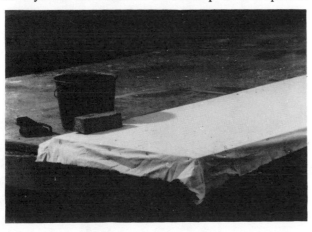

a small amount of water onto the fabric along the glued path. Using a wet wood block, go along the glue path with an ironing motion. The water will break down the filler in the fabric and the ironing motion will allow the glue to penetrate the fabric instead of just gluing the filler to the lumber.

If the space is available, let the frame dry horizontally. It can be set vertically but this often produces too much pull on a newly glued surface and the bond is broken.

Once the glue has dried (a twenty-four hour period is recommended) place the flat back on the work surface. Remove the nails and/or staples and, using a utility knife, make a cut parallel to and quarter-to-half an inch from the outside edge of the frame through the covering and into the wood. As the cut is made the excess should be pulled out away from the cut, not up. If the cut has not been deep enough, this method of pulling will result in a small tear in the muslin while pulling up from the cut might tear the fabric free from the lumber. In the process of cutting the knife blade will imbed the threads of the material slightly into the lumber and provide a smooth edge which will resist pulling free even when it rubs against another item.

In covering a window flat use the same procedure, but coat the perimeter of the window opening with glue prior to placing the fabric on the frame. Glue the outside edges as in a regular flat, then use the wood block to rub down the fabric onto the window opening. For a door or fireplace use the same procedure with a full size piece of material and, when finished, cut out the opening.

There may be times when other materials are used for covering. The above steps will provide a method of application. It is possible that there may be instances calling for solid covering such as plywood. This can be tacked, nailed, or wood screwed into place. Gluing a solid material to a frame leaves no way to repair damage to the covering.

SCENERY

(Illustrations for plan, section and elevation views courtesy of AUTOMATIC DEVICES COMPANY, Allentown, PA.)

BIBLIOGRAPHY

(This is a basic scenic listing and the amount of material on different facets of the scenery phase of work will vary from source to source.)

B- 2, 3, 5, 8, 9, 10, 11, 12, 13, 14, 16, 18 19, 20, 21, 22, 23, 26, 27, 28, 29, 30, 31, 32, 33, 36, 38, 39, 40, 41
P - 1, 3, 5 ,6
S - 4
M - 2, 3, 8, 17, 18, 19, 20, 24, 26, 27

GLOSSARY

butt joint 66
canvas 68
corner braces 64
cornerblocks 63
cross section 61
door flat 66
Duck 68
elevation 62
end matching 68
fireplace flat 66
flat 62
flat covering 68
grain 64
isometric view 62
keystones 63
lap(ped) joint 67
longitudinal section 61
miter joint 66
mortise-and-tenon joint 67
Muslin 68
plan 61
plan view 61
plug 66
rails 63
rendering 62
running joints 67
scabbed joint 67
scale 62
scaled drawings 61
scales 62
section view 61
selvage 68
sill iron 66
sketch 61
stiles 63
template 64
toggles 63
tongue-and-groove joint 68
window flat 66

CHAPTER TEN

HARDWARE

In addition to the standard hardware that can be purchased at any local hardware store, there are items made especially for use in theatre. While they have slightly different names in various localities, they remain in much the same configuration and their general names indicate their common use. Like general hardware items, the use of each piece of stage scenery hardware is not limited only to one specific task. A good supply of these items will allow the technician the opportunity to find new uses in almost each show. Items may have to be slightly adapted, especially the strap steel hardware, but this is not difficult.

Having decided to build a set of flats, the method of attaching one to the other must be chosen. There are temporary and permanent methods.

A semi-permanent method is by the use of hinges. Two flats are butted together, making sure they are precisely aligned at the bottom and joined through the use of hinges. Hinges are available in two types, several forms, and many sizes. The most common are discussed here.

HINGE TYPES

The two general types of hinges are the loose pin and the tight pin. The hinge pin is the shaft used to join the plates of the hinge together. This pin is either locked into position by rolling the ends of it or closing the path into which it is inserted, making it a tight pin hinge. If the pin is left so that it can be slipped out of position allowing the plates to come apart, it is a loose pin hinge.

The *loose pin hinge* provides a good method of joining scenic items where a relative amount of precision and stiffness is required, where two pieces of scenery will be joined and parted several times during the run of a show, or where other methods of joining will not work. By placing opposite halves of a hinge on the two pieces to be joined and locking them with a pin, a secure yet flexible joint is made. If the joint is to be

a stiff joint that will not change angle, two or more hinges may be used on opposite faces of the material. Proper placement and pinning will make a stiff joint.

Loose pin hinges are available in most forms or, if not available locally, a tight pin can be removed by grinding or cutting off one end of the pin and replacing the pin with stiff wire approximately the same diameter. If the pin is replaced with a pin wire, use about a five inch length and bend a loop into one end. This method of pinning is recommended for fast shift or for uses on traveling scenery which must be set-up or struck in a short time. In some cases a nail will do the trick.

The *tight pin hinge* is found on finish work where there would very seldom be any need to detach one section from another. If such work must be separated, the screws or bolts holding the hinges in place would have to be removed.

HINGE SHAPES

Hinges are named by the shapes of their sections or plates. There are three shapes found most often in construction and they make up the three forms of hinges. The hinge section which has a triangular

shape is the *strap* plate. A rectangular section is

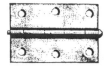

called a *butt* plate and the (almost) square sections

are *back-flap* plates. When pairs of panels, sections or plates are joined, the hinge takes the name of the plate shape. Thus two strap (triangular) plates make a strap hinge, two square plates a back-flap hinge and two rectangular plates, a butt hinge.

Combination of plates of different forms take on special names. A strap plate and a butt plate make up a "T" or "Barn Door" hinge. A butt and a back-flap make up a table hinge. There are others available in the hardware catalogs. So long as the knuckles of the leaves interlock, there is nothing to keep one from joining sections of two different hinges in a manner different from any found commercially, according to the need.

Hinge sizes are given in inches. Measurement will indicate the length of the joint, and either the width open or the width of the individual plate, dependent upon the form of hinge. In the strap hinge the usual reference is to the length of one plate (normally the plates are equal), thus a 6" strap hinge will mount 6" onto each piece of material.

Butt hinges and back-flap hinges are generally sized by their joint length. A 1-1/2" back-flap hinge will have a 1-1/2" joint and would show its other dimension as 3-7/16" which is its open measurement. The lack of positive pattern in measurement of hinges makes it important to be aware of the exact sizes needed or the space available onto which the hinge will mount.

There are many hinge forms available and many decorative forms are not listed here. Probably the most used hinge on a stage is the back-flap loose pin hinge like the No. 813 manufactured by Stanley. It is a 1-1/2" hinge and fills a great number of needs. Another multi-use hinge is the Stanley No. 900, light steel 3" strap hinge. Different designers will find uses for, and perhaps prefer, other forms and sizes.

JOINING FLATS

When joining two flats to make what is called a *book flat* the process is simple and it requires only that the bottom of the flats be aligned and the edges butted tightly together. To present an unbroken surface to the audience, the joint and hinges are often covered by a piece of fabric wide enough to cover the hinges and joint. This fabric piece is called a *dutchman*. It can be put on by painting the surface it will cover, then rolling the fabric into place while applying a coat of paint over the dutchman. The binder in the paint will offer sufficient holding power to keep the dutchman in place, yet allow easy removal. If the unit is to be permanent, the hinges should be recessed into the wood and a seamless covering used over the entire book.

If more than two flats are joined, there are other points of concern. The first two are joined as above, but if an unbroken surface is desired, yet there is a need to fold the package tightly for movement or storage, provision must be made to allow the third plate leaf to lay flat. To do this a piece of lumber the thickness of the prior package is added between the second and third flats. This is called a *tumbler* and is secured by hinges on each side. A wide dutchman is used to cover the joints. If the finished design is such that the joint would not show, the third flat could be hinged on the back, allowing it to fold back-to-back with the second flat. If this is done, compensation must be made for the thickness of the cornerblocks and keystones by adding strips of plywood under the hinges.

SCENERY HARDWARE

Another method of joining flats is through the use of the traditional scenery hardware. Such hardware has been designed to provide a relatively fast and secure method of erecting a set. With a trend today toward fewer full sets, this method is in less demand commercially. In schools, where a group of flats may be stockpiled, then utilized to make up a number of shows during the year, this permits a plan which allows complete interchangeability of flats. Through this method any two flats can be taken from stock and joined easily.

This process of set erection is called *lashing*. The key is the *lash line* which should be *sash cord*, a heavy-duty cotton cord which has relatively little stretch to it. It is superior to cotton clothes line, but is a little more expensive. Sash cord is referenced by number. The number is the diameter of the cord in 32nd's of an inch. Available in numbers 6, 7, 8, 9, 10 and 12, the number 10 provides a good strength and a convenient size to handle. The line should be about two feet longer than the flat is tall so it can be easily lashed and tied off.

From top to bottom, the traditional hardware starts with some means of holding the lash line to the flat. This can be a *lash eye* which mounts onto the stile, but some carpenters use a screw eye while others simply nail the top end of the line into the inside of the stile. The least expensive and simplest method is to drill a hole which is an eighth of an inch larger than the line into the cornerblock (being careful not to puncture the covering of the flat). Insert the line, and tie an overhand knot in the end. The knot pulls up inside the corner block to secure the line, yet replacement of the line is very simple.

Going down the lash line side of the flat the next piece of hardware is usually a *lash cleat*. This is simply a piece of steel around which the line passes.

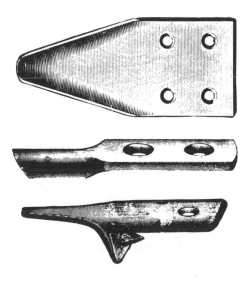

It should lay as flat as possible in line with the rear face of the flat so as to eliminate possible damage to adjacent flats during storage.

Some available cleats are simply flat steel plates, others have a slightly rolled edge. Others are cast iron, offering round shafts or even hooks for holding the line. Experimentation will provide the one best suited to a specific set of flats and the people involved with them.

The next piece of hardware, except on very tall flats, will be a *brace cleat*. This must be placed above the middle of the stile. While it serves as a lash cleat, it also provides a socket for the use of a stage brace to keep the flat erect.

If placed at the middle or below, the flat will be top-heavy and have a tendency to fall over in spite of the brace. On door flats or other flats which might have a tendency to flap at the top, additional brace cleats can be used in place of lash cleats and braces provided to stiffen the flat.

Additional lash cleats are provided down the side of the flat until the *tie-off cleat* is placed about two feet from the the line to slip. Tie-off cleats have squared or narrow sides to keep the line from slipping when it is passed around them.

On the opposite side of the flat a lash cleat is placed about six inches lower than each piece of hardware on the line side. There is no brace cleat used on this side, unless one is desired on a door flat to provide additional bracing. The tie-off cleat is placed at the same level as its partner.

During storage the lash line is looped around the tie-off cleat and, through the use of a slip knot, tightened to hold it in place against the back of the flat.

The number of lash cleats used on a flat is dependent upon the height of the flat and the desires of the designer. There can be so many that a weight/ cost problem is created or so few that the joint is weak and inefficient. Spacing of from two to three feet seems to work best in most instances, with the top lash cleat perhaps two feet from the top of the flat, the tie-off cleats about two feet from the bottom, and the remainder of the space divided into two-to-three-foot sections.

The exact vertical location of the hardware is a choice of the individual shop. The important thing here is that a plan be decided upon and that hardware be set according to that plan to assure the interchangeability desired. The choice of which side the lash line goes on is optional. When the hardware is placed, it should be set back from the outside of the flat like the cornerblocks and keystones are – that is the thickness of the material used for the flat frame.

An example of spacing, on fourteen and twelve foot flats for instance is: On the line side the tie-off cleat is at 2'-0", the lash cleat at 5'-0", brace cleat at 8'-0" and lash cleat 11'-0". On the opposite side the tie-off cleat is at 2'-3" and lash cleats at 5'-6", 8'-6", and 11'-6". On the twelve foot flats the top lash cleats are dropped to 10' and 10'-6" for easier access. Spacing may have to be altered slightly to allow space around toggles.

When spacing the toggles for a set of flats, care should be taken so that the toggles match in height as much as possible. This will allow the use of a *keeper hook*, a piece of hardware designed to allow a

stiffener to be placed behind a wall. The keeper hook drops over the toggle usually using two hooks per flat; a long piece of lumber is then dropped into the hook opening. This will batten the flats together.

It was indicated that the brace cleat should be placed above the middle of the flat to keep it from being top heavy. The *stage brace* which fits into the brace cleat is a hardwood, extendable shaft with hardware at the top designed to lock into the brace cleat and with several options at the other end to allow it to be fastened down to the floor.

The *rocker heel*, a curved metal strap with several holes, is probably the most common. This provides

locations for the insertion of a stage peg or stage screw which will be discussed next. Straight and hook foot irons are also shown in catalogs. In instances where the stage flooring is made of concrete, or there is some reason that it cannot be penetrated with a stage peg, a stage brace is made with a piece of rubber-backed plywood hinged to the bottom. When this is placed on the floor and stage weights or other weighting materials placed on it, the brace is secured.

We have made *floor plates* using a 16-inch square of plywood with a rubber sheet glued to it. To this has been glued and screwed a 2" X 4" with a 3/8" carriage bolt through it. This leaves two inches of threaded rod sticking up to accept the rocker heel of the stage brace. This is secured with a washer then wing nut. Stage weights are placed on the sides to hold the unit in place on the tile floors of classrooms.

The *stage screw* or *stage peg* is available in many forms, including a relatively new one which provides a double threaded plug and mated peg. Older forms have a rather wide hand-hold with a coarse wood-screw-like thread below. The tip is started into the flooring and, with pressure downward while turning, will work into the floor to hold the brace. Insert a stage screw into a joint between floor boards, preferably at a "T" where edges and ends of boards meet.

For the newer model stage peg a hole is first drilled, then the plug is set into the floor and the peg then placed into the plug. These are of value in hardwood floors or in locations where scenery is going to be set in the same location several times and the reinsertion of a standard peg would enlarge and thus weaken a hole in the floor.

Flats can often be suspended from battens to help in scenery changes. There are hanger irons provided for this. Both kinds use a metal rod formed into a "D" at one end to provide a location for attaching a rope, chain, or cable to support the flat. The strap iron of the hanger iron is passed around the flat side of the "D" and riveted in place.

The *flat hanger iron* is secured to the back of a flat or piece of scenery. To be sure of secure fastening it is best to use at least one bolt instead of using all wood screws in fastening the iron to the surface.

The *hook hanger iron* is similar, but has one end formed into a hook that will fit under the bottom of a flat or a piece of scenery. This provides support for the entire piece and is safer. It can be secured with wood screws since the weight rests in the hook.

In the event that a ceiling or some other horizontal piece is required, a *ceiling plate* is made. It is a flat piece of steel drilled to accept a number of wood screws, plus a larger hole for a carriage type bolt.

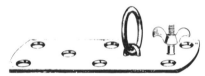

The bolt is passed through the scenery, then through the plate and secured in place. A loop is welded to the plate and has a ring in it to accept a supporting line.

A *trim chain* is of great value in supporting scenery from a batten. It is made from a piece of heavy chain and has a hook at one end and a ring at the other. The ring can be either slipped around the batten, or it can be dropped over the batten and the chain passed through it. The hook is then snapped into the

supporting device. Using the many coupling possibilities, the distance between the batten and the scenic piece can be easily adjusted. In this manner the scenic piece can be placed parallel to the floor in trim – hence the name trim chain.

Catalogs of stage hardware suppliers offer many more pieces of hardware for special purposes. Usually there are pictures and the technician can determine what is needed for a job. The limitations of a piece of hardware lie in its strength due to thickness, or its means of attachment to other elements of scenery or hardware.

BIBLIOGRAPHY

(See the basic bibliography at the end of Chapter 9. Hardware illustrations courtesy of J. R. Clancy.)

GLOSSARY

back-flap 71
book flat 72
brace cleat 73
butt 71
ceiling plate 75
dutchman 72
flat hanger iron 75
floor plates 74
hook hanger iron 75
keeper hook 74
lash cleat 73
lash eye 73
lash line 72
lashing 72
loose pin hinge 71
rocker heel 74
sash cord 72
stage brace 74
stage peg 74
stage screw 74
strap 71
tie-off cleat 73
tight pin hinge 71
trim chain 75
tumbler 72

CHAPTER ELEVEN

PLATFORMS, PARALLELS, STEPS AND RAMPS

In addition to vertical and horizontal scenic items, levels may be built to help present a more interesting picture to the audience. In working with levels there are platforms, parallels, and ultimately ramps, step units, and stairways to reach these levels.

PLATFORMS

A *platform* is a unit whose frame and top are thought of as being relatively permanent by virtue of being nailed, bolted, or held together with screws. Platforms can be any shape or size and their construction is nothing peculiar to the theatre. Usually they are a foot or less in height, since the frame is made from a piece of lumber on edge. There are larger ones. Some presentation platforms, called stages, are made as a group of very heavy platforms. For the most part, stage platforms will be smaller so that they can be handled by several stagehands, or *grips*.

A platform has a frame and a top. The top is usually some lumber by-product attached to the frame permanently with nails, screws, or bolts. Making the top detachable is unnecessary since the frame is stiff. This type of unit requires a lot of space for storage.

WAGONS

Platforms placed on wheels or casters are called *wagons*. They have been in use since the Greek "Eccyclema," their wheeled cart used to display the bodies of fallen heroes in the plays. Wagons are usually low units providing single direction run through the use of wheels or casters whose swivel mechanism is locked, or multiple-direction when provided with swivel casters. The weight of a wagon is rather great due to the size of lumber necessary to support from one caster to the next, therefore the type of caster or wheel must be carefully chosen after a study of the total design load of the frame. Metal or hard plastic wheels will mark floors, while a tire which is too soft will flatten out under a load.

PARALLELS

If storage space is a problem, it is suggested that the use of *parallels* be considered. A parallel is a unit having a folding frame with a detachable top. The top, temporarily secured for use, can be removed and the frame folded for storage. Because of this a number of parallels can be stored in a small area. While size is not limited, a modular unit seems to work best. Using 4' X 8" panels of plywood for the tops, a series of frames can be built of say, four each of 6", 12", 18", 24", 30", and 36" tall. These and their tops can be stored on a cart 4"-2" wide, 10' long, and require 12'- 6" of vertical space. The frames stack on end in the center and the tops stack at the ends.

The term "parallel" is taken from "parallelogram", which is what the unit must be in order to work. Each of the five sections: two sides, two ends, and one center, are made in a manner similar to small flats with exception of toggles. The rails, top and bottom, run full width. The vertical stiles, four on the sides and three each on the ends and center, run rail to rail.

Each joint is reinforced through the use of a cornerblock to help prevent side sway.

The finished dimension of the frame must match the perimeter of the tops. Care must be taken during design of the parallel units to make sure that the laps at the corners are figured properly. If the side sections are to be the full length of the top, the ends have to be the top width minus the thickness of BOTH sides. Another way of designing is to make each of the sides and ends the top dimension less one board thickness.

To fabricate the frame the outside (sides and ends) must be put together first. Find the proper location for one end of the center section and attach it, then fold the frame flat and mark the location for the hinges of the other end of the center section. Open the frame and attach the second end of the center section. Whether the center section is or is not square with both sides is immaterial. The limiting factor for a proper fold is the location of the hinges so that the frame will collapse entirely.

When folded, the parallel frame will be about three inches thick, as wide as it normally is high, and as long as the length plus the width of the erected parallel.

If storage is more limited, it is possible to build a parallel frame with a "continental fold". This uses end and center frames which are built in two sections each and fold in the middle as well as at the ends. The sides of this parallel are built the width of the unit less two side thicknesses. During fabrication one end and the center are collapsed one direction and the other end opposite. This makes a shorter but thicker package when folded.

Even more care must be taken in cutting lumber for parallels than for flats. If one vertical member is too short, it will not carry its load. Often the thickness of the top material is not deducted from the height before computing the length of the stiles. Less labor is required, and there is little weight difference, if 1' X 6" and 1" X 12" are ripped to proper width and then used as solid sides and ends for 6" and 12" parallel frames.

STAIRS AND STEPS

When platforms and/or parallels are used, one is presented with the problem of getting from one level to another. This can be accomplished in either one of two ways. The first is to place a series of small platforms at advantageous levels so that a person can move easily from one level to another with minimum effort. This, of course, is a *stairway* or *set of steps*. The second method is to build a slanted plane of a small enough slope that a person can maintain traction. This is a *ramp*.

There are a number of variables in building a set of steps or a stairway. These must be taken into consideration in order to fulfill the purpose – to get easily from one level to another.

Two types of step units are in use on the stage. The *practical steps* are those in view of the audience, and must fulfill a visual as well as a physical task. Because of this they must be designed to fit a given period of time, specific locale, etc. On other hand, the *escape stair* merely provides physical access. It must be safe, but not seen. Thus, it can be a series of several step units locked together or perhaps a stepladder.

Both practical and escape steps are found in one of two forms. They can be either dependent or independent. The *dependent stair* requires something to hold up the top end, as an extension ladder would. The *independent stair* is self-supporting like the step ladder. Both provide access from one level to another and can be of equal rise, but they differ in their own support.

Regardless of type or form, a staircase has three main parts. The supporting member which runs the length of the stair is called the *carriage*. This forms what could be called the side of the steps. If it is a solid piece and covers the ends of the steps it is called a *closed carriage*. If the material is notched so that its top edge resembles saw-teeth, and each step opens out into space at the end, it is an *open carriage*.

What is usually referred to as a "step" is actually made up of the other two parts. This often provides some problem in communication regarding step units, especially when talking about how long or how high they are. It is better to identify the unit by numbering its individual parts rather than the number of steps. One of these parts is the *tread*, the portion upon which the foot is placed. Here, again, it can be open or closed. An *open tread* is perforated to let moisture or other foreign material fall through, while the *closed tread* is solid. Stage units are most often solid while fire escapes and access ladders are usually open.

The third part is the *riser*. This is the vertical portion of the step. If there is no riser, just space, it is referred to as *open riser*. The use of some material to fill this space for either safety or strength makes a *closed riser*. Risers of ladders are open and instances of both open and closed risers may be found around most buildings and homes.

The most usual step unit found on stage is probably the independent staircase with open carriage, closed tread and closed riser.

In home construction the material used is mostly two inch thick lumber since the traffic is long lasting and constant. For stage use a one-inch thickness (actually a fraction less) is sufficient if the unit is designed properly. This results in less expense and weight. There are several concerns in building step units. One is that the riser must always come up under the front edge of the tread to provide support.

The strongest design is to have the riser drop below the back edge of the tread below. It is glued or nailed at this point, again to provide strength.

Both tread and riser must be fastened securely to the carriage. This joint is the one which takes the most punishment and is most likely to fail. If the unit is expected to last a long time and get hard use, a short piece of 1" X 2" should be placed under the end of each tread and glued and nailed to both tread and carriage. While the risers will provide some lateral support, it is best to put a solid back or an "X" brace in the unit from the top step to the floor. This will take out the possibility of side-to-side sway.

In planning a step unit, there are two measurements that must be checked first. One is the *total rise*, the distance from one level to the next, the vertical distance that the unit must span. The second is the *total run*. This is the distance (available) from the back edge of the top tread, to the front edge of the bottom tread. For people to be able to use the unit there must be a "landing" at the bottom which is as long as the step unit is wide.

In planning and construction it is important that each of these dimensions be equally divided into the steps. The average step will have a rise of 7 to 9 inches and a run of 9 to 10. The sum of the rise and run of a comfortable step should equal about eighteen inches. The normal 8" rise is quite high for stage use. A 6" rise will be more useful in that it is more graceful, especially in a period costume, and gives the illusion of going higher. With this use a 12" run which allows the performer a larger and more comfortable tread area.

Again, the equality of all of the rises, and all of the runs within a unit must be stressed. It is human nature to accept mentally the equality of these dimensions in a stair and, if one dimension of a series differs, a fall may be the result.

One problem encountered in the use of platforms and step units on a stage is that a set of steps will fit only two heights – one equal to the level of the top tread and the level one riser above that. For this reason a modular measurement should be chosen. If your module is six-inches, then all platforms, parallels, steps, and stairs should be built with six-inch multiples for height. This will allow the interlocking of units to provide the most flexibility in planning.

The author has experimented quite successfully with an adjustable stair. It provides access to any level from three feet to ten feet by being adjustable in its height. The unit uses a 1" X 12" tread supported on a one-foot piece of 2" X 4" at each end. A 1" X 4" riser is glued across the front of the tread and its supports. Each carriage is made up of two pieces of 2" X 4". These are bolted with carriage bolts centered in each of the carriage 2" X 4"'s and set 2" in from the front and the back of each step support. The carriage lumber is joined at the bottom with sections of 2" X 4", and at the top by 3/4" plywood which acts as a pivot point while forming a "foot" at the bottom and a pad to match the supporting wall or level at the top.

The top tread has two straps of steel protruding from it to rest on the upper level. Screws are placed through the metal to hold the unit to the upper level and a screw also secures the foot to the floor. With the treads placed 12" on centers, the unit gives a 12" rise when it is set up vertically. This rise drops down to a 4" minimum as the run of the unit is increased. The unit is obviously a dependent staircase with open risers, closed carriage, and is used primarily as an escape stair.

RAMPS

The second method of moving from one level to another is by ramp. A ramp uses a frame which has triangular side supports (carriages) and a deck (tread). Here again, one inch thick lumber will work for the carriages, especially when 3/4" plywood is used for the *decking*. If the decking is made from a number of pieces of lumber, then the carriages will have to be increased in number or size.

The limitation of a ramp is its incline. For the actor to maintain a safe footing, it is recommended that a one in five rise be not exceeded. This means that for each five feet of run, there should not be more than one foot of rise. It is possible to use a steeper rise than this, but the tread surface will have to be treated in some manner to provide more traction. Sand in the final coat of paint, or rubber mat well secured to the surface would provide better traction.

BIBLIOGRAPHY

(See the basic scenic bibliography at the end of Chapter 9.)

GLOSSARY

CHAPTER TWELVE

PAINTING

With the flats, platforms, parallels, steps, drops, and other items constructed, the final steps in making them objects to trigger the imagination of the audience can be taken. These steps are the processes of painting. Painting is done to cover a surface or to hide its real identity by making it look like something else.

Painting is, in essence, gluing a coating of colored powder onto a surface. This could be accomplished by applying glue to a surface then placing powder over it. Paint manufacturers have made it easier for us by combining ingredients so there is a one-step application.

PARTS OF PAINT

Paint has three parts: the pigment or color; the vehicle, which keeps the paint from drying prematurely; and the binder, which provides the method for holding the pigment to the surface. As compounded, the pigment and the binder are surrounded chemically by the vehicle, thus sealing them from the air. When air reaches the paint the vehicle evaporates, leaving the binder to dry and cause the pigment to adhere to the surface.

Not all paints will stick to all surfaces. This is because a given glue will not stick to all surfaces. Therefore, paints are compounded using different binders to be applied on various surfaces.

Likewise, different vehicles are used for different circumstances. The limitations of combinations of vehicles and binders dictate that there are limitations to the adherence of some paints. For instance, few water soluble paints will adhere directly to a metal surface. An example of this is trying to paint a piece of galvanized metal with paint from a child's watercolor set. Since the binder is weak, the paint will bead and not adhere.

Commercially, vehicle and binder combination is loosely referred to as base. On stage this is referred to as "size." In talking of "rubber-base paint," the indication is that the binder is from the rubber family and the result is a thin coat of colored rubber. This paint is cleaned out of brushes and rollers with warm water and soap, so it is water soluble. It has a water base – and water is a vehicle. A word of caution: read the label of any paint new to you. Those paints allowing water clean-up should use water as a thinner.

Most scenery shops purchase their paints in a form which is concentrated and must be mixed to the desired consistency and color. These forms offer some advantage. More elaborately equipped shops may stock all forms of pigment. In working in a shop one of the first decisions that must be made is which form of pigment will be used.

Dry *pigment* is the oldest form. It is available in many colors, dependent upon the individual source. Gothic Color Company, probably the leading source, lists over forty colors of dry pigment. Dry pigment in its many tints and shades offers more latitude in choosing a color for use in highlighting and shading. It also offers a greater flexibility for mixing to match an existing color.

When pigment is mixed, as is done for instance for a size coat, it is mixed dry. Dry pigment dries on the surface to almost the same color as when mixed dry. It will also accept a number of vehicles and binders. This provides more flexibility. Mixed in an approximate proportion of one part pigment to three parts of base or size, it does not affect the surface quality of the finished coat.

Some colors of dry pigment settle out more rapidly than others. It is a good idea to get into the habit of stirring with the brush each time it is dipped into the paint. Other dry pigments do not mix well with water. In these cases a small quantity of denatured alcohol or some commercial wetting agent is mixed with the dry pigment to form a paste, then is added sizing. Some of these are Raw Umber, Burnt Umber, VanDyke Brown, Prussian Blue, Black, and Violet.

A newer form is the wet pigment or pulp colors. This is a paste form in much the same color range as the dry pigments. It is more easily mixed with the binder, but does change color slightly upon drying. Mixing is accomplished in the same manner as with the dry pigments.

One form of wet or pulp pigment is *casein paint*. This has the binder with the pigment. There are more than 20 colors offered. The mixture is generally two quarts of water vehicle to one gallon of color/binder. It can be thinned more for color wash and colors can be mixed. Generally, the colors are not as strong and there are no real primaries available. Of more concern is the fact that casein dries with a slight sheen. This does not allow maximum absorption of light.

As indicated earlier, paint actually leaves a film of coating over the surface being painted. In the case of material which is to be flexed or bent often, such as a backdrop that must be folded or rolled for transport, the paint may eventually come off of the surface.

For uses where colors need to be transparent rather than opaque, aniline dyes are available. Aniline *dye* is a highly concentrated pigment in liquid form. When mixed with boiling water, a small amount of the dye will make a large quantity of the color, dependent upon the intensity desired. Aniline dyes are also available dry. In this form they can be extremely toxic and must be used with great care.

Aniline dyes actually penetrate the fiber of the fabric to which they are applied and "lock in." Because of this, care must be taken in application lest a dark color be placed in a square where a light color is wanted. The dark color is transparent and IN the fabric so the lighter color will not cover it. Bleaching is the only way to get the color out. Aniline dye is a material like that used for dyeing clothing. Clothing can be inspected to see if it is dyed – the fabric penetrated – or if the pattern or design has been stamped onto the surface using an opaque paint.

With over thirty colors of aniline dye available, the designer has a full spectrum at hand and can easily mix any color desired. The cost of using dyes compares favorably with that of using paint.

Some theatres, particularly those located some distance from cities with a scenic supply house, will use the paints offered at the local hardware store. Usually these are rubber base, or a casein paint. They will leave a relatively thick coating which cannot be scrubbed off. If this is done, then plans must be made to re-cover the flats sooner than would be done if scenic type paints were used.

Vehicle, the second part of paint, is the element that keeps pigment and binder in suspension and allows their transfer from container to surface. The *vehicle* for dry pigment, pulp paints, casein, and rubber-base paints, is usually water. Since water evaporates faster than oil, a water base paint will dry faster than an oil-base paint. Sometimes a small amount of ammonia is used to cause even faster evaporation in commercial water-base paints.

Binders for paints, in addition to holding the pigment to the surface, indicate whether the surface will finish flat, semi-gloss, or glossy. The quality of the *binder* indicates how well and how long it will stick.

The oldest scenery paint binder is *hide glue*. It is found in the forms of ground, flake, and gelatine glue. The ground glue is a granulated form that varies greatly in strength from lot to lot and will sometimes darken paint colors as they dry. It is the least expensive. The others appear as larger flakes, or in cakes. The latter are more uniform and a little stronger, showing less tendency to stain or darken. They are more expensive.

Scenery shops using hide glue establish a ritual of turning on the glue pot when the day begins so they will always have their binder ready. The preparation of this glue takes a while, so plans have to be made ahead of time. A quantity of the dry material is put into a container with enough water to cover it, and left overnight. The following day the resultant glob is placed in a double boiler with an equal quantity of water and heated to form a rather thick liquid. This is what is called "strong size."

"Size water" or "binder" is achieved by adding water to produce a sticky liquid. A small amount of size, when pinched between the thumb and forefinger, should result in a slightly sticky feeling. This is the only method of judging available since the original material varies greatly in its strength.

Some shops today use plastic-resin glues such as Mend-All and Elmers by cutting them them with water to make binder. The amount of water seems to vary with the pigment used; if the ratio is strong to the glue side, the result will be a glossy or semi-glossy surface when dry.

Mixing Latex Liquid (M.L.L.) is a successful scene paint binder. It can be prepared in quantity without danger of spoilage; it is used cold, hence is ready at a moment's notice; it compares well in cost to ground glue; and it dries to a flat finish. It also seems to mix well with most dry pigments. It is available in paint stores or concrete supply houses and is a white liquid the consistency of milk. It is manufactured for use with cement in making a wash of concrete that will adhere to other concrete surfaces. By cutting it 10 to 1 with water, a very good paint base is made.

It is, of course, possible to use any glue-like material as a binder. Any limitation would be that imposed by the desires of the designer or the demands of the material with which he is working.

Some general comments for the preparation of paints would be: mix all the paint that is going to be needed for the job, and keep track of the precise mixture ratio; keep your mixed paints in labeled containers with tight fitting lids; add binder or vehicle to that amount of paint that is going to be used that day.

PAINT APPLICATION

In painting the base coat of a set, be sure that each total wall surface is the same color. There can be a shade or two difference between one wall and another because of the difference of the angle of the audience's vision, but you cannot change the color even slightly in the middle of the wall.

Application of paint on sets is done with brush, roller, or spray. Brushes are available in many qualities and the tendency is to buy the cheapest. This is an error, for the proper brush will speed the job and provide for a better quality of work.

Priming brushes are wide, from eight to twelve inches, and have long bristles. They hold a lot of paint but do not do well for painting a sharp edge. A laying-in brush is narrower, from two to five inches, holds a good quantity of paint, and the bristles are shorter, thus allowing a sharp edge to be cut.

Foliage, lining, and round brushes are all of smaller dimensions and hold less paint. Their purpose is to provide more control of the color during application so that detail can be obtained.

All *paint brushes* must be cleaned thoroughly after each use and should be spun dry or hung with the bristles down to dry. It is possible to dry them horizontally, but this is second-best. In cleaning the brush, take care to see that the color is out of the heel of the brush – that part where the bristles are secured to the handle. Spin or shake the moisture out of the brush as much as possible. If you leave water in the ferrule – the metal band around the base of the bristles – it will begin to deteriorate and will ultimately rust out. A brush should never be

immersed in liquid up to its ferrule. Dipping a brush into paint half the bristle length is sufficient to fill it.

Paint rollers are useful at times, but often have to be pressed against the surface with so much force that the covering of the flat is stretched out of shape. For this reason they do not have the flexibility of a brush. Patterned rollers will often require support beneath the fabric covering of the flat to maintain contact and get a full print.

Spray tanks or guns will deliver effects different than those that can be accomplished with brushes or rollers. Experimentation will reveal many of these. The paint must be strained well before use, and the gun or tank cleaned with extreme care after use for the application to be effective. This additional work often keeps technicians from using these tools.

COATS OF PAINT

The application of paint to a (set of) flat(s) to make scenery is a three-step process in working with new scenery. The first coat is the *size or prime coat*. It is to fill the pores of the wood and fabric and does not need to be a specific color. Studios used to do it with only size water, which is which is the derivation of the name "size coat." However, the glue-water combination did not have much color, and it was easy to leave unpainted portions. These unpainted portions would affect the later coats of paint. For this reason a handful of color is usually added to the size water to provide a slight coloration to indicate where the paint has been spread.

The first coat should be applied to all surfaces of the flat except the back. Usually a flat is painted horizontally on the template, floor, or saw horses, then placed upright to dry.

The second coat is the *base or ground color*. This is used to bring all the flats to the same color. If older flats are used, this is their first coat for the current show. If new flats are used, it will be their second.

In the event that flats being used have been painted for a prior show and have not been scrubbed, the base coat must cover the previous colors. At times an earlier color will bleed through the new base. This will happen especially when trying to cover a dark color with a light one. A double-handful of granulated alum cooked in about four quarts of water until dissolved, then mixed in size, will form a smooth skin over the offending color. If the color still bleeds and recovering the flat is not practical, a wash of slightly thinned shellac can be used. The last alternative is to strip the covering and put on a new one.

The ground or base coat, like the prime or size, must be placed on all surfaces of the flat other than the back. It is important that the paint cover the edges. The painters do not always know which flat will be placed so that its edges show to the audience, and painting edges with the face of the flat is much easier and quicker than touching up on stage after the set is in.

The final or third coat is the *texture coat*. Its purpose is to make scenery visually attractive. To do this it must be made to resemble a specific item or to have depth and/or texture. This texture coat also helps to hide defects in the surface covering. The latter is important since dents and abrasions are often made during the final set-up.

There are a number of methods of texturing. Each of them breaks up an otherwise flat surface. Some are used to represent specific building materials such as brick, tile, concrete, wood molding, etc. Listed here are some of the more common methods. Texturing is limited only by the imagination of the painter.

PAINT TEXTURES

Spattering, or *sprinkling*, is probably the most common form of texturing since it is the simplest. It is achieved by flipping small drops of paint onto the surface. Usually several colors are used, and they will often be complementaries of the base coat or darker shades of the base hue. A more dense spatter of fine droplets can produce shading under a painted architectural item. A quantity of paint is held in the brush and the brush is flipped at the surface. The length of the bristle, length of the stroke in flipping the brush, the thickness of the paint, all cause a change in the texture of the spatter. Some painters prefer to strike the brush against a stick to produce a spattering effect.

Stippling is applied with a relatively dry sponge, brush, feather duster, or anything of a rough texture. An imprint of the applicator is left on the surface so it is important to keep turning or rotating the applicator while doing this so a pattern is not produced. Care must be taken that pressure with a fresh load of paint is less than that with a lesser load so that the same visible density may be maintained.

Scrumbling, or *wet blending*, is the softening of the edges of two adjacent colors so they blend. It is done while the colors are still wet. They are applied, then a third brush is used to blend them together. This is used to form highlight or shadow or to indicate a rounded surface.

Dry brushing, *dragging*, *combing*, or *wood-graining* are also done while the initial color is slightly wet. They produce narrow lines of color to represent wood grain. It is done with a short-bristled, rather coarse brush. The brush is dampened with paint of a contrasting color to the base, and drawn over the surface. Care must be exercised while setting down and lifting the brush from the surface so that a reasonable consistency is maintained to produce the desired effect.

Puddling is accomplished while the base coat is still wet and is done in a manner like spattering. The drops of paint are larger and upon striking the wet surface, have a tendency to spread and mix with the base, thus producing larger splotches of color with blended edges. Lifting an edge of the flat while these colors are still wet will produce runs of color not unlike those found in marble.

Rolling, either *rag roll* or burlap roll, uses a coarse fabric or even a piece of carpet secured around a cylinder, or perhaps simply rolled and tied. When saturated with paint and rolled lightly on a surface, it presents a textured pattern with a subtle repetitive design. The frequency of repetition is dependent upon the diameter of the roll and the control of the quantity of paint on the roll.

Lining is used to produce the effect of molding or other architectural items. In addition to being mechanical, it is a method that requires some patience and skill. The brush must carry a sufficient quantity of paint and a straight stick, called a lining stick, must be held adjacent to the line to be painted and a little distance off the surface. The brush is drawn along the stick to produce a straight line. Beginning painters often place a stick on the surface, but soon find that the paint works its way under the edge and spreads out. While the general width of a line must conform, the density of the line is of lesser importance. The density can vary during the run of the line as long as it does not change abruptly. Often hours are lost by attempts to make a lining project a perfection job. A good-looking line can be run in a short time with practice. Additional lines are joined alongside the first to present highlights and shadows to give the representation some three-dimensional form.

Flogging a flat with a piece of fabric whose ends have been cut into strips, or with the feathers of a feather duster, wet with paint, will present a nice combination between stippling and rag rolling. With care and practice a somewhat repetitive pattern can be achieved. This often will provide the effect of a fabric or tapestry background.

Stenciling uses a waxed paper, metal, or stencil-paper cutout. The paint is then applied through the openings with a damp sponge or brush. Stenciling is used to repeat a precise pattern several times. Care must be taken to apply the paint vertically to the surface – an extreme "brushing" action will force the paint under the edges of the stencil and blur the final result.

Stamping is another method of producing a pattern. A relatively soft material, such as a block of Styrofoam, is cut to the desired shape. Paint is applied to the block by dipping it into the paint or using a brush to coat the desired block surface. The block is then placed against the material to be stamped. Again, as in stenciling, make sure that a minimum amount of paint is applied. For both stamping and stenciling it is best to place a rather solid backing under the surface being painted so that all portions of the face of the stencil or stamp will come in contact with the surface. One example of the use of stamping is the production of brickwork.

Spraying will allow the painter to produce a smooth solid coat, or a spatter of either fine or coarse texture, dependent upon how he has the spray device set. With a spray gun – either the commercial type with a motorized compressor, or a hand-pump type as is used in a garden, or one of the airless type guns - the painter can practice and produce some effects that cannot be achieved easily with paint brushes. Probably the greatest problems in spraying will be in making sure that all the paint is the same consistency and well strained, and that the spray gun and other equipment is well cleaned after each use.

Appliques can be used to add interest because they actually present a third dimension to the set surface. In this method of texturing, something with a depth is actually placed onto the surface of the flat. An example would be the pouring of rather coarse wood shavings onto a wet base coat. Once the base coat has dried, turn the flat up and let the excess fall off. A wet brush of contrasting color is dragged over the texturing. Wet newspaper can be applied also and drawn into slight ripples and ridges. In either of the appliques stated, as well as in most others, the binder in the base coat will probably be sufficient to hold the applique to the surface. Since appliques are difficult to remove, flats or other surfaces treated in this manner can seldom be repainted and used again.

Glazing is used to produce a shine on paint which otherwise has a flat finish. Glazing is used to help set off woodwork from painted walls and to give depth to the entire setting. It will also help differentiate an industrial looking interior from a home interior. Utilizing shellac thinned with denatured alcohol,

sugar water, or the binder M.L.L. straight, will produce a surface which is reflective of light.

Other methods of texturing are known and used. As the demand arises, there is nothing to prohibit experimentation. The discovery of any number of materials for application techniques to produce specific desired effects is possible.

In addition to brushes, a number of other items should be included in the scenery painting area. *Lining sticks*: straight sticks – which are lightweight and available in varying lengths – are an adjunct to brush lining. Thin bamboo sections are taped to the handles of paint brushes used for lining, foliage, or other detail work, to let the painter get perspective by viewing his work from a distance while painting. These are a "must" when painting a drop or other scenery that is laid out on the floor. The scenic artist usually will remain standing while applying detail work. Even when drops and flats are painted while vertical, it is best that the artist stand back.

A *snap line*, described in the chapter on tools, will be invaluable. The line can be chalked with scene paint and snapped onto a wet base coat to present a thin, straight line. There will be a slight haze around the resultant line due to the pigment flipping off, but the result will be a straighter and thinner line than can usually be accomplished with a brush – and it is much faster.

Chalk and charcoal are used to lay out the work on a flat or on a drop. Whether measuring a molding or transfering a drawing from a sketch, the chalk or charcoal will provide an outline to be followed. Choose the one that will show least on the surface being painted; there will then be no concern about erasing or covering unwanted lines later.

If a more intricate design is desired, or one is to be drawn several times, try a *tracing wheel* and *pounce bag*. The desired design is drawn on wrapping paper; then a tracing wheel is used to follow the pattern, thus perforating the outline. The paper is placed over the surface on which the final design is to appear, and the pounce bag is patted along the perforated line. A pounce bag is a piece of muslin tied in a bag form and filled with powdered graphite, powdered charcoal, or scene paint. From this bag the powder penetrates the holes and leaves a dotted-line design outline.

Paint rollers and pans can be used for prime and size coats and for applying paint to hard surfaces such as platforms, parallels, and step units. By securing a rope in a pattern around a paint roller, a repetitive pattern can be produced. This is just one more example of the many application techniques that can be used – employing what most people accept as a "normal" piece of painting equipment.

BIBLIOGRAPHY

Special attention is called to B-1 and S-4 for reference in this area.

(See also the basic scenery bibliography at the end of Chapter 9.)

GLOSSARY

Paint Schedule

North Central
High School
Indpls., IN.

Production

Form

C - 1

Designer:_____   Date:_____

Color Number	USE	Square Feet	MIX								Total Quantity	Initial Mix by
			Color	Amt	Color	Amt	Color	Amt	Whtg			
	Base 1											
	Base 2		*PURPOSE OF THIS FORM:*									
	Base 3											
			To provide a precise listing of the mixes and their uses.									
			USE OF THIS FORM:									
	Texture 1											
	Texture 2		Spaces are provided to list the quantities of various hues required to make the final color for the different coats.									
	Texture 3											
	Texture 4											
	Texture 5		In this manner the final container needs be given only a color number for reference.									

SPECIAL INSTRUCTIONS :

CHAPTER THIRTEEN

LIGHT SOURCES

In most modern instances the light used on stage emanates from a *filament lamp*. The incandescent lamp is the most popular source because it is the most economical and the simplest to operate. To use lamps most effectively the user must be able to differentiate between the parts of the lamp and their respective purposes, limitations, and variables.

Many different types of lamps are manufactured and each has its purpose as defined by a number of variables in the lamp. The primary parts or variables of the filament lamp are: the base, the filament, and the bulb. While each part has its specific task, the total package is known to the manufacturer as a "filament lamp" and to most users as a "light bulb."

LAMP BASES

The *lamp base* is used to hold the filament and the bulb in their respective locations or positions and to make electrical contact with a power source. For different jobs the bases come in different sizes and in different forms.

The size of a base is measured at its largest diameter or, in the case of the bi-post type lamps, center-to-center of the two pins.

Different applications place restrictions on the base of a lamp; therefore, the forms of the base are varied.

For general service installations where the exact position of the filament is of minimal concern because there is no critical reflector or lens used, a

Skirted

Minia-ture Cande-labra Inter-mediate Medium Admedium (Mercury Lamp) 3-Lite Mogul

screw base is used. In a living room lamp, there is little need for the filament to be in a precise location – just so long as it is within the shade of the lamp. This form of base is the least expensive, allows secure fastening with a minimum of effort, and places the filament generally in the correct location. Screw bases are made in all the listed sizes.

Miniature Bayonet   Miniature Flanged   Bayonet Candelabra

It is a bit more critical that the tail lamp of an automobile be set in a precise location since there are often two contacts – one providing power for the tail light filament the other for the brake light filament.

This *bayonet base* is used for automotive lamps, flashbulbs, and many panel lights in electronic equipment. It is a smooth cylindrical shape with two pins protruding from the sides – often at different levels so as to prevent the base from being put into a socket in more than one way. If the pins are set opposite each other, the base fits in two ways, 180 degrees divergent. The reason for position concern will be explained later when filaments are discussed. The bottom of the bayonet socket is spring loaded so the lamp must be pushed in, then turned counter-

NAME	SIZE	VOLTAGE	USES
minature	3/8"	low	flashlight; Christmas tree (series)
candelabra	1/2"	low/high	Christmas exterior; interior parallel
intermediate	5/8"	high	Christmas exterior; decorative
medium	1"	high	common general service
mogul	1-1/2"	high	high wattage general service

clockwise to remove it from its socket. Due to the rather small contact surfaces provided by this type base, it is used only on low current lamps.

Medium Prefocus   Mogul Prefocus

For medium or high-current lamps whose filament must be located precisely, a *prefocus base* is often used. This is similar to the bayonet base in that it is a smooth cylinder, but instead of the pins there are two "ears" at the top of the base. Their outside radius is concentric with the radius of the base and one of the ears longer than the other so the base will fit into the socket in only one way. During manufacture the filament is set at a designed relation to this base so that the lighting instrument for which it is made will function properly. Again, the reasons for this concern will be covered later.

Medium Bipost   Mogul Bipost

Another base for medium and high current lamps is the bi-post. The *bi-post base* consists of a pair of shafts, cylindrical in shape, which fit into either a pair of clamps, or a two-hole base with a locking collar. This base will allow two filament positions and also, due to the clamp or snap fitting of the socket, one of the more positive contact methods for electrical current.

LAMP FILAMENTS

Incandescence is defined as: Getting something hot enough to give off light. It can be produced in many ways and the most common is the sun. Most commonly on stage electricity is passed through a thin wire coil of tungsten alloy called a filament. This produces light and its byproduct, heat. The purpose of the second part of the lamp, the filament, is to turn electrical energy into light.

Since the finely drawn tungsten filament actually gets white hot it would soon destroy itself if it were not in a controlled environment. This may be either a vacuum, as in the case of most lamps below 25 watts,

or in an inert gas atmosphere of nitrogen and argon for example. There are other combinations used (the newer tungsten-halogen will be discussed later), but these are the most common.

To satisfy different brightness requirements, varying lengths of filament material are used by the manufacturers. To keep the filament in the area most advantageous for the designated use, the filament material is most often coiled like a door spring. For spotlight applications (maximum light control), it is important that we have the smallest light source possible. For this purpose the coiled filament is sometimes coiled again – thus producing a coiled coil. With the entire filament material now within a compact area, we can determine the light source location.

For further identification, especially in spotlight lamps, there is a stated *light center length* (LCL). This is a measurement from a point on the base of the lamp to the center of the filament. This is necessary when relamping an instrument which has a reflector included in the optical system to assure us that the light source is in the center of the reflector. As long as the bases of lamps are the same, the bulb will physically fit into the housing, and the circuitry will provide sufficient current, all lamps of the same LCL will operate efficiently in a given lighting instrument. Varying lamp wattage is a way of changing the brightness of an instrument if you do not have control equipment for dimming available.

The filaments are supported by *lead-in wires* which form a stiff frame to support the filament in its proper position and carry current from the base. The shape (and size) of a filament will change from lamp to lamp to meet specific demands. The filament of a general service lamp will be spread over a rather large area because the lamp should put out light with a minimum shadow – therefore we can have a larger source area. In a spotlight where we would like to have the brightest and most controlled light possible, the filament will be condensed into as small a physical area as possible. The many filament shapes available can be seen in the lamp catalogs published by lamp manufacturers, but generally speaking, the filament for a spotlight (maximum control) will be

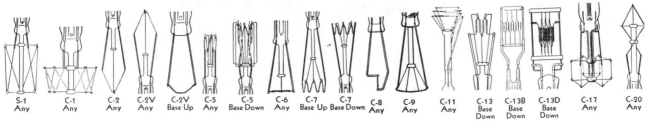

S-1 Any   C-1 Any   C-2 Any   C-2V Any   C-2V Base Up   C-5 Any   C-5 Base Down   C-6 Any   C-7 Base Up   C-7 Base Down   C-8 Any   C-9 Any   C-11 Any   C-13 Base Down   C-13B Base Down   C-13D Base Down   C-17 Any   C-20 Any

within a small area, while the general service (minimum control) filament will be spread over a larger area.

LAMP BULBS

In order to enclose the filament and keep air from it, we have the third part of a lamp which is the *bulb*. Bulbs vary in shape, size, and surface treatment.

Different *bulb shapes* are made to conform to specific instrumentation or uses. These shapes are designated by a letter code to show general shape, and an associated number which gives the width of the bulb at its widest point in 8ths of an inch. Examples would be: The "A-19" which is a general service lamp – the shape "A" is the typical or most often used shape encountered, and it is 19/8ths of an inch in diameter at its widest point. Most spotlight lamps are of "T" or tubular shape and their diameter is also stated. There are many other shapes made and these, too, are shown in manufacturers' catalogs along with their diameters and other technical information.

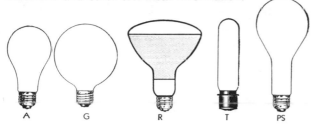

The smaller vacuum lamps are only incidentally found around stages. Because of their slight vacuum they produce a somewhat yellowed light and not much heat. The general service lamp which is gas-filled produces a whiter, but hotter product. The gas-filled spotlight lamps transmit heat to the bulb and, since they are higher wattage in a smaller envelope, have a stated burning position. This is found in the order code. It is also stamped on the top of the bulb.

LAMP ORDER CODES

The *lamp order code* is a series of letters and numbers which give the buyer and user specific information about the lamp. The first information given will be the wattage of the lamp. This may be in numbers: 60, 100, 500 etc.; or number-letter: 1M (1000), 2M (2000). Next is the shape of the lamp given by a letter code of one or more letters. Some letters stand for words which define the shape: R = reflector; B = bulb shape; T = tubular; PS = pear shaped; FE = flat end; F = flame, etc. The numbers following the lamp shape letter designation will tell the diameter of the lamp at its widest part in 8ths of an inch. A "T20" lamp is tubular shape, 20/8ths of an inch, or 2 1/2" in diameter. A "G40" is globe shaped, 5" diameter. The

diameter code is most often followed by a slant line (/) after which special information is given. This may be done with letters: IF = inside frost; R = red; Y = yellow, etc., or with a key number. The key number will refer you to a catalog footnote which will give you some technical information about that specific lamp.

The American National Standards Institute (ANSI) has created a *three-letter code* which is used to identify lamps. This is used for projection and photographic lamps as well as stage lighting lamps. Unfortunately, neither the letters nor their sequence stand for any specific measurement or detail in the lamp as nearly as I can discover. Manufacturers' catalogs cross-reference these identifications with the older order codes in most cases.

Spotlight lamps have a somewhat shorter life than general service lamps due to the more concentrated heat. Their life will be shortened even more if the lamp is burned in an incorrect position. Some spotlight lamps are designed to dissipate their heat through the bulb and must be burned base down (in relation to the filament). Incorrect *lamp burning position* will cause premature failure of the lamp and may cause it to shatter perhaps scarring the reflector surface in the instrument.

The surface treatment of a bulb is done to allow another facet of control. The clear bulb is used for the most control, but if a smoother and larger light source is required which is not so harsh, the bulb will be frosted or color treated.

One of the problems of the incandescent lamp derives from the fact that as tungsten burns it gives off a residue which gathers on the bulb. This can be noted on an older lamp which has spent its life in one position. The higher portions of the bulb are blackened. This is not so much of a problem in stage lighting, but with the advent of color television and its extremely sensitive color cameras, something had to be done about the color change in the light output caused by these deposits.

The answer came through the use of more expensive quartz glass. Its ability to dissipate more heat without fracturing allowed smaller bulbs for one thing. Another advantage of this type of bulb is that it is compatible with halogen gas. By using a halogen atmosphere inside the bulb, tungsten burn-off combines with the halogen and, as it moves around inside the bulb, is redeposited on the filament, thus providing a longer life and consistent color. This type of lamp is called by several different names by various producers: *quartz-halogen lamp, tungsten-halogen lamp* or *quartzline*.

Some stage lighting instruments are now designed for this type of lamp and the bulb is much smaller than its equal wattage standard incandescent counterpart, so lighting units can be made smaller. It should be noted that the wattage (heat) must still be dissipated. The quartz glass also dissipates heat better, so there is seldom a specific burning position required for a quartz bulb.

With the quartz bulb the acid of the perspiration on a person's fingertips can cause etching of the glass. For this reason a warning appears with each lamp to handle it with gloves or with the provided paper or plastic wrapper. Due to etching, these lamps have been known to explode within a fixture because of bulb failure.

OTHER LIGHT SOURCES

Incandescence is not the only source of light. Since it gives us the most light at the smallest point, it is the one most used. Other forms and sources will, no doubt, be developed in the future.

At the moment the fluorescent lamp offers more brightness for less current consumption than the incandescent. For this reason it is used for classroom lighting and other large area coverage where precise control is not necessary, but high brightness and smooth coverage are desired. Unless it would be used for general coverage work light, *fluorescence* has no practical value on stage except in its form we call "black light."

Often called by other names, "black" light is used as a gimmick. It is really using ultraviolet wave lengths of light. Some items accept ultraviolet wave lengths, change their wave length, and send out these rays thus becoming illuminated, while others absorb the rays and stay dark. In the regular fluorescent tube electrons bombard a powder on the inside surface of the tube and it glows brightly. In stage use the tubes emit ultraviolet rays which travel to items which have been treated to reflect them, not just to a powder in the same tube. Many people erroneously refer to this as "luminous."

A luminous article is one which has been exposed to radiant energy and has stored enough energy to shine after the exciting source is gone. Luminous surfaces actually glow, while the fluorescent surfaces will react only while an ultraviolet exciting source is present.

A relatively new form of light is produced by *electro-luminescence*. It gives off little light in terms of brightness, but also utilizes very little electricity;

therefore, there is little heat. It is being used for exit lights and clock faces and has been successfully employed to provide a glowing panel offstage to direct an actor who must leave the stage after a complete blackout without endangering himself. It has also been used to provide a lighted strip below a lock-rail to illuminate instructions. Small units are on the market for home night lights.

BIBLIOGRAPHY

B - 8, 16, 25, 27, 28
P - 2, 4, 5, 6
S- 1, 2,
M - 1, 4, 7, 12, 13, 14, 15, 19, 22, 23.
    Chapter illustrations courtesy of General Electric Company, Nela Park, Cleveland, OH.

GLOSSARY

bayonet base 89
bi-post base 90
bulb 91
bulb shapes 91
electro-luminescence 92
filament lamp 89
fluorescence 92
Incandescence 90
lamp base 89
lamp burning position 91
lamp order code 91
lead-in wires 90
light center length 90
prefocus base 90
quartz-halogen lamp 91
quartzline 91
screw base 89
three-letter code 91
tungsten-halogen lamp 91

CHAPTER FOURTEEN

CONTROL OF LIGHT

From any light source the rays of light emanate in all directions. With actors on one side of a light and the audience on the other, there is need to control some of the rays to keep them from blinding the audience. The designer of a piece of lighting equipment can call upon one or more of three methods of control of light rays: absorption, reflection, and/or refraction.

ABSORPTION

Absorption is the stopping of a ray or rays. It has a by-product which is heat. This control is accomplished by using a shell, casing, shutters, louvers, etc., to block the ray.

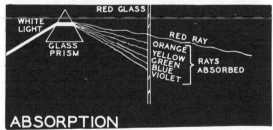

In the next chapter some specific lighting instruments will be discussed. You will find examples of absorption in the housings of many of these lights, in the framing shutters installed in the ellipsoidal spotlight, the *barn doors* that can be added to the front of the Fresnel spot, the blinder at the front of the lamp in the beam projector, and the iris diaphragm in the Trouper or other follow spotlights.

By placing a hand in the beam of light emitted from a projector aimed toward a surface a shadow is produced because the hand is absorbing the light. If you are close enough to the projector, and the source is strong enough, you will feel the heat caused by this absorption.

If a source is placed inside an absorptive sphere, and only a small opening is left for some light to escape, most of the light is wasted by being turned into heat. To utilize some of this otherwise wasted light, a second method of control is used – reflection.

REFLECTION

Reflection is the re-direction of rays of light by bouncing them off of a surface. If reflection were 100% efficient, there would be no heat, but it is not

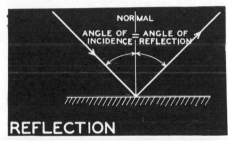

so. The efficiency depends upon the type of surface treatment. While surfaces may be finished in many ways, they can be classified in three general surface finishes.

REFLECTOR FINISHES

A *specular finish* is mirror-like and polished. This is the most perfect reflector finish, thus it is found in instruments in which the greatest amount of control is desired. While offering the most control, it is also the most harsh in quality.

A smooth, flat, specular surface will allow you to see the "angle of incidence equals the angle of reflection" theory. This theory means that if you look into a mirror from an angle of 45 degrees to the mirror surface, you will see what is 45 degrees to the other side of a line perpendicular to the mirror surface.

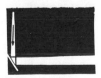

Thus, the only way to see yourself in a mirror is to stand on front of it (90 degrees). Apply this theory to the specular reflecting surface, and you will begin to understand the use of the different reflector shapes, a facet covered later in this chapter.

The least control and softest quality is given by a *diffuse finish*. This can be obtained by providing a rough surface, or one that is painted white. Either will cause the rays to be broken up and scattered. This type of reflector finish is used in flood lights.

An example of this reflection can be seen during the presentation of slides or movies. While you see a perfect pattern on the screen caused by the focused projection of the film, the reflection from the screen to the rest of the room is one of soft light with no hint of the shapes on the screen. Projection onto a mirror would deliver a perfect reflection back toward the projector.

The third reflector finish is the *spread finish* and is the result of an etched or scratched surface which produces a combination effect. Some of the rays are reflected perfectly, while others are scattered. The result is that there is more control than with diffuse finishes, but a softer quality than with specular surface finishes. Reflector surfaces with this finish are found in borderlights where some control yet soft quality is desired.

Since control is the key word in the use of light, the instruments which exert the most control will use the specular-type reflector finish. With this finish and its resultant precise return of the ray various shaping can be used to allow the rays from the back of the source to be utilized. These rays would normally be lost as heat by being absorbed by the housing.

A word of warning lest you think that the reflector is the most important part of the lighting instrument: at least one college instructor used to have the reflectors removed from his Fresnel type instruments. He had discovered that they, when properly aligned, only increased the light output some 25% and only a small percentage of the instruments came with the reflector properly installed. Manufacturers have re-designed the mounting for this reflector now, and it does do the job for which it is intended. Regardless of the reason for the mis-alignment, improper positioning of the

reflector/light-source combination will result in less efficiency.

REFLECTOR SHAPES

There are three geometric shapes which are the basis for reflector design in stage lighting. By analyzing the perimeter/center-point relation in these shapes it is possible to see just what control the reflector shape will place on the rays of light. In each case it will be assumed that the light source will be present at the center or focal point. We know that the smaller the source of light, the better the control. This is the reason for the discussion earlier on the area required for the placement of the filament, and why the manufacturer attempts to get as small a light source as possible.

One of the simplest shapes to draw is the circle. In three dimensions it is a sphere. Its construction requires only a point and a radius. The *spherical reflector* is merely a section of a sphere. We know geometrically that a radius line is perpendicular to a tangent touching the sphere at the same point.

SOURCE AT **CENTER**

Therefore, a ray of light traveling on a radius line, will return along that line. With the light source at the center point rays of light will be returned to the center point by a spherically shaped reflective surface.

SOURCE AT FOCUS

A *parabolic reflector* results from taking a section of a cone which has been cut by a plane parallel to one of its sides. The result of starting rays of light at the center point is that they will strike the surface of the reflector and be redirected so that they emerge parallel to each other.

An ellipse is constructed by using two center points and defining a curve in which the distances of any point on that curve from the two center points always have the same sum. Offering the most control of any of the reflector shapes, an *ellipsoidal reflector* will send its reflected rays through the second point. Being the most efficient, this also concentrates a lot of heat at that second point, and provision for dissipating this heat must be made.

SOURCE AT FOCUS

The uses of these shapes (and combinations of them) will be covered in the next chapter, Lighting Instruments.

REFRACTION

The third method of control is *refraction*, which allows a ray to be directed by passing through a more dense (than air) medium, usually glass, thus changing its direction slightly. Here again some light is lost since there is not 100% transmission due to the quality of glass used. This is the reason that heat-resisting lenses have to be used in some equipment. The purpose of refracting light is to allow an increase in intensity by gathering rays into smaller groups or beams than they would usually travel. The refraction tool, the lens, therefore changes the path of a ray slightly.

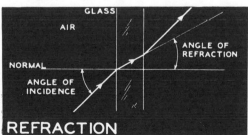

REFRACTION

The principle of refraction is that light, as it passes from one medium to another of greater or less density, changes direction. If a ray approaches a surface perpendicular to that surface, it does not change direction. If it approaches at an angle to the surface, then as it enters the denser medium, it bends away from the surface. As the ray leaves a denser medium, it will bend toward the dividing surface.

The purer a lens is, the less will it spread a ray of light in its interior. Eyeglasses are made from the purest glass because their result must be more nearly perfect. Most stage lighting units use a poorer grade of glass because the quality of control is not so important. This is one reason for the spill from lights and the resultant requirement of masking.

LENS SHAPES

As in reflectors, we have several shapes of lens available to do different jobs. The most popular today are the *Fresnel lens*, (pronounced Frueh-nel'), named for the Frenchman who developed it, and the *plano-convex lens* or *condenser lens* which is named for its manufactured shape.

The direction of a ray of light is changed by the angle at which it strikes the surface of a denser medium. The angle of the glass is critical. Obviously, the angle relation between the two sides of a piece of glass can vary widely. Reference to the opposing sides is made by using combinations of terms. To determine the shape of a lens, you start with a vertical line perpendicular to the axis of the lens as you look a it from the side. If a surface of the lens is parallel to this vertical line, that surface is a plano, or flat. As you look at the lens, and a side curves away from the vertical line, that surface is convex. If a side curves in toward the line, that side is concave. Thus, the plano-convex lens has one flat side, and one which curves out. A contact lens or eyeglass lens has one surface which curves in, and one which curves out, and it is concave-convex. A sheet of regular window glass is plano-plano.

The radius upon which the curve of a lens is plotted will tell just how thick a lens will be and, as an end result, exactly how it will control light. Physics texts go into a deeper study of the details of lens uses and will give formulas on how to figure precisely which lens one needs. In theatre a number of different lenses are offered for pieces of lighting equipment, and the manufacturers' include tables indicating what each lens will provide.

Each of the lenses gives the light rays a slightly different quality in addition to having a different control effect. The plano-convex lens provides a more precise, but harsher edge on the beam.

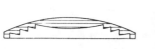

The *step lens*, which actually started as a convex-convex lens, softens the edge a little. This lens looks as though it is concave-convex, but close examination will show that its sides actually curve away from each other. The glass was designed out of the center of the lens to cut down on its thickness and weight.

The Fresnel lens actually started as a plano-convex lens and by adaptation the glass amount was cut down until the lens was relatively thin but maintained its control. In the process of manufacture the back or plano side of the lens is slightly roughened and this, plus the concentric risers on the front, projects a soft-edged beam of light.

Lenses will defined by two dimensions. One will be the diameter of the lens, the second will be the focal length. Thus, a 6" X 9" lens will be 6" in diameter and will have a 9" focal length. Substituting lenses of different focal lengths will change the diameter of the beam as well as its consistency of light distribution. The 6" X 9" plano-convex is one of the most popular lenses used in the ellipsoidal spotlights today. Most of the 6" Fresnel instruments use a 6" X 3" lens.

The primary uses and terminology of lenses stated above are just that – primary. Any unit can be given any lens – and the resultant light pattern output will change. Experimentation by the lighting technician will show final results better than words.

BIBLIOGRAPHY

B - 4, 7, 8, 11, 12, 13, 15, 16, 20, 21, 22, 23, 24, 25, 26, 27, 28, 29, 30, 31, 34, 35, 37, 41.
P - 1, 2, 3, 4, 5, 6,
S - 2
M - 1, 4, 6, 7, 9, 10, 13, 14, 15, 19, 22, 23, 25, 28, 29

(This is a basic electrical listing and the amount of material on different facets of the area will vary from source to source)

Control illustrations courtesy General Electric.

GLOSSARY

CHAPTER FIFTEEN

LIGHTING INSTRUMENTS

The selection of a specific lighting instrument for a given task can be made from a wide field of choices. Within the pages of almost any manufacturer's or distributer's catalog are a number of items, each of which will direct light toward an area. Without even straying from manufacturer to manufacturer, we have what seems at best to be a difficult choice – one which may be more a matter of chance since we often see only a picture in a catalog.

Personal contact is the best way to choose a piece of lighting equipment. If you are purchasing equipment, try to get a sample piece of that equipment to see if it will do what you want, unless you are familiar with the specific unit. If you own equipment and it is a question as to which unit to use to do a certain job, experimentation is the answer. Keep in mind that equipment from different manufacturers, while seemingly the same in design, configuration, and indeed using the same lamp, will not necessarily place the same amount or quality of light in the area to be lighted. This can be due to the quality of materials, the precision of design, and/or the amount of care taken in manufacture and assembly of the unit.

Lighting instruments make use of the forms of control of light rays available – absorption, reflection, and refraction. Being aware of these forms and their interrelation will help in selection. The type of lighting job to be done will be the deciding factor in choosing an instrument with one, two, or all three forms of control. The following looks at some of the common pieces of equipment used in theatre today.

LIGHTING INSTRUMENTS

Judging by units in use, the most common today is probably the *Fresnel* (Freh-nel') type spotlight which is named for the Frenchman who designed the lens. This unit is used on the stage itself since it has a relatively short throw and presents a beam with a soft edge. Due to that soft edge a number of beams can be rather easily blended together to give the stage the look of illumination from one angle, all from one source.

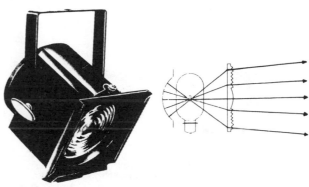

courtesy Decor Electronics Div.

The Fresnel uses all three methods of control by having a housing which blocks or absorbs the greater portion of the rays, a reflector which really increases the efficiency of the instrument only about 25%, and a lens to provide final gathering of the rays.

The Fresnel is available in several sizes from 3" to 16" lens diameter, the most common being the 6" and 8". The 6" units are generally lamped with 500 watt lamps, although 250, 400, and 750 are available. The 8" is usually 1000 watts. The unit is limited in its burning position by the type of lamp installed. Check the top of the lamp for limitations. If a quartz lamp is used, any burning position is usually acceptable.

The units allow the lighting designer to change the diameter of the area covered. This is done by moving the *burner assembly* (the combination of socket, lamp and reflector) closer to the lens to widen or flood the beam or, away from the lens to narrow or spot position.

The Fresnel lens sends a number of extraneous rays of light outside the major field of light; hence, there are masking devices such as *funnels* and *barn doors* available to attach to the front of the unit to help cut down these rays spilling onto scenery and/or curtains.

The usual problems with the Fresnel come from lack of maintenance. The lens gets dirty and the focus mechanism sometimes rusts. Lenses can be cleaned easily with any good glass cleaner and a cloth – I suggest a diaper since it is soft and can be easily washed. Lubrication of the sliding burner assembly should be done with dry graphite.

Similar to the Fresnel is the *plano-convex lens spotlight*. While its shape may be different it functions just as the Fresnel, but the plano-convex lens provides a hard-edged beam of light. It has the same characteristics, limitations, and problems. These units were popular in the 20's and 30's but many are still around.

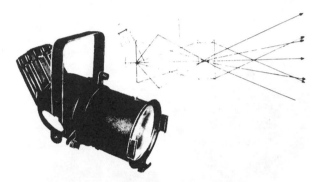

The second common unit is the *ellipsoidal spotlight* used for lighting stage areas which must be strictly defined. Named for its reflector shape, this unit also uses all three control forms. Its housing absorbs fewer rays than that of the Fresnel because the reflector surrounds more of the source and, due to its size and relative shape, is the most efficient in lighting equipment. This results in a greater quantity of light reaching the optical system. The light is thus concentrated in a smaller area which in turn allows more exact control. This type unit is ofter referred to as a "*Leko*", which is the patented title owned by Century Lighting.

In the ellipsoidal spotlight the optical system includes shaping devices within the unit. These devices can consist of: *framing shutters*, which allow a number of straight-sided shapes from triangles to almost any four sided shape; an *iris diaphragm* to change the diameter of a circle; or a slot to accept a piece of metal perforated in any shape the designer desires. It is called a "*gobo*". Note that at the point of shaping a great amount of light thus much heat is concentrated. This often leads to the premature failing of the shaping devices unless they are kept free of rust and corrosion and lubricated with a heat-resisting dry lubricant.

Since the unit is designed to provide a shaped beam, we want maximum control most of the time. Therefore, the plano- convex or step lens is most often

used. If the lighting designer wishes to soften the beam somewhat, it can be done by changing the length of the lens tube – an adjustment built into the instrument. Changing from a lens of one focal length to another focal length will change the area covered by the basic beam. It must be noted that the brightness of the lamp-reflector system will stay the same and spreading the beam over a larger area distributes the same amount of light over a large area resulting in a proportional drop in brightness. Substitution of another type of lens can also soften the edge of the beam for other purposes.

The ellipsoidal is most often found lighting the stage from the ceiling of the auditorium. The beam can be shaped exactly to the contour of the proscenium arch or kept out of the front rows of the house in other forms of stages. Due to its high brightness and controlled beam, it may also be found backstage lighting windows, doors, or other openings in the sides of the settings.

Some problems come from the high heat concentration which tends to rust the shutters in place. Dry graphite seems to last longer and work better than other lubricants. DO NOT USE OIL since it is subjected to high heat and will smoke. Since there is so much heat, the air movement is greater so grime accumulates on the lenses faster, calling for more frequent cleaning.

Another unique problem associated with the ellipsoidal is the necessity to adjust carefully the position of the lamp each time a new lamp is installed. If the filament of the lamp is not PRECISELY in the center of the reflector, the light output is adversely affected. Each ellipsoidal instrument provides a method of adjusting the lamp position in all planes.

At times technicians will use a larger wattage lamp than that for which the unit is designed. The lamps will fit, but the unit is not capable of dissipating the heat and the result is that the socket will ultimately fail. This often happens by freezing the tip contact in the retracted position where it will not contact the lamp so you think the lamp is burned out. Test lamps before you discard them. One design of sockets manufactured in the 1970's was defective and allows the retainer ring for the ears of the medium prefocus lamp to slip up which also disconnects the lamp from power. This happens in the burn-base-up or angled-lamp-housing ellipsoidals of several manufacturers.

An additional unit in the ellipsoidal category is the variable focus or *zoom focus ellipsoidal*. It is similar in design and capability to the "standard" ellipsoidal, but provides a number of advantages. The materials used in fabrication as well as the design of the instrument allow a broader use of an individual spotlight. Units are on the market which will allow you to change

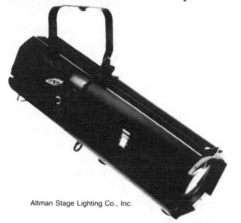

Altman Stage Lighting Co., Inc.

beam spread from 20 to 40 degrees, thus allowing you to stock only one model to cover the uses which once required a multitude of instruments from 4-1/2" to 8" lenses. This covers most of the average uses. Specific descriptive literature is available from the manufacturers.

Floodlights utilize housings which usually are designed and finished as reflectors and emit a minimallly controlled, very soft edged, flood of light. As one would expect, this is used where control is of least concern and a very general wash of light is required. With this type of lighting instrument almost all of the rays of light are used, but they come from a large-area filament and are returned by a diffuse or spread finish reflective surface, and are only generally directed.

Since the flood is a lamp, socket, and reflector only, it has minimal problems. A dirty reflector surface is about the only thing that can create a problem.

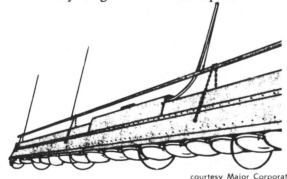

courtesy Major Corporation

Today's borderlights, *strip lights*, or *footlights* are collections of floodlights. With their individual lamp/ reflector/color-media units they offer a general wash of light controlled in intensity and color. Dependent upon size (length) and circuitry, they have variably limited uses. Traditionally they are included on most stages, although they are priced in such a manner that

a technician could own one spotlight in lieu of two feet of borderlight and have a lot more control of the light.

For stages designed for multiple-type presentations, the *borderlight* is still a good light and can be depended upon to light the entire stage area with a wash for concerts or large choral works. For musicals and dramatic presentations the lighting designer usually wishes to more specifically point out individual areas and therefore uses spotlights.

Borderlights today have few problems. The individual reflectors seal out most of the dust and dirt to keep it from collecting on the roundels. Broken or missing roundels and improper or burned out lamps are about the only problems. In relamping make sure that you use the lamp for which the unit was designed. Even with the general service lamps used in most borderlights, a different light center length will lessen the amount of light. Shorter L.C.L. lamps sometimes will not fit into the deeper reflectors and cannot make electrical contact.

Another portable lighting instrument used on and around the stage is the *beam projector*. This unit is named for the job it does. It utilizes a housing for absorption and a parabolic reflector shape to control the rays. It is more efficient than the Fresnel and less efficient than the ellipsoidal. Its beam control is also between the two. The instrument offers the designer the choice from a tight area to a medium area and either one is rather intense.

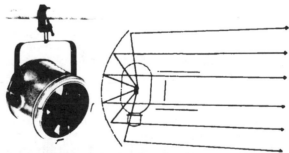

The softness of the beam edge is, as stated, betweeen the softness of the Fresnel and the hard or exact edges of the ellipsoidal. Often referred to as a *sunflood* or *sun tub*, this unit can be used from the auditorium ceiling position to cover a lectern area, or backstage to cover doors, windows, or other setting openings.

Any beam projector needs to have its reflector and lamp cleaned occasionally and its focusing device lubricated with graphite.

Recently, more use has been made of the *PAR can*. This unit utilizes an adapted automobile headlamp to provide a bright, non-variable pattern of light. The lamps are available in narrow, medium and wide patterns in several different diameters. The glass housing includes the reflector, filament and lens and is very strong. Road concert groups use them since they will withstand physical abuse, including transport while still hot, without shaking the filament loose. With all of this in one package, there is nothing to get dirty and nothing to get out of line so it is almost trouble-free.

BEAM CHARACTERISTICS

With a background of information indicating the specific capabilities of the different types of lighting instruments, the technician must be able to choose a unit to satisfy the needs. There are basically two conditions to satisfy: a unit must produce certain beam characteristics, and one must be able to locate the unit where it will do the job best.

Beam characteristics of a lighting instrument are size, shape, intensity, and quality. As indicated earlier, instruments offer the means to alter these characteristics. An early decision is the size of the area to be lighted. If this area is to be occupied by only one person, the limit of movement within that area during the time it is illuminated indicates the size of the area. Intensity must also be kept in mind at this point, since distance changes both intensity and size. If our area is to contain a speaker at a lectern, one light, or perhaps one from each side, might be enough to light the performer in a satisfactory manner. If he is going to move from the lectern during the talk, then perhaps a second area concentric with, but larger than, the first should be considered. If, however, the area being lighted contains one firm object such as a picture in its frame, the minimum and maximum limits of the area are immediately defined.

The shape of a stage lighting area will most often be the oval pattern produced when the round beam of an instrument is projected upon a surface which is not perpendicular to the axis of the beam of light. If other shapes are desired, they can be obtained by using absorptive devices such as exterior barn doors, interior shutters, iris, or pattern devices.

Another method of pattern change is to modify the angle of projection. This can produce undesirable effects, such as accentuation of highlight areas, deepening of shadows in recessed areas, or the almost complete elimination of shadows which will be the hot spot caused which will make an object look flat. The most common problem which calls for change in beam shape will be the hot spot caused when the beam strikes a piece of scenery or a curtain close to the instrument.

While most people think of intensity control done with dimmers, it is possible to make permanent change through the use of either a grey color media, or the relamping of the unit with another lamp which meets the basic requirements of the instrument. In changing from the initially specified lamp(s), one must make sure that the lamp base will fit the equipment socket and that the filament of the new lamp will rest in the focal point of the reflector. The latter can be checked by consulting the manufacturer's catalog and comparing the light-center-lengths of the lamps in question. A third but obvious point of concern is that the shape of the bulb will allow it to enter the instrument and/or other obstructions in the unit. If the above things are equal, then you can change lamps to different wattage.

Instrument manufacturers generally state design wattage and will designate maximum wattage. Since it is common to want more light from a unit, a final check must be made to insure that the instrument was designed to dissipate the amount of heat created by the lamp. Wattage rating is heat rating (not light output), and even though a unit will physically accept a higher wattage lamp, we can anticipate shorter lamp life, premature deterioration of component parts of the instrument and the overheating of adjacent materials.

Lamp choice today must take into consideration the relatively new light source: the tungsten-halogen, or quartz-line, or quartz-iodine lamp. This light source offers such things as a longer life span, no restriction on burning position of the lamp, and the maintenance of purity of color during the life of the lamp. The initial cost is sometimes higher, but the cost-per-hour-of-life will be less. If there is an access problem to some of your units, then this longer life is a real boon. Most quartz lamps, unlike the usual incandescent spotlight lamp, can be operated in any position without decreasing efficiency or life. This allows units to be mounted in places heretofore not possible. The quartz lamp will also keep its color temperature during its life, while the normal incandescent lamp becomes more yellow as it gets older. This is of less concern on stage than it is in the color television studio.

The most updated source of information on the quartz type lamps will come from the manufacturers: Sylvania Lighting Products (M-23), and General Electric Company (M-12).

Both have current information and descriptive pamphlets on their lamps. Through the use of the included tables, photos, charts, and diagrams, one can do a rather complete comparison on the interchangeability of these lamps with others in the incandescent line.

Experience has shown that in changing from incandescent to quartz in instruments designed for incandescent lamps much more care must be taken in aligning the filament, especially in the ellipsoidal type instrument, to produce a smooth field of light. This is, I believe, due to the slightly different configuration of the filament of the lamps, hence the altered pattern of reflection. Prior to a complete change I suggest the purchase of a sample number of lamps, their installation into existing instruments, and analysis of the results in your own equipment.

The quality of a beam of light projected into an area often determines whether the area stands out as a lighted area, or if it blends in such a manner as to focus attention, yet not be obtrusive. The sharp cutoff of a beam of light, such as high intensity light representing sunlight coming through a window, represents a harsh quality which is desirable. On the other hand, as a person approaches a portion of a set which includes an operating floor lamp, he should walk into gradually increasing light. This obvious change in light level calls for a softer quality beam edge.

Floodlights, borderlights, and Fresnel lens spotlights all deliver beams with soft edges, while instruments with ellipsoidal reflectors and/or condenser or step type lenses are designed to present a hard edge. For some installations the hard edge will be desired most of the time, but when needed this can be softened through the use of the focusing lens tube on the ellipsoidal, or the use of additive media such as frosted gelatine or plastic placed immediately in front of the instrument.

INSTRUMENT LOCATION

With the beam characteristics determined and the general configuration of the required instrument selected, attention must be turned to possible locations in which the instrument(s) can be mounted. In the consideration of possible locations we must assume that the owner either has or will supply the proper electrical service or electrical control to expedite the use of the lighting equipment.

The ideal *lighting angle* for an area falls between 35 and 45 degrees above the horizontal line of sight in the area being lighted and about 45 degrees off to either side. This optimum angle is based on the assumption that the area lighted will contain movement, a three-dimensional item, and/or will be seen basically from one side. In situations where a two-dimensional item is being lighted, a still life is

the subject, or the area is viewed from a horizon width of more than 120 degrees, additional instruments will have to be considered.

In lighting thrust or arena stages lighting areas must include instruments spaced around them to produce lighting for each of the viewers. This is done by utilizing additional sections of the area with the instruments placed on the 90 degree marks around the area. This would indicate about four instruments per area for theatre-in-the-round. If you are short on instruments, it is possible to go up to 120 degrees apart and use three units, but your job is harder.

If you must place instruments in such a manner that the beam angle is greater than 45 degrees to the floor and the object being lighted is three-dimensional, you may find that the contours of the article will cast undersirable shadows. If you are forced lower than 35 degrees above the horizontal, the resultant loss of shadow has a tendency to flatten the contours of the object being lighted. Note that the recommended lamp burning position must be kept in mind when selecting the instrument and placing it.

As has probably occurred to you by now, many of the considerations are interdependent and what one may allow, another may limit. This is the case with distance. The distance at which you place an instrument from its area has been somewhat calculated for you during your consideration of angle, intensity, and perhaps quality, the latter due to your choice of lens in the instrument.

Certainly consideration of location must be made concerning the availability of something from which to support the weight of the unit. The means of clamping, securing, or fastening the instrument to a structural member or ceiling device are many and varied. Not only are stock items available from manufacturers, but their engineers are available to assist in the design of specific support devices. Your own inventiveness helps, but make sure that the support is safe.

Any lighting instrument available today will have to have its lamp replaced, its lenses and reflector cleaned, or its focus or shutters changed from time to time. Make sure that the unit will be accessible to you – enough so that you can perform these tasks as simply and as safely as possible. This has been a matter of too little concern to some who design lighting installations. The end result is that total utilization of the equipment has been restricted. When units designed for accent lighting of areas cannot be focused simply, lamps in others cannot be changed without extensive scaffolding arrangements, lenses cannot be cleaned, the utilization of the equipment toward the task it was designed to perform cannot be done due to the lack of a safe, relatively simple access for these purposes.

The question of placing a unit in an exposed or concealed location depends upon the formality of the area in which the unit is to be used and upon the prior consideration, accessibility. Many of the instruments which are available today are visually acceptable if mounted in full view of the audience. They are well enough masked in their venting that they send out very few extraneous rays of light. On the other hand, there are people who find it distasteful to see lighting instruments before or during a production. Arguments either way can be stated, but I feel that this question can only be answered by those who actually will have to use the units. They should take into consideration all the other variables, saving this until last.

Remember, for maintenance purposes that units placed above the audience ultimately draw the heat, dust, smoke, etc. from below and there is a rapid accumulation of dirt on the lenses and reflectors.

Through consideration and analysis of the requirements of the job to be done, an understanding and application of the basic principles of equipment design and utilization, you should be better able to approach the task of selecting the lighting instrument that will serve best.

OPERATION OF FOLLOW SPOTS

Many people feel that they must have at least one follow spot to make a stage effective, especially with musicals. The most common *follow spots* today are incandescent. These use either a filament lamp, or a *Xenon* lamp which allows electrical current to jump a gap or an "arc." Older units may still utilize the arc carbons but these units are no longer being manufactured.

Once the unit is ignited, operation is much the same whether it is a lamp or an arc light source. Often operation is left to chance, and it turns into a visual circus detracting from rather than adding to the performance on stage. Good follow spot work will result in the lighting of the performer with the audience hardly noticing the existence of the light.

With the incandescent lamp light source the unit has only to be switched on. The Xenon units also switch on, but care must be taken to make sure that the fans are operating up to speed before igniting the lamp.

With the light source ignited, most follow spots have similar adjustments of their optical system, and experience and desire of the operator will do much to

decide the quality of the operation. It is strongly suggested the operators have the opportunity to practice until they are completely familiar with the unit. They need to attend rehearsals so they know what to expect from the performers.

A follow spot usually provides a means to increase and decrease the height of the beam of light. This is most often done with *horizontal framing shutters*. With these open all the way the projected light is round and a second means of control comes into play – the *iris diaphragm*. This allows the increase or decrease of the diameter of the beam of light. The iris is somewhat restricted in its size, therefore a method of additionally increasing the size of the beam is provided. This usually allows the lens(es) to be moved closer to the light source spreading the area lighted. Note that you are spreading the same amount of light over a larger area, so you will get less intensity overall. On most larger units the horizontal framing shutters and iris are operated by knobs on the top of the unit, while the *lens control* is done by means of a large handle along the right front side of the unit.

Somewhere in the optical system of the follow spot will be a means for introducing color called a *color boomerang*. In the incandescent lamp units this is usually in the beam between the light source and the lens system. In others it is in front of the front lens, after the light has gone through the lenses. These devices are equipped with either gelatine or plastic color media and most offer a means of setting an ultra-violet (black light) filter. Incandescent lamp sources lack ultra-violet output, but the carbon arc or Xenon sources are very rich in u-v wave lengths and so work well.

Through a slight adaptation, an 8" iris diaphragm can be added to a follow spot in front of the front lens. This will allow the achievement of a dimming effect with the unit. In this way the light can be brought up slowly rather than having to be suddenly turned on with the horizontal framing shutters.

Other adaptions that can be made to follow spots include the labeling of handle functions and a reference numbering along the handle run. This will provide an operator with a method of pre-setting some functions of the unit, rather than finding that there is a three-hand cue and only one hand available to do the job.

Some suggested practices for operators include:

1. When firing the unit, keep it aimed into your booth (if operating in one) in case the optical system is open.

2. Leave the unit and the area around it clean.

3. In arc operation make sure that ALL pieces of carbon are removed from the unit. The short end of the rear carbon often falls into the bottom of the lamphouse and may jam the carbon feed mechanism if left there.

4. Keep as clear a cue sheet as possible so others can read it if necessary.

5. Report any malfunction immediately and do not attempt any repair unless specifically authorized.

In general operation it has been found that: a spot that covers the floor about 2' in front of a performer and about 1' above his head is the best, unless there is a lot of fast movement; when using two follow spots, keep their beams the same size; be set on the performer's entrance location and open as he enters it – don't open up then swing to the performer; if two units are covering the same performer and the performer is close to the background, keep the beams of the units concentric if possible; with two spots working, cover the performer on the side of the stage opposite your position, make any adjustments in position as smooth and subtle as possible; keep the beam off the front lip of the apron or off the back drop if possible; check quality and other operational items before the house is opened for the audience. Follow spot work is to enhance a performance, not be an obvious thing unto itself.

Instrument photos courtesy:
ALTMAN STAGE LIGHTING

BIBLIOGRAPHY

(See the basic electrical bibliography at the end of Chapter 14.)

NOTE: The major portion of this Chapter originally appeared as a series of three articles by the author in DRAMATICS MAGAZINE in December 1970, and January and February of 1971.

GLOSSARY

barn doors 93
beam projector 95
borderlight 95
burner assembly 93
color boomerang 98
ellipsoidal spotlight 94
Floodlights 95
follow spots 98
footlights 95
framing shutters 94
Fresnel 93
funnels 93
gobo 94
horizontal framing shutters 98
iris diaphragm 94, 98
Leko 94
lens control 98
lighting angle 97
PAR can 95
plano-convex lens spotlight 94
strip lights 95
sun tub 95
sunflood 95
Xenon 98
zoom focus ellipsoidal 94

Follow Spot Cue Sheet

North Central
High School
Indpls., IN.

| Production | Form L-4 |

Page _____ of _____   Cue sheet written by:_____Date:_____

Cue Number	Action	Location	Side hndl	Iris	Cut off	Gel
	PURPOSE OF THIS FORM:					
	To provide a listing of the location of the action as well as the settings for the light so the cues will be precise, even with a replacement operator.					
	USE OF THIS FORM:					
	During technical rehearsals the operator will enter the appropriate information in the blanks.					
	During dress rehearsal this will be checked for accuracy and any adjustments made.					

CHAPTER SIXTEEN

ELECTRICITY AND DEVICES

In order to utilize lighting equipment it must be connected to a power source. This power source today is *electricity*, though it has been gas in the past. A physics course will provide an in-depth study of this subject, so our purpose here will be to gain a basic understanding of the subject and some concept of the characteristics, nature, and terminology of electricity.

DEFINITION OF ELECTRICITY

Electricity is energy flowing in a complete, or closed, circuit. It cannot be seen, tasted, smelled, or felt, but it does produce a reaction in most of the things it contacts and we do sense this reaction. To exist electricity must flow and it flows in a circle or *circuit*. It must always return to the point at which it started and, unlike other forms of energy, it becomes a part of the material through which it flows. Since we cannot see it, it is best to treat each conductor as if it does contain electricity until proved otherwise. This will greatly lessen the chance to feel the reaction of current passing through you on its way back to its starting point — the phenomenon we call shock.

If you receive a shock, you are completing a circuit. A circuit is the complete path of electricity from power source to and through its use and back to its source again. Your shock was caused by the electrical current making your muscles respond — an act which they perform each time you use them since they are controlled by small electrical charges sent from your brain. The massive jolt (in relation to brain current) they received produced a predictable effect, not just a reaction.

MEASUREMENTS OF ELECTRICITY

As any other form of energy, electricity has its measurements. The terminology of these measurements differs slightly from one area of study to the next, but they still measure the same things.

The rate or volume of flow is measured in *amperes*. The amp is to electricity what the gallon-per-minute is to water or the cubic-feet-per-minute is to gas. Just as a pipe can only deliver so much water or gas regardless of pressure, due to its diameter, a wire can only deliver so much electricity. If we put too much pressure through, or demand too much of a pipe, it will split. If we demand too much of a conductor, it gets hot and will ultimately melt.

The pressure applied to push electricity through a conductor is rated in *voltage*. In gas or water we talk of pounds of pressure. Just as these other forms of energy will rupture their conductors if too much pressure is applied, electricity will jump out of its conductor unless we insulate it from taking the shortest possible route and causing what is called a short-circuit.

Wattage is probably the most misunderstood rating. Since electric lamps are rated in *watts*, most people consider it a rating of quantity of light. It is not. Instead it is a rating of the amount of current used — the amount of heat given off by the consuming item. Electric toasters, irons, heaters, are all given wattage ratings, yet people do not expect them to give off light. Your electric bill is figured in watts. To expedite billing the meter reads in Kilowatt hours (KWH). A *kilowatt hour* is the amount of electricity it takes to produce 1000 watts of heat for one hour.

This kilowatt hour can be one 1000 watt lamp burning for one hour, a 100 watt lamp burning for 10 hours, a 750 watt iron and 250 watt toaster working for an hour, etc. Your electric meter is devised so that the more current is flowing, the faster it runs. It simply keeps track of the quantity passing through it, regardless of the amount of time it takes.

While we are not too concerned with kilowatt hours on stage, we are concerned with other elements of current so that we do not overload conductors or dimmers. Since lamps are rated in watts, the figuring of circuit wattage does not present anything more than an addition exercise. All of the dimming equipment manufactured today has a wattage rating and we simply add together the load to assure the proper limitation. Conductors in the form of wire or cable, however, are rated in amperage capacity identified by the National Electrical Code as ampacity.

Circuit protection devices which are discussed later have limitations. Wires, too, have limitations. If an attempt is made to draw too much current through a wire, it will get hot. To figure the characteristics we can use a formula which is nicknamed the "West Virginia" formula since if uses the initials of that state: W=VA. W (watts) equals V (volts) times A (amperes). This is the base formula and it can be applied in different ways to get different values. As in other formulas, we must know two of the parts to get the third.

A fourth measurement which is necessary to the engineer planning equipment is the measurement of resistance to electricity by an item. This is measured in *Ohms*, but it seldom affects the user of stage lighting equipment in such a manner that we would need the equipment to measure it.

TYPES OF ELECTRICAL CURRENT

Current with which you are likely to deal on stage will be *alternating current*. This electricity is the most common found in the U.S. today and is so named because it pulsates. In the U. S. its most common transmission form is 60 cycles per second. The trade will indicate "60 Hertz (Hz)". Although we do not see the result of this pulsation in the incandescent lamp, this type of current requires a specific type of wiring within electric motors and some other electrically operated items.

The other type of power, *direct current*, comes from batteries. Autos, flashlights, portable radios, etc. derive their power from batteries, and these items cannot operate on A.C. without special converters.

D.C. will always flow in the same direction. It is a constant flow and a positive and negative can be labeled. A.C., on the other hand, does not have a simple positive and negative. The two sides of the alternating current circuits are referred to as the hot and the neutral sides – the hot coming from the power source and the neutral returning to the source. Until recently electrical appliances in the U.S. have had two wire cords and were manufactured so that the hot/neutral connection made no difference. If either conductor became bare and came in contact with the case of the appliance, there was danger of electrical shock.

To help eliminate this potential shock hazard a third wire is now used in the power cords. It connects to the appliance shell and to a ground. If there is a current leak, it is thus grounded and the danger to the user is lessened. These third pins are also appearing in stage equipment and since the plug can only be placed in the receptacle one way, the polarity or relation of wires in the circuit is always the same.

Ground fault circuit interrupters are now required in locations near sinks or other water sources and for outside use in new construction. These sense tiny amounts of current flow between hot and ground and turn current off very quickly to lessen the possibility of harm.

CONTROL OF ELECTRICAL MOVEMENT

A number of different devices are used to handle electricity. By sorting them into categories it can be more easily seen how they help in the transmission and control of electrical current.

Any material which will allow electricity to pass is called a *conductor*. Each conductor does have its limitation as to how much current it can handle, due to its size and/or the material from which it is made. If its primary job is transmission, then it is a conductor. Almost all metals, some plastics and even specially made rubber materials, are conductors. Pure water is a poor conductor, but a tiny bit of salt makes it a good conductor.

On the other hand any material which will not allow electricity to pass is called an *insulator*. Here, too, each material has a point at which it will break down and allow current to pass, dependent upon the pressure of the current. While there are many insulating materials, ceramics, glass, most rubber, and most plastics are considered the better insulators.

Some items will allow only a measured amount of electricity to pass. These are called *resistors*. The by-product of a resistor is heat. A 100 watt lamp is a 100 watt resistor. Toasters, irons, electric frypans are all using resistance elements which consume their rated number of watts of current. Any electrical conductor that is subjected to handling more current than its capacity becomes a resistor because heat will begin to build up.

The *semi-conductor* is being seen more and more in theatrical lighting control equipment. This device allows part (or all) of the available current to pass part (or all) of the time. The amount passed is easily controlled by the altering of "signal" or "control" current fed into the device from a second source. The use of the semi-conductor has led to a reduction in size and expanded capability for stage control systems. Since only a small amount of current is required to control the semi-conductor, the controller can be remotely located from the dimmers.

WIRE AND CABLE

In handling electricity you will likely use several items, the most common being *wire*. The term "wire" actually refers to the individual metal strands which make up the conducting portion of a cord or cable, but many times the word "wire" is used to mean more.

To deal with wire you need to know at least three things. One is: as a wire increases in length and/or decreases in diameter, it increases in its resistance to electricity. Example: an extension cord rated to carry 15 amps. maximum, when connected to several others to make up a long run, will not carry that much. Tables are available in many books and in some hardware stores, so it is wise to make sure any run over fifty feet is rated to carry your load.

Resistance is friction. Friction causes heat. If the extension cord gets warmer than the air around it, the chances are that you have an overload.

A second aspect of wire is that it is classified by an arbitrary number system. The larger the number, the smaller the wire diameter. Arbitrary means that the number does not stand for a specific value. The number is simply an indentifying mark which allows reference to the National Electrical Code charts to find the cross sectional area of the conductor.

The third factor is that each of these numbered sizes is rated in its *ampacity* (current carrying capacity). This rating indicates the point where the conductor will begin to heat up. A hot conductor will not carry as much current as a cool one, so the cycle begins. While a slight overload will not cause the insulation to melt or cause a spectacular short, any heat will cause the insulation to begin to dry out and the drying out will shorten the life which means that the insulation will crack sooner.

Since an electrical circuit must provide for current to come from a source, pass through a use, and then return to the source, we must have two conductors for each circuit. Due to the nature of alternating current it is possible to use the same return path (neutral) in some cases for more than one circuit. This is referred to as a common neutral. For the most part, though, our devices for extending electrical circuitry have at least two conductors, each of the conductors made of wire.

Two or more lighter duty (ampacity less than 17 amperes) conductors in the same casing are referred to as *cord*. As a rule you can generalize ampacities:

Conductor Size	Ampacity
18	7
16	10
14	15

These are the sizes usually found feeding sweepers, lamps, televisions, and other small home appliances.

Heavier duty conductors, two or more in a casing, are referred to as *cable*. An extension cable, therefore, would be considered heavier duty than an extension cord. Individual conductors making up a cable are:

Conductor Size	Ampacity
12	20
10	25
8	35

Conductors are made in larger sizes, but will probably not be found in use as extensions in most theatres.

The sizes listed above are only for the most common copper alloy conductors. There are many other metals used in conducting current and they differ in capacity. Insulations around these conductors also vary, so the total outside diameter of the extension should not be taken as an indication of the current carrying capabilities of the conductors. To be sure, the size of the conductor must be known as well as its metal content.

Conductors are insulated for various purposes. The common zip cord is a plastic covered pair of conductors. It shows an impression between the conductors and will pull apart on this line like a zipper. It is usually a number 18, although it may be obtained in larger sizes. It is satisfactory for home interior use.

This plastic would not be satisfactory if used to run power underground to a post light in the middle of the front yard. The insulation would deteriorate in a short period of time. There is a different plastic available which is used for the casing of what is called burial cable. This plastic is impervious to moisture and most ground acids.

Neither of such insulators would stand up well to a large amount of heat. Thus, for cords or electric irons, stage spotlights, etc. the primary insulation used to be made of asbestos. Asbestos is easily frayed, therefore, will be carefully protected where it is close to metal which might cause abrasion. Asbestos, on the other hand, will stand all the heat it can be given. Today these cords and cables are being replaced with fiberglass and some high-heat plastics. If you have the older asbestos covered wires you can obtain fiberglass sleeving to cover them to keep them from fraying.

An older form – still in use but no longer made – was called *Type "K" cable*. This consisted of two (or more) conductors with individual rubber, then cloth braid insulation, a piece of hemp or jute which actually became rope, then a double woven casing over these, and a coating of tar. This type of cable could be suspended by itself for long runs or could be subjected to a great deal of physical damage due to heavy equipment running over it. If damaged, the outside casing was cut and left a telltale break.

This Type "K" has been replaced by flexible rubber or thermo-plastic covered cables of types "S", "SO", and/or "ST". With this rubber insulation it is possible to subject the extension to such a sharp blow that it will sever the copper conductor and not cause enough of a cut in the outside jacket that the cut is visible. Also, since both the jacket and the copper will stretch if a long run is made and any tension applied for any period of time, it is possible to stretch the conductor and actually change (lessen) its ampacity – (conductor gets longer and thinner...).

Of course, there are a great number of other types of insulations used for different purposes in the electrical industry. A copy of the current National Electrical Code charts these insulation materials, their purposes, and their limitations.

Within the insulation the conductors will differ slightly according to whether they are flexible (a number of individual strands of wire), or solid (a single strand). Using a number of strands allows the bundle of wires to be bent without changing the physical diameter of the total conductor, therefore not altering its ampacity. The multiple strands also allow the conductor to bend more easily and not retain a kink. Extension cords and cables should always be of flexible conductors. Wiring used for permanent installation (through walls, in conduit, etc.) can conform to its environment one time, then will rest in that location with no movement and so is usually solid.

ELECTRICAL CONNECTORS

Having at our disposal the electrical current, conductors to carry it, and devices to utilize it, there is need for a method of attaching these items into a complete circuit. Twisted conductors with taped or otherwise locked joints are used for permanent fixtures. On stage we are concerned with a quick means of attaching or detaching wires or cables. The means used is a set of *connectors*.

Connectors are made to allow the quick and easy attachment or detachment of wires, cords, and/or cables. They provide a safe and sure means of doing this job without having to interrupt the current flow to a circuit, although connecting an item which is "on" to a live circuit is not good practice.

What we term a connector is actually a part of a connector set. To be complete the set must have two parts. Correctly these are the line and the load.

The *line* portion of the set, also referred to as the *receptacle, socket*, or *female connector*, is the portion of the set which contains the electrical power. It should always be on the conductor from which the power is being taken. It is designed so that its contacts are shielded from accidental touch.

The *load* connector portion, also called the *cap*, *plug*, or *male connector*, is that portion which will receive the power. This is the portion of the set which has exposed contacts. These contact surfaces will not be electrically charged until they come into contact with the line portion of the circuit, thus they will be covered.

The obvious purpose for this arrangement is safety for the user. In some electronic applications which have very small amounts of current there may be a deviation from this arrangement. In handling household or stage current this arrangement should never be violated.

As indicated earlier, if there is an abnormal amount of heat present in an electrical conductor, there is a problem. If a connector gets hot something is wrong. The current flow may be too great, or there may be a loose connection which is causing the electricity to jump a gap creating an arc and thus, heat. The termination of a wire inside a connector should be checked with the circuit off to make sure of a good, firm, clean, contact.

Wires should always be wrapped under the head of the securing screw with the end of the conductor pointing the same way that the screw is turned to tighten it. If this is done, the action of the tightening is to pull the wire more tightly under it. If the wire is wrapped counterclockwise, the action will be to force the wire out from under the head and leave a loose connection.

To complete the installation of a connector it is best to have a cord grip. These are built into many connectors. If a grip is not available, the conductors should be tied or wrapped around part of the connector so that any strain is placed on the conductor, not on its connection. Many people disconnect a cord by pulling on the cord itself instead of taking hold of the connector. This ultimately results in the stretching of the conductor or, especially in the case of molded on connectors, the breaking of the strands of wire at the point where the cord enters the connector.

CONNECTOR TYPES

There are many types of connectors available for use on stage. These appear anywhere from light duty household types to extra-heavy special stage connectors. A specific stage may use one or more of these types, but each has its strengths and weaknesses. The most well known is the *Edison, household,* or *parallel blade connector.* There are many forms of this type available and they can be found in almost any price category. The tendency

seems to be that people will purchase an inexpensive connector because they feel that it will carry the same amount of current that the more expensive one will. They pass up the life-lengthening additional cost options of cable grips, heavier materials, and more secure installation of current carrying portions. Most of the less expensive Edison connectors are made of molded rubber or Bakelite and have no real method of adjustment for wear.

An adaptation of the Edison is the *Twistlock.* It has a slightly curved blade on the male portion usually with an "L" shape to it so that it is inserted into the female and rotated clockwise about 1/8th turn to lock the connection. These are used on many stages since they

look heavier and supposedly lock the connection firmly. An additional argument is that they will always be interlocked with the same polarity since one blade is larger than the other. The Twistlock is a little more expensive than the Edison.

It is possible for the Twistlock type connector to come apart, especially when used on floor cables. The greatest problem comes from the fact that there are many manufacturers of this type connector, and not all makes have always been interchangeable. There are also a number of sizes (amperage ratings) and they look so similar that it is hard to tell them apart. Different sizes will not always interconnect. Again,

there is no provision for adjusting contacts, although there is less need for it in this type of connector.

The *pin connector* or *slip connector* is specifically made for stage use. It is a little more expensive than the others, but it is practically indestructible, and it does allow for adjustment of the contacts. This type has a built-in cable grip and is made from a plastic which will not shatter under impact. The material

courtesy Union Connector Co.

used for the contacts is heavy duty and the contacts are spaced so as to provide more than ample division of conductors. The method of manufacture is such that all makes are interchangeable and even the older two-pin form will fit into the now-required three pin form. There is now a locking mechanism available in some pin connectors.

This type connector is one thing for which you can price-shop and not seriously reduce the quality. Pin connectors are available in several amperage capacities which are not interchangeable.

The heaviest duty type connector found around stages is the *block plug* or *stage connector.* These are even stronger, have a greater electrical capacity, and cost more than the pin connectors. Mostly found in the older equipment of professional touring companies, this type of connector was the earliest manufactured

courtesy Union Connector Co.

for stage use. With its spring-loaded contact on the male portion it compensated for wear automatically. Due to the size of the opening in the female portion of the set, there was some danger of accidental electrical shock.

With these different types of connectors available, we often find two or more types in use on a stage. This requires that *adapters* be available. If the types of connectors on the ends of a cord are of the same type, that is, they can be plugged one into the other, then it is an *extension.* It is used to lengthen a run of cord or cable. If the connector types differ, one is line, the other load but they cannot be plugged together, it becomes an adapter. This allows a device with one type of connector to be plugged into a receptacle with a different type. Stages which house productions by outside groups who bring their own equipment often have a number of different adapters available in addition to extension cables.

At times there is need to operate more than one item on a circuit. The Edison type connectors provide a *cube tap (3- way plug)* which will allow three devices to be plugged into one outlet. One or two manufacturers mold a multiple receptacle in the Twistlock type, but these are hard to find and rather expensive. The pin connector provides the *multiple branchoff* or *"spider"* which is built the same as other portions of the connector and, while rather expensive,

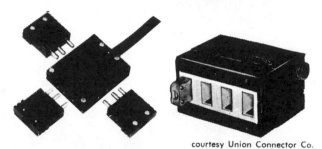

courtesy Union Connector Co.

is almost indestructible. In the block type there are steel-boxed packages of female connectors which are extremely heavy, expensive, but allow a number of devices to be plugged in.

SWITCH TYPES

To control current in electrical circuits there must be a way to turn it on or off. For this we use a switch. We are familiar with switches – but perhaps not their different types.

One of the earliest types made and still in use today for high-current circuits is the *knife switch*. It consists of a jaw and a blade with an insulated handle. When the blade is moved into the jaw, the current will flow, and when the gap is opened the current will not flow. This type of switch is used often as the main or primary switch in stage switchboards. It must be operated quickly when opening or closing the circuit. If operated slowly, the current will jump the gap or arc as the two pieces of metal get close together. The arc causes great heat and can literally weld the pieces of the switch together.

Switches which are operated for general service in the home or on the face of a switchboard are usually the *toggle* or *tumbler* type, having a spring activated blade. This will snap into one position or the other, thus making or breaking the circuit quickly and eliminating an arc.

A third type of switch is used in locations where the noise caused by spring activation would be a problem. By enclosing a small amount of mercury in a tube with two contacts spaced a little ways apart, a *mercury switch* is created. As the tube is tilted, the mercury rolls to one end and makes (completes) the circuit. If the tube is tilted the other way, the mercury rolls away from the contacts, breaking (opening) the circuit. There is no sound. Not all silent switches are mercury switches and may not require that they be mounted in a specific manner as the mercury switch does.

In electronic equipment and in some theatrical electrical control equipment *rotary switches* may be found. As the name implies, the operation is circular rather than in-line. An example is the channel selector switch on a television set. This, like others, is an adaptation of the knife switch.

SWITCH FUNCTIONS

Each type of switch can come with different capabilities as to the number of currents or circuits it can control and the number of directions it can send each of these currents. The number of currents or circuits that is kept separate in a switch determines the number of *poles*. A single-pole switch controls one current, while a three-pole switch controls three.

Assuming that the off position is the home or starting point, the number of directions a switch can send a current, or the number of other positions the switch has, determines its *throw*. A normal household switch is single-pole (one current), single throw (on). For ordering purposes these functions are often given in initials: SPST.

A switch which is rather common in the home today is called a *"3-way"* switch and is used to provide a method of turning lights on or off from two locations. This is a single-pole, double throw switch. There is actually no "off" position but it is figured into the circuit, thus making "3" ways. This type of switch is also used in stage lighting control boards. When it is wired so that it allows a device to select power from one of two sources, it is called a *selector switch*. When it is used to assign current flow to one of two paths, it is called a *transfer switch*. These last two names are functions, not forms.

CIRCUIT PROTECTION

As indicated several times in this and in preceding chapters, the amount of electrical current flowing in a circuit is of concern. Since a conductor can become overheated if too much current flows, or a switch can weld itself together if the gap is closed too slowly or if too much current is passed through it, there must be some built-in way to limit the amount of electricity in a circuit. For this purpose the industry has available current limiters called *circuit protection* devices.

The local generating station has these at their generators and all along their lines to protect them from damage by too great a demand. Homes and schools have main service limiters to restrict the total amount drawn. From these large devices current flows through smaller conductors and smaller limiters out to the individual branch circuits. Diagrammatically the electrical network of a home or school would look like a large tree. The trunk is the large capacity feed conductors, the larger branches carry power out a ways, then fan out into a great number of small branches.

The purpose of a circuit protection device is to open a circuit in case of an overload or a short. An overload is the demand for more current than the circuit is designed to carry. Circuit protection devices are of generally two types.

FUSES

A one-time device which must be replaced when it has opened or blown is a fuse. Employing a soft metal in the form of a thin wire link, the fuse provides the weak link in the chain and, if too much current flows through it, it simply melts due to the heat and interrupts the current flow. By inspection, usually through the clear window provided, one can see the link is no longer intact, and, once the problem has been cleared, replace the fuse. These fuses will often "tell why" they gave up.

If the problem was a simple overload, the link will have melted. If the cause was a short circuit, the link will have literally exploded and the result will be the residue of the "blast" on the inside of the transparent surface. The case of the fuse will remain intact in either case.

Fuses can be found in several forms, the most common being the *plug fuse*. Having a medium screw base, the plug fuse shows its rating both on the face and on the tip. All amperage sizes of the plug fuse are manufactured in the same physical size thus are interchangeable from smaller to larger amperage. Since the purpose of the device is to protect the

courtesy Bussman Mfg.

wiring in the circuit, it is of no value to have a fuse of larger capacity than the wire it is meant to protect.

A newer form of the fuse of the *Fustat*. It is similar in size and looks like a fuse. Its various amperage sizes are color-coded and the threading of the base is designed so that you cannot install an increased

Fustat Fuse

Fustat Adapter

courtesy Bussman Mfg.

amperage substitute. The receptacle adapter for the Fustat is too small to allow the insertion of a coin – a method used by some to keep a circuit operating until another fuse is available. This practice is extremely dangerous since the cross-section of a penny is sufficient to carry 100 amperes and never even get warm. Fustats have a face window, like the fuse, and the instructions in the box tell how to ascertain the difference between a short circuit or overload cause of failure.

The third form is the *cartridge fuse*. The cartridge fuse is a tubular shape with metal ends. Some simply have collars at the ends, others have a flat strap projection to provide insertion into the circuit. The cartridge fuses found in home current applications have a fiber tube while the smaller ones found in electronics and automobiles are glass.

courtesy Bussman Mfg.

Cartridge fuses come with the ends sealed for one-time use as well as with provision for opening the unit and inserting a new link. Either will be marked on the outside with the amperage rating.

CIRCUIT BREAKERS

In newer installations the other type circuit protection device will be found – the circuit breaker. This device senses a demand for too much current and turns itself off. Once the problem has been cleared it simply has to be reset. With some circuit breakers a small sign appears when the breaker has tripped. Others provide that the handle goes to a middle position – neither on nor off, while on others the handle simply goes "off." In any case, the handle position will give indication as to which breaker has tripped.

Again, there are different forms. Most often found around stages is the *magnetic breaker*. Working with the theory that the more current there is in a circuit, the stronger the magnetic field induced, this breaker is manufactured so that a coil of wire inside becomes an electro-magnet. As more current is drawn, the magnet gets stronger. At a pre-determined point the current strength mechanically trips the handle.

A *thermal breaker* senses heat and, when a given temperature is reached, a physical reaction takes place and opens the circuit. The household heating thermostat is an example of a thermal switch/breaker. The thermal breaker should not be used on stages due to the varying demands of the lighting circuits. One circuit may be operating at full capacity and the heat from that breaker could heat up the adjacent breaker, lowering the current flow capacity of the second breaker.

Many home breakers today are *thermal-magnetic*. As the name implies, it is provided with a means of tripping to either heat or magnetism.

Regardless of which type or form encountered, the method of restoration of electrical service to a circuit is the same. Make sure that the current is actually off. If a fuse, remove the old one and ascertain the reason for the disruption of service. If a breaker, make sure that the handle is off. Then eliminate the short or lighten the load to clear the problem. Finally restore service by replacing the fuse or restoring the breaker. Keep in mind that a protection device will only fail if the demand on it is too great. A 20 ampere device will not protect a 5 amp conductor.

BIBLIOGRAPHY

(See the basic electric bibliography at the end of Chapter 14)

GLOSSARY

CHAPTER SEVENTEEN

DIMMING AND DISTRIBUTION

In an earlier chapter there was discussion of control of rays of light in order to illuminate areas. Attention is now turned to the overall control of a group of lighting instruments and their relative intensities.

The combination of dimmers and the method of controlling them into a stage lighting control system, or switchboard, are the things which set the degree of flexibility available to the operator.

For years it was said that the ultimate in lighting control would be to have individual intensity control over each lighting instrument, independent of all others on the stage. In the past this has been too expensive and, due to the limitations of the types of mechanical control devices available, almost impossible. With the introduction of the semiconductor as a variable current control device and the use of low voltage control circuits, this is now an economic reality. To help things along computers are in operation to keep track of the greater number of circuits, their groupings, and their settings.

Essentially there are three parts to a stage lighting control system. There will be some overall method of controlling the signal power to the dimmers, the dimmers themselves, and a method of grouping the dimmers for control or grouping lights to respond to given dimmers. The possible combinations are numerically fantastic, and it is impossible to discuss each each of them here.

At the end of this chapter there is a dictionary of terms used in memory systems. As of this writing there is still some discrepancy from manufacturer to manufacturer in terminology. A committee of the U.S.I.T.T. is working on standardizing the terminology throughout the industry.

CONTROL SYSTEMS

One part is the *control section*. In direct control boards this function was sometimes spread all over the face of the board, but could be mechanically incorporated into a smaller area. There usually was a means of turning off all power to the board – a total power blackout. From this point power was fed, perhaps through other selector switches, to the dimmers. Often included in this section were contactors – electrically operated heavy duty switches which controlled a large electrical load, but operated from a remote location by a small amount of current.

A board using either of the direct control dimmer types usually provided a method of locking handles of individual dimmers together. This mechanical mastering or interlocking caused a group of dimmers to react together. Often associated with this in later boards was electrical mastering which was the use of a large wattage dimmer to feed power to several dimmers of smaller wattage. This allowed the operator to pre-arrange the settings of the smaller dimmers, then bring up the handles of the large dimmer resulting in several circuits achieving their own setting with the movement of only one handle on cue.

Electrical mastering of a sort is used in the multiple preset electronic boards. In this type board, using low voltage control circuits, a row of controllers for each dimmer available exists for each "pre-set." A board can be designed for any number of presets – from one to infinity. Two, five, and ten seem to be popular. There must be a row of controls for each pre-set and each row will have at least a master control for each preset. When the master control is brought up, each controller will respond to its pre-set level. For the next cue, the first master is taken out and the next brought up. This is repeated for each cue in the show with someone changing the individual controller readings on the pre-set row as soon as the operator is finished with that cue. There are innumerable variations on this theme that can be built into a board, and the refinements of the circuitry seem limitless.

Today the lighting designer has available memory systems utilizing computer memory to allow the presetting of each dimmer for each cue, then committing this to the memory. Once the cue is entered, it can be automatically, totally recalled by the system at the command of the individual at the console. Exact designs and capabilities are as numerous as the systems themselves, since they can be programmed to do whatever the person purchasing them desires. Due to the extreme number of combinations and even the manner in which the recall is done, be cautious in comparing the different systems available because each will be unique.

Also in the control section will be some means of controlling the house light levels. This can be a device to use one of the dimmers in the board, later allowing it to be used for dimming stage lights, or it can be a separate system which is operated from several locations. If motor controlled, the system will have a run time which is the elapsed time from full up to full dim. Probably there will be a provision for halting the motor run at any point so the total time can be lengthened, or the lights left at some pre-determined intensity. The time of the run cannot be instantly altered in most motor controlled systems.

There may also be one or more non-dim contactor control switches. These provide circuits into which a group of lights can be plugged and then switched on and and off. This is handy for meetings or lectures in an auditorium where the lights can be on when the audience arrives and left on until it leaves. It sometimes eliminates the need for an operator during such a program.

TYPES OF DIMMERS

The second part of a system is the *dimmer*: a means of varying the amount of current available to a circuit. In reviewing dimmers past and present, three types are evident. Each has its advantages and disadvantages, but even these defy precise identification because what may be an advantage in one facility is a disadvantage in another. For this reason only the general characteristics of the different types will be treated.

If the board contains resistance or autotransformer dimmers, they will be adjacent to the control area because they are the direct or manual control type, requiring physical change in mechanical position. The physical size of the dimmer will place a limitation on the size of the board. Within the board there may be dimmers of varying electrical capacity, especially if it is designed for electrical mastering. If the board has this feature, there will no doubt also be associated selector and transfer switches to route electrical power and give the operator flexibility in operation. The input of each dimmer will also have a circuit protection device.

The great advantage of the electronic board is the capability to place the dimmers in one or more out of the way locations and the control point(s) in locations where the operator can see the stage. Here again, the dimmers will have protective breakers or fuses with them and may also have pilot lights to indicate when the dimmer is activated. A full control board will usually be located out in the house and a partial control panel at the stage manager's location.

The earliest means of control was the resistance dimmer. Electrical current takes the path of least resistance – and when it reaches the point of most resistance in a circuit, creates heat (and/or light). By providing a device in a circuit so that the resistance could be changed, the point of most resistance could be altered. If the lamp was the point of most resistance, it glowed. If the dimming unit was the point of most resistance, it heated up instead of the lamp. The resistance dimmer circuit always consumes electricity and gives off heat.

The *resistance dimmer* is found in both the slide (straight) and radial or circular forms. The chosen form only aids the equipment designer in accomplishing his packaging task—the end result is the same. In either form the resistance dimmer is a manual dimmer. To cause the lights to dim a physical change must be made in the location of a pick-up or slider. In an attempt to allow more freedom of placement of the actual dimmers, motors have been used to position the pick-up, but these imposed a number of limitations.

The resistance dimmer was for a long time the only one which could be used for both AC and DC. Recently a semi-conductor circuit has been developed to deliver DC.

The "*rheostat*," a synonym for resistance, which is used to control the intensity of the dashboard light on most automobiles, is a resistance dimmer. The least expensive in price-per-watt of the dimmers, the resistance dimmer always consumes electrical current in its operation, thus becoming the most expensive to operate. Another limitation of this dimmer is that it can only be UNDERloaded by about 10% of its total capacity and still function properly.

The next type of dimmer added was the *auto-transformer*. unlike its predecessor it will control only AC. It uses alternating magnetic fields to effectively cause a stalemate in the flow of current. In other words, it actually causes the current to block itself from flowing, allowing only the desired portion to flow. In this type, the only current used is that which reaches the lamp. This dimmer changes the voltage reaching the lamp.

Like the resistance dimmer, the autotransformer dimmer requires a physical movement of a contact. It, too, is available in either slide or radial form. As indicated, it will operate only on alternating current but causes no heat. Of all the types, this is in the middle as far as price is concerned and it can be used with almost any size load from 1 to 100% of the rated capacity. Like the resistance dimmer, it has sometimes been motor operated. This type is no longer manufactured and packaged as a theatrical dimming device but many of them are still in use.

The third and newest category of dimmer is the *electronic dimmer*. Using one or more electronic circuits this type is the only really remote control dimmer available — one in which the actual dimming unit can be placed in one location and the operator in another and still have complete control and all control variables. One of the earliest forms of electronic dimmer was the *thyratron* which used a series of electronic tubes to control current in a circuit. The tubes were expensive, gave off a great quantity of heat, often failed during a show, and were at times unstable.

During the Second World War the *magnetic amplifier* was developed and after the war came into use as a circuit control device. A heavy unit utilizing a number of transformers or chokes reacting to a control voltage, this provided a stable dimmer with relatively little heat.

The latest generation and the one which seems to answer most of the needs of stage lighting control is the *semi-conductor*. The early units used Silicon Control Rectifiers hence were called SCR's. This gave the industry a small, lightweight, remote control dimmer at a price which became affordable. Additional research in the field has added new devices and made the dimmer even smaller and lower in price. The cost dropped to the level of the autotransformer a few years ago. That fact coupled with the physical size and control possibilities led to the demise of the auto-transformer as a theatrical dimmer.

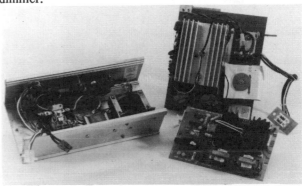

courtesy Decor Electronics/Hub Electric

Due to the small physical size of the dimmer plus the capability of using computer control as well as computer cross-connecting of control circuits to group dimmers we now see *dimmer-per-circuit* systems which allow that ultimate control about which I spoke at the first of the chapter.

In general, the electronic dimmers will operate only on AC. Their generated heat is minimal, varies, but must always be taken into consideration. There are very specific load limitations on these dimmers, especially on the semi-conductors themselves. The control circuitry can be as simple or elaborate as the designer wishes. This is where the cost comes in, because unlike the manual boards, the electronics use a low voltage signal current to in turn control the higher voltage. With the low voltage small controllers and switches can be used. This allows more combinations of controls than ever before.

Most of the electronic dimmers will not control loads such as fluorescent lights, motors, or flash pots. They can be specified to have the capability of being turned into contactors to handle these on/off loads.

All dimmers, past and present, have one feature in common. None can be loaded above its rated capacity without causing damage to the dimmer itself. Some are more sensitive than others. The early resistance dimmers could be and often were overloaded, but the life of the dimmer was sacrificed slowly. Because it was a slow sacrifice, it made little difference. With the semi-conductor an overload of 1% for 1/120th of a second will cause permanent loss of the semi-conductor. Some circuits have been developed to slow down or eliminate this possibility. While the semi-conductor itself is inexpensive, the surrounding control circuitry to operate and protect it is what increases the cost. There are fuses or breakers included in the circuits which will react in less time than it takes the device to blow. This allows the operator to replace a fuse or reset a breaker rather than have to replace a dimming component.

CROSS CONNECT

While it is possible that the output of a dimmer may be run directly to an assigned load, the most flexible arrangement of the mechanical control systems was to provide some means of selecting and/or varying the loads. This is the third part and is done with a cross-connect or patch panel. In this manner a means is provided to allow any dimmer to control any load or combination of loads appearing on the panel. In this arrangement a dimmer controls the current to one or more receptacles on the panel.

The receptacles will be labeled to identify which dimmer or contactor controls them and perhaps a pilot light to indicate that the receptacle (group) is activated. This is often true when the cross-connect is remotely located from the dimmers and/or control section. Inserting a load into a live receptacle, called "*hot patching*," is not a good idea. It damages the cross-connect and can cause dimmer failure.

Elsewhere in the area is represented a number of loads. These are actually a group of extension cords which have been built into the board and the building and run to specific locations. The operator can then select which load or loads are to be controlled by which dimmer – the combinations being limited by the electrical size of the load in relation to the electrical capacity of the dimmer.

There are various forms of cross-connect panels. One is the captive-cord form on which only the end of the cord is free. It is equipped with a plug which fits into the power receptacles. A patch-cord form provides a panel with both line and load jacks and cords with line and load connectors. In this case several different lengths of cords may be provided. In either case the physical weak point of the system is at the junction of the cord and plug. During insertion and removal the operator should handle the device only by its plug. In the captive form system the plug should be escorted gently back into the storage hole. Neophyte operators often want to drop the plug and watch the cord disappear into the hole, but this will eventually rip the

cord out of the plug. With the free cords the tendency upon removal is to grab a handful of cords and pull. Here again there is danger of divorcing cord and plug.

There are other forms of circuit connection, but none are as economically flexible as these for a large number of dimmers and a large number of loads. Included is the rotary switch form. A rotary switch is provided for a branch circuit and thus the operator can select power from a number of sources. Most common is the choice of 8 power sources. Another form uses a row of push buttons to accomplish the same thing and provides a somewhat greater number of power source selections. Slider and pin cross connects are used also. With a number of vertical slots and horizontal positions, one representing dimmer outputs and the other load circuits, these are connected to assign control. They do get rid of cords and plugs. As their advocates claimed, they looked neater, but they also allowed the possibility of placing all the stage loads on one dimmer – something that was impossible with the cord plug form. If more than ten power sources were used, either of these became more expensive than the cord- plug system.

Whichever form is used, each of the load circuits will be breaker protected and the breakers will probably appear in a collection called a magazine and be individually identified as to the circuit each controls.

In electronic boards today many systems assign dimmers to controllers and some allow you to assign a dimmer to more than one controller and ask it to respond at a different maximum level. In this case the patch or cross-connect is made in the control (low voltage) circuit and allows a number of dimmers to be operated by one controller. This may be in addition to or in place of the cross-connect system described above. An advantage of this is the ability to group any number of dimmers onto a single controller without concern for overloading a circuit.

The three sections of a stage lighting control system do not have to be spread around, nor do they need to be permanent. For smaller theatres, traveling groups, theatres with small budgets, or groups just starting, there are portable switchboards on the market. These are now of the semi- conductor type.

Portable switchboards combine the three portions into one or two packages and require a place from which to draw power and a series of cables to lead to the lighting equipment. These provide a simple, portable control. Each of the makes has its own strengths and weaknesses. The right one for any group can only be indicated after the group has evaluated the characteristics of the dimming device, the necessary portability of the total unit, the power source(s) available, and the amount in the budget. It is possible to rent these boards in many places, and one could be tried in a production prior to purchase.

DISTRIBUTION

In control systems equipped with built-in power distribution there will be locations on the stage and in related areas which will allow lighting technicians to plug in instruments. In well-planned theatres these receptacles will be all of the same type and will be located in areas where the lighting equipment will be needed. It will remain for the lighting designer to locate the instruments and plug them in, then gather the circuits at the cross-connect, if one exists, into groups for control purposes.

Receptacles will most often be found in the *beam or ceiling position* above the seating. Perhaps they will be on the front of the balcony and / or in the side walls of the auditorium (called the *splay area*).

Usually you will find them at the front edge of the apron and above the playing space just behind the proscenium. Some planners provide them at the sides of the playing space just behind the proscenium in a vertical row (*tormentor position*) in the stage floor at either side of the playing space and upstage of the playing space. Dependent upon the exact facility, there may also be receptacles above the deeper playing space.

Tormentor tower

Often there will be plugging arrangements close to or within a borderlight. Usually the first row of spotlights behind the proscenium is called the *teaser position*, although if it is tied with the borderlight, it is referred to as the first *electric*, the term "electric" indicates that the pipe has both borderlights and spotlights on it. If a walkway is provided above either, it becomes a *lighting bridge*.

Receptacles recessed into the floor will usually be contained in metal covered boxes called *floor pockets*. A similar box may be recessed or surface mounted on the walls or ceiling. Reference then is to a *wall pocket* or *ceiling pocket*.

Receptacles located in the beam position, splay ports, tormentor towers, or teaser positions are usually provided in a *plugging strip*. This metal raceway with receptacles spaced along its length and usually has an adjacent pipe for mounting portable lighting instruments.

Such a strip may have flush mounted receptacles or perhaps they will be at the end of a short length of conductor called a *pigtail*.

Such arrangements allow lighting crews to locate equipment with a minimum of extension cable thus allowing maximum freedom of movement for scenery and personnel.

DICTIONARY OF MEMORY SYSTEM TERMS:

ACTIVE: Referring to dimmers, settings, and lighting visible on stage.

ANALOG: Control by varying voltage signals to the dimmer.

AUTO MODE: Facility to modify automatically recorded information in a playback when required without altering permanent memory.

BLACK-OUT: Action or switch which turns off all dimmers.

BLIND RECORD: Operation carried out through the keypad, not seen on stage at the time.

CASSETTE / DISK / TAPE: A "library" storage device onto which cues are stored, later retrieved for use in the performance.

CHANNEL: An individual controller within a pre-set row which can control one or more dimmers.

CONTROL CONSOLE: The main central control point for the dimming system.

CONTROLLER: A device to adjust the intensity of the lights assigned to it.

CROSSFADE: A gradual change from one lighting look to another.

CROSSFADER: Usually a pair of potentiometers to perform the crossfade action.

CRT / SCREEN / VDU: Cathode Ray Tube - commonly a TV monitor used to display system information.

CUE: Commonly a memorized scene or look.

CUE INSERT: Ability to record an additional look into a sequence without having to change other cue designations.

CUT (dimmer): To stop that dimmer from functioning.

DIGITAL: Information to the dimmers sent by (usually binary) codes.

DIPLESS CROSSFADE: All channels change from old to new level without going below the minimum level set in either cue.

DISC: (see cassette).

DOWN FADE: A lighting change involving only dimmers that are decreasing in intensity.

FADER: A device used as a master intensity control for a group of controllers – usually a potentiometer. Can be straight line, rotary, or wheel configuration.

HIGHEST TAKES PRECEDENCE: The highest of several signals to the same dimmer sets the dimmer level.

HOUSE LIGHTS: Auditorium / audience lighting.

KEYBOARD: Group(s) of numeric and other push keys to allow data entry – similar to a calculator.

LATEST TAKES PRECEDENCE: The latest signal to a dimmer sets its level.

LEAD-LAG FADE: Incoming (or increasing) channels change before, or faster than, outgoing (or decreasing) channels.

LED: Light emitting diode - a semi-conductor device that gives off light and is used as a pilot or indicator light.

LEVEL: An indicator of intensity.

LIVE: A look which is showing on stage.

LOAD: To enter a cue or cues into memory.

MEMORY: A system which can receive, store, and then playback lighting looks.

MICRO-PROCESSOR: A small computer programmed to control the functions of the system.

MIMIC: Use of pilot lights or CRT to display a lighting look.

MOMENTARY: A switch which performs when pushed and then returns to its normal state upon release.

NON-DIM: An on / off switching device.

NUMERIC DISPLAY: Digital indicator to provide information to the operator.

PANIC / RESET SWITCH: Brings houselights to full intensity.

PLAYBACK: Method or process of bringing a cue up on stage.

POWER SUPPLY: Source of low voltage for the control console.

PRESET: A row of related controllers; a memorized look.

PREVIEW: A method of seeing, usually numerically, what a cue will contain without showing it on stage.

READ: Copying data from one storage into another without affecting the stored material.

RECORD: Copying data from one storage into another perhaps changing data.

REMOTE: Operation of one or more functions from a location other than the control console. May be wired, wireless, or infra-red.

SCENE: Typically, a group of dimmer signals setting their levels.

SCREEN: See CRT.

SEQUENCE: Next cue in line is automatically brought up when the preceding cue is completed.

SOFTWARE: The program fed into a computer to set its operation.

SPLIT CROSSFADER: A pair of controllers allowing independent control of incoming (increasing) channels and out- going (decreasing) channels.

STAGE RECORD: A method of recording the stage picture as a cue.

STORE: To hold a look for later recall.

TAPE: See "cassette."

TIMED FADER: A device to complete automatically a fade at a pre-arranged rate after being started by the operator.

UP FADE: A change in which levels only increase.

VDU: Video Display Unit - see CRT.

VOLATILE: A memory device which will hold information only while power is on, but which will clear upon loss of power.

BIBLIOGRAPHY

(See the electrical bibliography at the end of Chapter 14.)

GLOSSARY

CHAPTER EIGHTEEN

COLOR AND LIGHT

Another form of control of rays of light is color. *Color*, by one definition, is the physiological reaction by the retina of the eye to certain wave-lengths of light. As this implies, color is an individual experience. What a color does for you is your reaction, and yours alone. This chapter is an attempt to indicate some of the why and how this happens, not precisely why or how one responds.

The *visual spectrum*, the wave-lengths of the radiant energy spectrum which will trigger this reaction by the average optical nerve, is precise, definable, and divided into specific parts. These parts are given the names of various hues and appear in an order. Visual experience of this is presented each time a rainbow is observed. The rainbow is the refraction of rays of sunlight and their division into the basic colors of the spectrum. Since visual reaction is both physical and mental, the ultimate response to a color is personal.

COLOR TERMINOLOGY

To attempt to explain light and color the variables must first be set. There are hue, brightness, and saturation. Other sources will perhaps give these different names, but the division remains essentially the same.

The term "*hue*" relates the position of a wave length in the total spectrum. Red indicates that the position of the wave length is toward the upper end or longer wave-length end of the spectrum. Blue indicates presence near the lower or shorter wave-lengths.

If all wave lengths of light are present in equal quantities, *white light* is experienced (full response). If no wave length of light is present, the result is *black* or darkness (absence of response). In between are combinations, each of which produces a color.

Hue is spoken of in two categories: spectral and dominant. The *spectral hue* is the presence of a single wave length of light. A *dominant hue* is the presence of several wave- lengths of light, and it is given the

name of the most dominant, or most easily seen. This is somewhat akin to the musical scale or audible range of the energy spectrum. As we are aware, we can produce a number of tones or vibrations which have been given representative letters on the musical scale. It is possible to produce one wave-length or note (spectral hue), but more often we hear a number of notes combined into a chord (dominant hue) which is given the name of the predominant note in that chord.

As we listen to music we are aware mostly of what it termed as the melody or predominant portion of the pattern. The harmony is present but it takes concentration to be determined. The same is true in hue. We note an item for its dominant hue and it takes a concentrated analysis to determine what its component hues are. This often creates a personal problem, since it is possible to have a personal visual apparatus which will not respond to one or more wave- lengths of light. If this happens, we say that a person is "*color blind*" in that area. If one person cannot receive a certain pitch, we say that he is deaf to that pitch.

The second variable is *saturation* – the purity of a hue. An absolutely pure hue is saturated. As any other hue or hues are introduced into the first, it becomes unsaturated (diluted). It thus becomes fainter and less obvious. From a saturated hue of red, as white is added, the result moves toward pink.

Brightness is the third variable of color and is the capability of a hue to reflect or transmit light according to the qualities of the source of illumination used. Brightness is used to measure the amount of light present, or the amplitude of the light waves. Usually we are dealing with reflected light, thus we see a series of hues under the same light source and refer to one as being the "brightest" by which we mean that it is reflecting the most light. On the other hand, we may be looking at several light sources of equal output but with different filters. We may indicate that one is "brighter," meaning that its filter is allowing more strength to be transmitted.

Color, then, is a combination of all three properties and a study of color is a study of these combinations and their reactions to each other. Color analysis can be made very accurately in a scientific laboratory. With the proper equipment a graph indicating the exact properties of a color can be made. These graphs will show the precise amount of each wave-length of light present.

Stage lighting is not a laboratory experiment and the colors with which we work will very seldom be pure. While the response of a given pigment to a certain light may be estimated, the actual response can only be experienced through trial.

COLOR MIXING

We deal with two methods of controlling or mixing colors in stage work. These are the additive method and the subtractive method. An understanding of the inter-relation of the two will allow the lighting designer to determine what visual stimulus can be presented to an audience.

The *additive method* of color mixing indicates that two or more colors are projected onto a neutral surface and are thus mixed so that the person viewing the result will, if the colors are smoothly projected onto the same area, see a combination. This is the process that allows us to direct lights of different colors onto a neutral backdrop, change their relative brightness, and obtain a change in coloration so as to produce a representation of a sunset or a sunrise.

Representative of the total visual spectrum are the three additive *primary colors*. The term primary is used to indicate that this color cannot be achieved by adding other colors. We must start with it. Since these are representative, the addition of all three in equal quantity will produce white light. The additive primaries are red, blue, and green. Border and cyclorama lights are often equipped with these filters. Theoretically, by providing each color circuit with a dimmer and adjusting the brightness of each, the operator can achieve any color in the visual spectrum. In actual practice this is somewhat limited by the fact that incandescent lamps produce a relatively small quantity of short wave-length (blue) light and tend to lose even that as they are dimmed, causing them to go yellow, then orange, then red.

If two primaries are combined, a *secondary color* is obtained. The secondaries are blue-green, yellow (sometimes called amber, or orange), and violet (sometimes called magenta or purple). If instruments projecting the three secondaries are focused on the same location, the result will be white – because equal quantities of the three primaries are present. The yellow contains one part red and one part green, the blue green one part blue and one part green, and the violet one part blue and one part red. The total is two parts of red, two of green, and two of blue. As could be expected, this will be a brighter light than with three instruments projecting primaries.

An unbalanced mixture of the three primaries results in a *tertiary color*. For the most part these are the colors with which we will actually deal in stage lighting, since color media in use today is not spectral in hue.

In stage lighting we must actually deal with *subtractive control* before we deal with additive in that our lighting sources give off, in varying purity, white light. From this we absorb the unwanted colors by filters and allow the desired hue(s) to pass on to a surface where it is then mixed and reflected for the audience to see. Our final visual response is dependent upon three things. First, the presence of a wave length in the source; second, its transmission by the filter; and finally, its reflection by the surface which it strikes. Light rays themselves are invisible. It is only when they strike a surface and are reflected that we can "see" them. Our seeing is actually their reflection from the surface they illuminate.

In any form of the subtractive method a pigment is used which is capable of absorbing certain wave-lengths of light. This may appear in the form of transparent media which can absorb many wave-lengths of light while allowing others to be transmitted; it can also be in the form of a paint or dye on a surface which absorbs some wave lengths and reflects (transmits) others. Pigment is named for the color(s) it reflects; therefore, when we attempt to determine what result will come from a given color of light on a given color of pigment, we have to think in terms of what color(s) of light will be reflected.

The subtractive method of color mixing applies to anything that is not light, and therefore encompasses almost everything that we see. Since subtractive is opposite of additive, it follows that the relation within the two methods will be opposite. In subtractive method, the combination of all colors produces black and the absence of all colors white.

We can use mathematical symbols to work problems in color if we think about absorptive factors of pigment in relation to the light (additive) rays since it is the reflected light that allows us to see.

SURFACE	REFLECTS	ABSORBS
red	red	blue, green
blue	blue	red, green
green	green	red, blue
blue-green	blue &/or green	red
yellow	red &/or green	blue
violet	blue &/or red	green
white	all	none
black	none	all

If a red light (+red) is projected onto a red surface (-green, -blue), the red is unaffected, resulting in a red visual stimulus. If a violet light (+red, +blue) is projected onto a blue-green surface (-red), the red is cancelled or absorbed while the blue is reflected and we see blue. Remember, for us to see a color, that color must exist in the light striking the surface, or it cannot be reflected. A surface cannot initiate a color.

Light is the key to our sight and to our concept of color. Pigment cannot initiate light; therefore, a color in pigment cannot be reflected (seen) unless that color is present in in the light. The fact that color and light are determined by physiological reactions is the very thing which keep the theories listed above from obviously working all the time. The human eye/brain does not provide for a good color reaction.

While the human is very good at color comparison, he is very poor at seeing a color, then having to match it after it has disappeared even for a short time. The eye can differentiate between about 2500 colors on a color triangle which represents all the possible mixtures of the three primaries. It can also differentiate between about 100 steps between black and white – that is, greys. Combining these indicates that the eye could differentiate between 250,000 colors. To differentiate there must be a stated norm, and this is where the human meets a problem. It can't always identify the norm. Few people can pick a primary red out of a group of reds.

According to the theory given earlier, the primaries of pigment should be the same as the secondaries of light. Yellow; violet, (called red but having a blue percentage); and blue-green, (called blue but having a high green content) are the most often stated pigment primaries. Likewise the primaries of light should be the secondaries of pigment – and again they are – but our eye does not identify them that way. Green, orange (which is usually close to primary red), and violet (which is usually close to primary blue) are known as the pigment secondaries.

Again, note that neither the stage lighting industry nor the artist deals with an exact science of color. The pigments are prepared by companies which must keep them at a marketable price. Since the precision of a color is not necessary, it is not a criterion in the production.

Precise colors can be obtained, and indeed are used. The dyes used in the preparation of color film and photographic color filters are very carefully controlled. The colors used in the transmission and reception of color TV is another example. Their cost would be prohibitive for the stage lighting industry. Since the dyes in clothing are not perfect and scene paint pigment isn't either, there is no real need for laboratory precision in light filters.

The chart below indicates the actual and orderly relation between colors and their methods of transmission. It should be especially noted that white pigment will show any color which is projected upon it. Black, on the other hand, will reflect nothing and, as a result, is always black. Any visual change in black comes about due to dust particles on the surface, so reflecting light colors.

ADDITIVE (light)	COLOR (Actual name)	SUBTRACTIVE (pigment)
+R	Red (O)	-B-G
+B	Blue,(V)	-R-G
+G	Green (G)	-R-B
+R+G	Yellow (Y)	-B
+B+G	BlueGreen (B)	-R
+B+R	Violet (R)	-G
+R+B+G	White	-O
+O	Black	-R-B-G

Notice that the primaries of light are the secondaries of pigment and that the primaries of pigment are the secondaries of light. Also note that the presence of or absence of colors in black and white are also opposites - just as the terms additive and subtractive are.

Some materials (pigments) possess the capabilities to cause a change in the wave-lengths of light rays striking them. This is what allows us to use ultra-violet rays, which are normally outside the visual range, for special effects. Since not all pigments "glow" when receiving these rays, the eye reacts as it would to black. Pigments reflecting ultra-violet rays glow, others absorb the rays. Ordinary soap and some starches fluoresce – the term given for an item that reflects ultra-violet bombardment into the visual range. Calcium deposits in teeth, fingernails, and eyes will glow with a greenish cast when excited by U-V rays. Other items can be found through experimentation. There are paints and dyes in the market made especially for U-V work.

COLOR MEDIA

In order to achieve the filtering of the white light of the standard electric lamp, there are several items available to the lighting designer. Dependent upon the equipment at hand and the environment in which it will be used, one can choose from colored lamps, glass filters, or consumable media.

Colored lamps fall into three varieties. *Natural color* lamps are those which have been manufactured using a stained glass for the bulb. This is colored, but transparent. These lamps provide a well controlled color which does not vary from one manufacturing run to the next. The color is in the glass, therefore it does not fade. The lamps do get hotter than the normal incandescent lamps due to the absorption of some colors in the bulb; therefore, the life is somewhat shorter.

A second method of coloring lamps is *spray painting*, either inside or out , during manufacture. This results in a translucent rather than transparent finish which eliminates use where careful control is required. The paint used is not as carefully controlled as the dye for the natural glass envelope.

A third method is *lamp dip*. This is used commercially to color some Christmas tree bulbs now available. It is a lacquer base dip which is recommended only on lamps of less than 40 watts. Others would get too hot and the covering would burn off. This lamp dip is still available from the color media manufacturers and can also be used in the preparation of effect slides which need a transparent coloring that goes on well with a paint brush, comes in several colors, is easily obtained, and is relatively inexpensive.

Many older borderlights depended upon colored lamps for obtaining color circuits, but this meant stocking lamps of each color for replacement. Methods were devised to allow the placement of a separate color medium between the lamp and its field and medium were designed to do the job. One of these permanent media is the *roundel*. Slightly convex, this circular piece of glass serves as a coloring filter and also provides a minimum of diffusion to the rays of light. It is possible to purchase these with a more controlling design, usually a 55 degree spread, but usually they are less precise.

In some instances a designer might want the permanence of glass in his filters, but have a greater amount of heat to overcome. *Stripped glass* color filters are available for use in spotlights. They are transparent and are made of strips of heat resisting glass set into a relatively thick frame. while they are brittle and rather expensive, they also are available in a good selection of colors.

The most common method of filtering light today is the use of *consumable color media*. Less expensive than other methods, and available in many more colors, these allow the lighting designer a large color range from which to choose. In this way a color to provide a specifically desired reaction from the pigment on set can be chosen.

Gelatine, probably the most common, has been available in over 70 colors. It is purchased in sheets which can be cut to whatever size is desired. A water-soluble material, gelatine does present something of a problem if used in a high- humidity area as it will absorb water, become flexible, and drop out of its holder. It is relatively inexpensive, but does fade rapidly and as a result is being replaced by more permanent media.

Its close cousin, the *plastic media*, comes in fewer colors but is not water soluble. It is about three times as expensive but it lasts longer. There are several of these made and each has its advantages. Mylar base lasts longer — but is the most expensive. Some plastics are coated on one or both sides, while others are permeated with their color.

The colors in both the gelatine and the plastic will fade more rapidly than those in glass. Your filters should be carefully watched and discarded as soon as there is a visible difference between the area through which the light has been projected and the area covered by the frame.

BIBLIOGRAPHY

(see the basic electrical bibliography at the end of Chapter 14.)

GLOSSARY

additive method 122
black 121
Brightness 121
Color 121
color blind 121
Colored lamps 124
consumable color media 124
dominant hue 121
Gelatine 124
hue 121
lamp dip 124
Natural color 124
plastic media 124
primary colors 122
roundel 124
saturation 121
secondary color 122
spectral hue 121
spray painting 124
Stripped glass 124
subtractive control 122
tertiary color 122
visual spectrum 121
white light 121

Color Frame Schedule

| North Central High School Indpls., IN. | Production | | | | | | | | | | | Form L-1 |

Instrument Location	Frame Size	Color No. & Designation						Instrument Location	Frame Size	Color No. & Designation					

PURPOSE OF THIS FORM:

To provide a planning list, then serve as a work list for the preparation and installation of the color frames for the show.

USE OF THIS FORM:

Enter the color numbers you plan to use in the show across the top under "color & designation".

List the locations of the instruments you are using down the left side of the columns.

For each instrument list its color frame size and the designation of how you want the color inserted.

Frames: A = 7 1/2" x 7 1/2"; B = 10" X 10"; C = 13 1/2" X 13 1/2" ; D =   E =

Designation: C=Clear; F=Frost; SF= Soft Frost; D= Double; S= Special (See back)

CHAPTER NINETEEN

PLANNING LIGHTING

With the knowledge of equipment, the methods of powering and controlling it, and the uses to which it may be put, the actual planning of the lighting for a show is the next step.

A method for planning was set down in 1929 by Mr. Theodore Fuchs in his book STAGE LIGHTING. His method is most complete and provides a thorough yet relatively simple way of going about the planning for a production. It is still a good way of stepping through planning.

FUNCTIONS – WHY LIGHTING

The planning must start with an understanding of the functions of stage lighting. What can we expect to accomplish with lighting? The functions answer the question, Why are we lighting the stage?

The first and obvious function of stage lighting is *visibility*. We owe it to an audience to see and hear a show. Without one or the other it becomes difficult, if not impossible, to maintain attention. Visibility allows identity and identity can be hindered by either too much or too little light or by locating the light sources incorrectly. Visibility is the most important of the functions and is the only one which is necessary for every show.

A second function is *realism*. The realistic period in drama was in the late 1800's. Almost everything on stage had to be very realistic. Today the realism is found in the motion pictures and some television since they have the budget, time, and capabilities to work for total realism. Without the vision-limiting characteristics of the camera, the technician on the live stage must accomplish realism for many different angles. This is extremely difficult.

Realism need not be carried too far. One of the wonderful things aiding the legitimate theatre is the imagination of the audience. They are ready to become emotionally involved with the actor – all that is needed is something to trigger that imagination. A simple red glow in a scenic fire-place suggests fire. It is possible, but unnecessary to go to great lengths to create a realistic fire effect in this case. Simple color changes; the use of dramatic angles of lighting – from the side or the back of an actor; limited use of moving or blinking light sources; all contribute to realistic suggestion.

The third of the functions is that of *composition and design*.

With the control capabilities of lighting equipment it is possible for us to aid the director in playing a scene where he may have a lot of people on stage, but wants only one to be outstanding. While he, too, has a number of ways to accomplish this, we can help by providing a pool of brighter light for this character. Elsewhere on the stage the lights can be dimmer, or even out completely. In this way we can assist with the focus of attention, much as one does when composing a photograph. Another task within this function is to make the lighting look good within itself. A stage set with scenery, but without the actors, should present a meaningful picture; a picture which gives a desirable visual feeling to the audience.

The fourth function is *plastic expression*, or three-dimensionality. This is the function which provides a visual depth. Here we achieve the addition of the dimension which is missing in television or in motion pictures. While depth can be accomplished with a single color of light, the designer will usually make use of the artist's concept that every item has a warm and a cool side. Lighting opposite sides with different colors will achieve depth. Different intensities of the same color will work, too.

Plastic expression adds life to the stage, and a visual reassurance to the audience of a full-scale visual experience. Light thus becomes a tool for the designer, like a chisel allows a sculptor to provide a study in depth.

Lighting can also function (number five) to create *psychological expression*, or mood. Lighting does, to some extent, affect the emotions. While the exact amount of reliability of mood creation is unmeasurable, we can depend upon some generalities. Tragedy is dim. Comedy is bright. The red end of the spectrum is warm, exciting, stimulating – while the blues and greens are more calm and smooth. Experimentation with light and shadow – relative brightness changes – will produce as many results as will color change. While music is a much more reliable terms of expression, light still provides a quick, silent way to achieve emotional stimulation. Music can be more efficiently defined in terms of voice, pitch, volume, rate, key, etc. by writing it on a scale. Light requires experimentation.

In lighting a presentation not all five functions have to be used. If they are, they do not require five different sets of instrumentation. There are times where one unit in the right place with the right color and at the right intensity will accomplish all five functions. As a beginning, only the first function is required; the others will follow as the designer becomes more accomplished in his work.

CLASSIFICATIONS – HOW TO LIGHT

After indicating the Why's of stage lighting, Mr Fuchs went on to list six *classifications of stage lighting*. These classifications present a check-list of How to light the stage. Taken on a step-by-step basis, these allow a person to work through a show item-by-item and to finish with a complete lighting layout.

Acting Area Lighting is used to make the area, and the people in it, expressive. Since we are normally used to seeing items lighted from above, the theatre light source(s) should be located somewhere between 35 and 45 degrees above the horizontal line of vision of the individual performer. Ideally the light for the stage could come from a single source, but that is impossible today. To keep shadow angles the same from one part of the stage to another a number of instruments are used.

The stage is divided into areas about eight to twelve feet in diameter, dependent upon the exact lighting instruments, and each area is then lighted from an angle of about 45 degrees off to each side. Thus, the area is lighted on the diagonals of a cube with the actor's eye level at the center of the cube. By using this layout the designer can achieve an individual treatment of areas through selective coloration of the shafts of light into that particular area. The areas can be located in any manner, but the arrangement to coincide with the nine basic acting areas seems to work best. Of course, there can be more or fewer

areas, according to the requirements of the setting of the show. It is recommended that an odd number of areas be used. In this way a well lighted center area is available, for actors and directors do like to work a lot center stage.

The areas are numbered in order for reference. The usual pattern is from down left, across the front, then left to right across the middle, then left to right across the back. The numbers are used for focusing, coloring, and blocking.

If the downstage areas are well forward on the stage, or even out onto the apron, they will be covered by light from the beam or ceiling position. If splay ports are available, they will be helpful in this area, too. These ports and their receptacles should have been designed into the proper locations. If so, then you need only place and focus lights. The second row of areas will get their light from instruments placed on first electric. Dependent upon the depth of the set, the third row of lighting might also come from there. In locating instruments, make sure that the primary or "key" light in each area comes into that area at about the same angle as in all other areas. A change in angle will often create a "dark spot". The intensity may be greater, but the angle change will create a problem. Try to keep the beams of the instruments as parallel as possible.

Since the lighting for the front areas will probably have to be shaped to keep it from "spilling" onto the proscenium and into the audience, it fairly well indicates the use of ellipsoidal type spotlights. In theatre-in-the-round, open stage, some thrust stages, or even some smaller proscenium stages, Fresnel type instruments can be used, but only if the throw is short. With the shorter throw the focus of the instrument can be held rather tight and will result in a minimum of spill.

When ellipsoidal spotlights are used from the front, an attempt must be made to blend the individual areas by softening the sides of the beams, or letting them overlap quite a bit. If this is not done, the actor's movement from one area of light to another as he moves across the stage will be obvious. This change will differ visually according to his up-down stage position since the beams will intersect only at one point and will overlap everywhere else upstage of there. Make careful note of where the upper edge of the beams will strike the floor or the rear scenery. This may have to be softened also to keep from getting a very sharp line in he middle of an otherwise smooth lighting job.

The directing of the beams of light with the Fresnels on stage also must be done with care. Again, attempt to produce rays which are generally parallel, thus keeping the actor in a relatively smooth light. Experimentation with the distance from the lighting units to the actors will allow the determination of the best range to keep the lighting smooth. The Fresnel spotlight manufactured today generally has a very hot center when pulled into a tight or "spot" position, and a slightly dark center when at full or "flood" position. Either extreme causes problems out of proportion and should be avoided if at all possible.

Many stages are equipped with borderlights. Some people use these for acting area lighting. These will give a smooth job of lighting, but large open fields and commercial establishments are about the only places that smooth light is found. For this reason a slight alteration in intensity is both natural and acceptable. The degree of differentiation allowable is between the designer and the director. The use of smooth lighting from borderlights or footlights erases most shadows, the very thing which helps three-dimensionally and recognition.

The colors for the acting area lighting should be motivated by the theoretical area. If it is an interior in early morning with sunlight streaming through a window (the sunlight will be discussed later in another classification) then the source of warm light would come from that side. At high noon any light entering a window probably would be reflected from the sky, thus actually would be a cooler color. The designer develops his own rationale for the placement of warm and cool by logic. According to the number and type of instruments available the designer may wish to use colors which are all in the warm range. In this case the terms "warm" and "cool" are in relation to each other, one warm color being slightly warmer than another.

The warm/cool arrangement adds credibility to the setting and, although the audience would not audibly complain if the acting area cool light came from the side of the stage on which there is a roaring fire, and the warm from the side with a window lighted by reflected moonlight, the total picture would be somewhat strange. This sort of lighting can be done with specific purpose and toward a given end, but should be planned and not just allowed to happen.

Cooperation with other members of the technical staff will allow the elimination of, or at least anticipation of, some of the problems often encountered in final rehearsals. Mental notes should be made: that some of the furniture has very light colored upholstery; that there is a large mirror located so that it will direct the rays of some of the spotlights back into the audience; that the costumer plans to use dinner-jackets and tuxedo trousers thus giving an adjacent black and white combination. With such problems noted the designer can begin to work around these future problems.

The notation of these things early will allow specific planning. The furniture can be reupholstered or covered with a dark nylon netting pinned tightly to the item. The mirror can be dulled with the commercial dulling spray, or rubbed with window putty which will leave a linseed oil film to kill the reflection. The dinner jacket could perhaps be dyed slightly (a cup of coffee in a gallon of water) if it belongs to the theatre, or the costumer convinced to use a dark jacket.

Simply making others aware of the potential problems early will smooth things out later.

The second classification of stage lighting is *blending lighting*. The purpose is to unify, blend, or smooth the acting area lighting – to fill in the areas between the pools of the primary acting area lighting. Some consider this as a part of the acting area lighting.

This classification uses flood or borderlights and is a lot like painting with a mop. It must be used at low level or it will negate any effect of the care and planning which went into the acting area lighting. The quantity will probably be about 1/10th of that in the first classification. Provision for two circuits, one warm and one cool, will allow the change of overall tone of the acting areas.

Since blending is done to help the acting area lighting the colors should be chosen from tints. Pinks, ivory, light amber, light blue are some possibilities. In all of the classifications, experimentation in both color and intensity will provide a number of interesting answers.

Even though flood type lighting instruments are used, care should be taken to keep them from lighting the scenery. The colors in these instruments are chosen to aid the expression of the actors and should not be limited by the color of the scenery. Blending instruments are the sources to use when a scene must be played "in the dark" with only enough light for the forms of the actors to be seen. The flood of light at a steep angle and a deep blue coloration, will result in the capability of visual realization, but practically no identification.

The third of the classifications, *tonal lighting*, is concerned with the setting. Its whole purpose is to control the color in the set. If a set needs to look shabby in one act and bright in the next, some of this can be accomplished with tonal lighting. The choice of a color which will grey the set for the first act will dull the set. Another color would be used in the later act to brighten the response of the paint. The instruments used for this would be floodlights, or spotlights with softened beams from the teaser position or tormentors.

The color chosen to tone the setting should be a deep or saturated hue. This way it will have little effect upon the actor in an area because the tints used for the acting area lighting will be lighter. Since the texture coat of paint on the set will usually contrast with the ground color, a media color can be chosen which will emphasize one and depress the other. Usually is will be the texture coat which will be emphasized; but by activating different colors during the show it is possible to actually change the look or "feel" of the setting if there is not too much stray light. Tonal lighting also aids the costuming by providing deep color lighting from a step angle thus illuminating the deep folds in the cloth and making a more interesting visual presentation.

Areas behind the set or outside of it should also be lighted. These are covered by the fourth of the classifications: *background lighting*. Included are walls, door backings, window backing, sky domes or cycloramas, and other items not previously covered.

The areas here represent another room or an exterior. The light should theoretically come from a single source – either a lamp or the sun or moon. The direction of the rays of light will help tell the audience part of the story regarding time of day, location of a lamp, etc. In any case the units must be placed so that shadows are not cast. Be especially careful of shadows caused by an actor waiting in the wings or by a piece of scenery being moved backstage during an act.

If the background is to be a sky illusion you have a choice of two methods of lighting: sheet or flood. *Sheet lighting* utilizes a strip of lights at the top and perhaps one at the bottom of a sky surface. These function to produce a sheet of light across the face of the surface without using much up-down stage space. Some designers feel that this is a poor method because of the higher intensity at the top and bottom of the surface. It seems to be rather realistic since the sky is visually brighter at the horizon and as one looks toward the light source (sun).

The other method, *flood lighting*, uses a number of instruments located some distance away from the surface. Each covers a specific area of the space and the areas covered are overlapped to prevent a "cloud" if a lamp burns out. If color change is necessary, as for a sunset, then a set of instruments for each color desired must be set. The flood method provides a smoother intensity overall, but the blending of colors

along the top or bottom for a sunset or sunrise becomes more difficult.

In lighting a sky, keep in mind that it becomes more interesting and more realistic as a contrast is produced by a ground row. A ground row is simply a scenic barrier at the bottom of the sky surface, set away from it a small distance. As a stage gets shallower, a ground row becomes more important since it is the thing which gives a three-dimensionality. To aid in this depth and to help break up shadows that might be cast on a sky surface, a scrim or gauze located a foot or so away from the sky surface should be used. The scrim here becomes effectively a piece of lighting equipment since the audience is unaware of it. To make the sky even more remote use several ground rows, each lighted differently and painted in less detail with more greying of colors as they get farther from the audience.

The fifth classification is *effect lighting*. Any lighting done for the achievement of an effect, either realistic or fantastic, is in this classification. It includes the projection of beams ostensibly from the sun or moon; rays of light from fire, candle, or lightning; and lighting scrims for transformations, disappearances, etc.

Any lighting instrument can be used. An ellipsoidal used to project a gobo pattern or a pattern which has been cut from a piece of heavy kitchen foil and inserted at the shutter point, a Fresnel type unit without the lens gelled with multicolored strips for striping, or an overhead projector borrowed from a classroom to project a drawing or cutout; all are examples of effect lighting. The concern of the lighting designer is to get close to the desired effect. If the effect is too realistic, the result is a light show with which the rest of the production probably cannot compete.

If sunlight is desired, analyze sunshine. The noonday sun is the whitest source of light seen by man. The direction or the angle of the sun's rays tell the time of day. The rays of the sun are parallel as they strike the earth, hence beams must be parallel if they come onto the stage through two windows on one side of the set. The sun, even in early morning or late evening, is of high brightness. Analyze the effect, then produce it simply and faithfully.

Moonlight is a reflection of sunlight. More often than not it is romanticized on stage as blue when actually it is a low brightness white. Lightning is very white and of short duration. To achieve a lightning effect use photoflood lamps. These should be on a circuit acivated by a specially mounted mercury switch.

Encase a mercury switch in an insulted housing and include a means of suspending it in the "off" mode. When the housing is picked up and shaken, the circuit is energized for short periods. It is quiet, of short duration, and a simple operation. It is much more satisfactory than snapping a switch or breaker on and off powering a borderlight circuit.

Mechanical devices can be used in conjunction with spotlights. A small fan blowing strips of silk or thin nylon in the beam from a spotlight will produce an offstage fire effect. A disc of plexiglass painted with smears of lamp dip in the warm colors can produce another fire effect.

Mentioned earlier was one of the most used effect lighting units today, the ultra-violet or "black light" source. Filters may be obtained for lighting instruments and some of the darker blue gelatines offer a degree of fluorescence. The most efficient source today seems to be the fluorescent tube with a integral filter (F40/T12/BLB). This provides a rather high U-V output with a minimum of light in the visual range. It creates little heat and can be turned off and on with little problem. Also available are vapor type lamps which require a cooling-off period between being turned off and being re-ignited. The vapor type lamp is more pure in its U-V emission, but due to heat has a restricted operating time. U-V can be used in addition to normal lighting if the scenery has been textured with a reacting paint so extra punch can be added.

Unusual angles used for pictorial effect are also in this classification. Perhaps the designer may wish to present a character in an unrealistic situation, yet have his features be most obvious. A strong backlight from high to the rear will frame this actor while another front light of cool color and perhaps less intensity can be used to define the facial features. A strong sidelight can act as an illuminator for the face yet be extremely dramatic in its effect. Lighting from below is pictorial. Often used inside cauldrons, coming out of wells, or simply up from the floor, this lighting inverts the normal shadow/highlight pattern of a face and creates an unusual effect.

The final classification is *motivating lighting*. Often lighting designers stop before they reach this classification and fail to present to the audience any item which would seem to be able to give off light. The result is an otherwise realistic setting, but one which has no lighting fixtures yet a lot of light in the room.

This is the do-it-yourself classification since the exact type, style, period, or form of source has to be found, then made to actually give off the light. Floor and table lamps are not too much problem, nor are fireplaces, or even lanterns – although the lantern would have to be equipped with a battery, lamp, and switch.

Ingenuity has to come forth when torches, candles, or other portable open-flame forms of lighting are called for. Not all of them really need to give off light. This needs to be discussed with the director, for it is a directorial decision if the effect produced will be worth the effort of building a special piece of equipment.

In any item used in full view of the audience the highest wattage source used should be 40 watts. A floor lamp normally uses at least a 150 watt lamp, but it is actually responsible for the illumination of an area. In this classification of lighting, use a small wattage lamp to produce an internal light sufficient to indicate that the fixture is on. With this, use a cover spot – usually a Fresnel – around the motivating source. Obviously, the cover spot will have to operate as the motivating source does. The end result of effort with motivating light is a final detailing of the stage picture.

PLANNING FORMS

To aid in the planning of the lighting for a show, a number of forms would be handy. A floor plan of the stage showing the outline of the set (several plans if there are several sets), is a place to start. On this *lighting plan*, the designer can sketch in the acting areas, then locate the instruments and associated key information. Information is then available to those who will hang, focus, gel and circuit the instruments. Starting with the basic symbol, add: a letter in the beam indicating wide, narrow, or medium focus for the Fresnel or a shape for the beam of the ellipsoidal; a number inside the equipment symbol to indicate color media number; a code at the rear indicating circuit. Additional details such as hanging height can be added in marginal notations so that others can share in the installation and can learn by doing.

The designer can continue through the classifications dealing with each as it comes until a full complement of lighting plans have been made for the production.

In conjunction with this, you may need a *color frame schedule* indicating for each unit which color of media should be installed. This is important if there are to be overlapping productions on the stage. (A copy of the form we use may be found at the end of Chapter 18.) A second set of color frames will allow the preparation of a set of media for one show while another is on the stage. This is a great saving of time during the tech period which is usually hectic enough as is.

A *switchboard set-up chart* will provide an operator with an indication of the plugging arrangement. Each circuit would be labeled with its code and would list what it controls, and how it relates to control from the rest of the board. The chart would indicate total wattage of the branch circuits so that after an early run-through, circuits can be added together if required. This would allow for fewer operations in running the show, hence fewer possibilities for error. In newer systems the chart will list the assignment of dimmers to controllers.

Just as a musician has music for a concert, the switchboard operator should have a *cue sheet* for the show. This will list the changes to be made, the speed at which they are to be made, approximately what the cue is, and at times an indication of the space between cues. The cue sheet also provides for a back-up operator in case of illness.

It is the responsibility of the stage manager to actually give the execution command but the operator(s) of the board will assist greatly by knowing the show as well as possible so they can be prepared for the cues.

The lighting crew needs to take down special instruments, coil and store cables, refocus, regel, store all color media used for the show and clean up around the control console. A listing of any defective or damaged equipment should be given to the person in charge. Copies of the forms for the running of the show need to be turned in to the stage manager. Those things completed, the lighting crew members are finished with their part in the production.

BIBLIOGRAPHY

(See the basic electrical bibliography at the end of Chapter 14)

GLOSSARY

Celebrity II - console set-up

North Central
High School
Indpls., IN.

| Production | Form L - 2 |

Page ___ of ___

Scene Masters-screen 1	Controllers	
1 _____	1 _____	25 _____
2 _____	2 _____	26 _____
3 _____	3 _____	27 _____
4 _____	4 _____	28 _____
5 _____	5 _____	29 _____
6 _____		30
7 _____	7 _____	31
8 _____		32 _____
9 _____		
10 _____		
11 _____		
12 _____	12	36
13 _____	13 _____	37 _____
14 _____	14 _____	38 _____
15 _____	15 _____	39 _____
16 _____	16 _____	40 _____
17 _____	17 _____	41 _____
18 _____	18 _____	42 _____
19 _____	19 _____	43 _____
20 _____	20 _____	44 _____
21 _____	21 _____	45 _____
22 _____	22 _____	46 _____

PURPOSE OF THIS FORM:
To show which dimmers are assigned to which control channels.

USE OF THIS FORM:
List the dimmers assigned, adjacent to the controller number.
In the Scene Master column list the controllers active in that master.
(NOTE: This form is for our 48 channel, dimmer-per-circuit control console. Yours will probably be require a different format.)

Cue Sheet

North Central
High School
Indpls., IN.

Production

Form
L - 3

Page ___ of ___

Cue	Channels @ full	@	@	@	other
1					
2					
3					
4					
5					
6					
7					
8					
9					
10					
11					
12					
13					
14					
15					
16					
17					
18					
19					
20					
21					
22					
23					
24					
25					
26					
27					

PURPOSE OF THIS FORM:

To provide a listing of the controllers and their levels contained in a given cue.

USE OF THIS FORM:

As a cue is written list those channels at full, then groups at their various lower percentages.

This provides a back-up in case of memory failure in a computer, or a running sheet if running a show manually.

BIBLIOGRAPHY

BOOKS (B)

This bibliogrophy lists books, old and new, in and out of print, because many libraries maintain older books and often do not have funds to purchase the newer publications. Most of the older books contain information which is still valid.

B-1
Ashworth, Bradford; NOTES OF SCENE PAINTING; Whitlock's, Inc.; New Haven 1952

B-2
Baker, James; ELEMENTS OF STAGECRAFT; Alfred Publishing; Los Angeles 1978

B-3
Beck; PLAY PRODUCTION IN THE HIGH SCHOOL; (Now part of PLAY PRODUCTION TODAY, 1983) National Textbook, Skokie

B-4
Bellman, Willard F.; LIGHTING THE STAGE: ART AND PRACTICE; 2d. Ed., Harper & Row; N.Y. 1977

B-5
Bellman, Willard F.; SCENOGRAPHY AND STAGE TECHNOLOGY; Harper & Row; N.Y. 1977

B-6
Bowman, Ned A. ; HANDBOOK OF TECHNICAL PRACTICE FOR THE PERFORMING ARTS; Scenographic Media; Wilkinsburg, PA 1972

B-7
Bowman, Wayne; MODERN THEATRE LIGHTING; Harper; N.Y. 1957

B-8
Bradwell, Eric; PLAY PRODUCTION FOR AMATEURS; Allyn & Unwin; 1952

B-9
Brywon, Nicholas; THERMOPLASTIC SCENERY FOR THE THEATRE; Drama Book; N.Y. 1972

B-10
Burris-Meyer, Harold & Cole, Edward C.; SCENERY FOR THE THEATRE ; Little Brown; Boston, 1971

B-11
Chilver; STAGING A SCHOOL PLAY; Harper -Row; N.Y.

B-12
Cornberg, Sol & Gebauer, Emanuel; A STAGE CREW HANDBOOK; 4th Rev. Ed; Harper-Row; N. Y.

B-13
Dolman, John & Knaub, Richard; THE ART OF PLAY PRODUCTION; Harper Row; N.Y. 1973

B-14
Friederich, Willard; SCENERY FOR THE AMATEUR THEATRE; McMillan 1950

B-15
Fuchs, Theodore; STAGE LIGHTING; Blom; N.Y. 1964 (A reprint of the 1929 classic)

B-16
Gassner, John; PRODUCING THE PLAY with THE NEW SCENE TECHNICIANS HANDBOOK (Barber); Dryden; N.Y. 1967

B-17
Gillette, A.S.; AN INTRODUCTION TO SCENIC DESIGN; Harper Row; N.Y. 1967

B-18
Gillette, A.S.; STAGE SCENERY: ITS CONSTRUCTION AND RIGGING; Harper Row; N.Y. 1972

B-19
Graves, Maitland; THE ART OF COLOR AND DESIGN, 2d Ed.; McGraw Hill; N.Y. 1951

B-20
Gruver, Bert; THE STAGE MANAGER'S HANDBOOK, Rev. Ed.; Harper Row; N.Y. 1972

B-21
Hake, Herbert; HERE'S HOW, Rev. Ed; Samuel French ; N.Y. 1958

B-22
Hewitt, Bernard; PLAY PRODUCTION; Lippincott; 1952

B-23
Lounsbury, Warren C.; THEATRE BACKSTAGE FROM A TO Z; Univ. of Washington , Seattle; 1967

B-24
McCandless, Stanley; A METHOD OF LIGHTING THE STAGE; 4th. Ed.; Theatre Arts, N.Y. 1958

B-25
Ommanney, Catherine; THE STAGE AND THE SCHOOL, 4th. Ed.; McGraw-Hill; N.Y. 1972

B-26
Parker, W. Oren & Smith, Harvey K..; SCENE DESIGN AND STAGE LIGHTING ed. Ed.; Holt, Rhinehart, Winston; N.Y. 1968

B-27
Phillipi, Herbert; STAGECRAFT & SCENE DESIGN; Houghton, N.Y. 1953

B-28
Selden, Samuelk & Sellman, Hunton D.; STAGE SCENERY AND LIGHTING; Appleton, N.Y. 1930

B-29
Selden, Samuel & Rezzuto; ESENTIALS OF STAGE SCENERY; Appleton, Century, Crofts; N.Y. 1972

B-30
Simon, Bernard, Ed.; SIMON'S DIRECTORY, 5th Ed.; Package Publicity; N.Y. 1976

B-31
Smith, Milton Meyers; PLAY PRODUCTION; APLETON; N.Y. 1948

B-32
Stell,Joseph; THE THEATRE STUDENT: SCENERY; Richards Rosen Press; N.Y. 1970

B-33
Welker, David; THETRICAL SET DESIGN; THE BASIC TECHNIQUES; Allyn-Smith; Boston 1969

B-34
Williams, Rollo G.; THE TECHNIQUE OF STAGE LIGHTING; Pitman, London 1952

B-35
Williams, Rollo G.; LIGHTING FOR COLOR AND FORM; Pitman, London 1954

B-36
Wolfe, Welby B.; MATERIALS OF THE SCENE; Harper Row, N.Y. 1977

BOOKS ADDED FOR SECOND EDITION:

B-37
Palmer, Richard H; THE LIGHTING ART; Prentice-Hall, Englewood Cliffs, NJ; 1985

B-38
Padgett, Allen and Smith, Bruce; ON ROPE; National Speleological Society, Huntsville, AL; 1987

B-39
Bigon, Mario and Regazzoni; THE MORROW GUIDE TO KNOTS; Quill, New York, NY; 1981

B-40
Sporre, Denis J. and Burroughs, Robert C.; SCENE DESIGN IN THE THEATRE; Prentice Hall, Englewood Cliffs, NJ; 1990

B-41
Arnold, Richard L.; SCENE TECHNOLOGY; Prentice Hall, Englewood Cliffs, NJ; 1990

PERIODICALS (P)

P-1
DRAMATICS MAGAZINE
International Thespian Society
3368 Central Parkway
Cincinati, OH 45225
513/559-1996

P-2
LIGHTING DIMENSIONS
135 Fifth Avenue
New York, N.Y. 10010-7193
212/677-5997

P-3
SECONDARY SCHOOL THEATRE JOURNAL
(Defunct)

P-4
TABS
(Defunct)

P-5
THEATRE CRAFTS
135 Fifth Avenue
New York, New York 10010-7193
212/677-5997

P-6
THEATRE DESIGN AND TECHNOLOGY
United States Institute for Theatre Technology
330 West 42nd Street
New York, New York 10036-6978
212/563-5551

SPECIAL PUBLICATIONS (S)

S-1
INCANDESCENT LAMPS (TP-110R)
General Electric Company
Nela Park
Cleveland, OH 44112

S-2
LIGHT AND COLOR
General Electric
Nela Park
Cleveland, OH 44112

S-3
MICROPHONE PRIMER
Electro-Voice
600 Cecil Street
Buchanan, MI 49107

S-4
SCENIC ARTISTS HANDBOOK
(Was published by Gothic Color Company)
contact: Gothic Ltd.
Box 189 Continental Hill
Glen Cove, N.Y. 11542
516 / 676-6600

S-5
THEATER WORDS
U.S.I.T.T.
330 West 42nd Street
New York, NY 10036-6978
212 / 563-5551

S-6
(Multiple publications)
National Fire Protection Association
Batterymarch Park
Quincy, MA 02269

S-7
Theatre Safety
DRAMATICS MAGAZINE
3368 Central Parkway
Cincinnati, OH 4525-2392

MANUFACTURERS (M)

(Theatre Crafts publishes an annual DIRECTORY which provides a complete listing of manufacturers and suppliers with current addresses and phone numbers.)

M-1
ALTMAN STAGE LIGHTING CO. INC.
57 Alexander Street
Yonkers, N.Y. 10707

M-2
AMERICAN SCENIC COMPANY
(not listed 1990)

M-3
AUTOMATIC DEVICES COMPANY
2121 South 12th Street
Allentown, PA 18103

M-4
(BERKEY COLORTRAN)
LEE COLORTRAN
1015 Chestnut Street
Burbank, CA 91506-9983

M-5
(BOSTITCH-TEXTRON)
STANLEY - BOSTITCH
Briggs Drive
East Greenwich, R.I. 02818

M-6
BUSSMAN MFG. CO.
PO Box 14460
St. Louis, MO 63178

M-7
Capitol Stage Lighting
(out of business 1981)

M-8
J. R. CLANCY
7041 Interstate Island Road
Syracuse, N.Y. 13209

M-9
Decor Electronics
(For older systems contact:)
MACRO ELECTRONICS CORP.
1611 Headway Circle, Bldg. #1
Austin, TX 78754-5137

M-10
(Electro Controls)
STRAND-ELECTRO CONTROLS
18111 So. Santa Fe Ave
Rancho Dominguez, CA 90221

M-11
ELECTRO-VOICE
600 Cecil Street
Buchanan, MI 49107

M-12
GENERAL ELECTRIC
Nela Park
Cleveland, OH 44112

M-13
(Hub Electric Company)
VARA-LIGHT/DIMATRONICS/HUB
6207 Commercial Road
Crystal Lake, IL 60014

M-14
KLIEGL BROS. INC.
5 Aerial Way
Syosset, NY 11791-5502

M-15
(Major Corp, Major Control Prod)
LIGHT CONTROLS INC.
PO Box 9276
Crystal Lake, IL 60014

M-16
Millers-Falls
No address available 1990

M-17
MUTUAL HARDWARE
5-45   49th Avenue
Long Island City, N.Y 11001

M-18
PARAMOUNT THEATRICAL SUPPLIES
(Alcone Corp)
5-45   49th Avenue
Long Island City, NY 11001

M-19
ROSCO LABORATORIES
36 Bush Avenue
Port Chester, NY 10573

M-20
(Stage Decoration and Supplies)
Not listed 1990

M-21
STANLEY TOOLS
New Britain, CT 06050

M-22
STRAND (Century) LIGHTING INC,
18111 So. Santa Fe Avenue
Rancho Dominguez, CA 90224

M-23
SYLVANIA
100 Endicott Street
Danvers, MA 01923

M-24
TIFFIN SCENIC STUDIOS
PO Box 39
146 Riverside Dr.
Tiffin, OH 44883

M-25
UNION CONNECTOR CO., INC.
PO Box H
300 Babylon Turnpike
Roosevelt, NY 11575

M-26
UNITED STAGE EQUIPMENT
PO Box 667
Hartselle, AL 35640

M-27
WENGER CORPORATION
PO Box 448
555 Park Drive
Owatona, MN 55060

M-28
ELECTRONICS DIVERSIFIED
1675 NW 216th Avenue
Hillsboro, OR 97124

M-29
LEHIGH ELECTRIC PRODUCTS
RD #1, Box J1
Wescosville, PA 18106

M-29
HOFFEND & SONS, Inc.
34 East Main Street
Honeoye, NY 14471

M-30
GOTHIC LTD.
PO Box 189
1 Continental Hill
Glen Cove, NY 11542

INDEX

F

W

X

Y

Z

ABOUT THE AUTHOR

EDUCATION: Northwestern Univerisity, Evanston, IL 1959,1960-61
                       M. A., Theatre, 1961
            University oif Evansville, Evansville, IN 1949-1953
                       B.A. Education; Speech/Theatre, 1953
            Benjamin Bosse High School, Evansville, IN 1945-1949

ORGANIZATIONS: Northminster Presbyterian Church, Indianapolis
                       Deacon 1958-60, Elder 1971-1973
            PROFESSIONAL: Indiana State Teachers Association (1958-1989)
               Speech Communication Association
               United States Institute for Theatre Technology
               Indiana Speech Associaton
               Indiana Theatre Association
               Construction Specifications Institute (1970-1975)
            COLLEGE: Lambda Chi Alpha - Social Fraternity
               Alpha Psi Omega - Honorary Dramatics
               Pi Delta Epision - Honorary Journalism
               Tau Kappa Alpha - Honorary Forensics
               Who's Who in American Colleges and Universities
            HIGH SCHOOL: National Honor Society
               National Thespian Society (Best Thespian 1949)

EXPERIENCE:Theatre Consultant: 1961-present, designing spaces and systems for
               stage electrical, curtains, and rigging systems for several architectural firms
               with over 200 projects to date.
            President: THEATER ASSOCIATES, INC., 1957-present - rctail sales,
               rentals, repair of theatrical lighting systems.
            Faculty: NORTH CENTRAL HIGH SCHOOL, Indianapolis, IN 1958 - present
               Chairman, Performing Arts Department, 1985 - present
               Teacher, Stagecraft, Speech;
               Production Supervisor managing 1500 seat auditorium
            Graduate Lighting Assistant, Northwestern University, 1960-61
            Graduate Scenery Assistant, Northwestern University, summer 1959
            Scenic Carpenter, WFBM-TV, Indianapolis 1957-1958
            Production Supervisor, AVONDALE PLAYHOUSE, Indianapolis, IN
               Summer stock Company summers 1957, '58, '60, '61, '62, '63.
            Manufacture, sales, installation of stage equipment 1955-1957
            U.S. Army, 1953-1955, Ft. Leonard Wood, MO., Infantry basic,
                  Engineer Basic, Engineer Leadership School.
               Gelnhausen, Germany, Batallion Troop Information and Education NCO,
               TDY Special Services to refurbish a theatre in Frankfurt, 1954
               TDY Special Services, Lighting Designer All Army Talent Finals,
               Deutsches Museum, Munich, Germany 1955.
            Technical Director, Evansville College Theatre, 1950-1953
            Lighting Director, Evansville Commuity Players, 1947-1953
            Student Lighting director, Bosse High School 1946-1949

PUBLISHED: Series of three articles (Appearing as Chapter 15 of this text) for
               DRAMATICS MAGAZINE, December 1970, January and February 1971
               INSTALLING A THEATRE LIGHTING SYSTEM, Indianapolis, 1977
               STAGECRAFT 1: Your Introduction to Backstage Work, 1978
               HOW TO: CHECK YOUR (STAGE) RIGGING, Theatre Crafts, May 1984.
               STUDENT WORKBOOK for STAGECRAFT 1:, 1985